Chin Nan Kuan Hua

The Guide to Kuan Hua

Chin Nan Kuan Hua

The Guide to Kuan Hua

ISBN/EAN: 9783337164249

Printed in Europe, USA, Canada, Australia, Japan

Cover: Foto ©Andreas Hilbeck / pixelio.de

More available books at **www.hansebooks.com**

南指話官

THE

GUIDE TO KUAN HUA

A TRANSLATION OF THE

"KUAN HUA CHIH NAN"

WITH AN

ESSAY ON TONE AND ACCENT IN PEKINESE

AND A

GLOSSARY OF PHRASES

BY

L. C. HOPKINS

H.M. Consular Service, China

SHANGHAI
KELLY & WALSH, LIMITED, THE BUND & NANKING ROAD
AND AT HONGKONG, YOKOHAMA AND SINGAPORE

1895

TRANSLATOR'S PREFACE.

Few foreign residents in China will, I suppose, challenge the proposition that to speak of a man as a Sinologue is to think of him as a fool.

Let me then hasten, in the interests of my publishers and myself, to assure the gentle, the candid, and the general reader, that the perusal of this volume need leave no one more foolish than he was before.

This firm confidence in the harmlessness of the present work may be had because from a sinologic standpoint "there is nothing in it."

Whether the Chinese of antiquity said "*hwei* 7 *guk*" or "*t'an* 5 *dam*;" whence they came—these ancient but objurgatory speakers— from Babylon, from Accad, or Assyria, and who they were, Chaldees or Hittites, Proto-Medians or Ugro-Altaics, the lost Ten Tribes or natives of some old-world Parish of Stepney; whether the *I King* is a phallic gospel or a pocket dictionary; where in the world Ta Ts'in and T'iao-chih could have been; and precisely how much remains of LAO TZU after being translated by BALFOUR and analysed by GILES, —on these and kindred topics the *Kuan Hua Chih Nan* will throw no gleam of light.

Mr. GOH's text is modern, work-a-day and practical, written in excellent Pekinese of the present time, not of two hundred years ago, and, by common consent of both northern natives and foreign students, is as useful as it is idiomatic. Having heard a good many of my friends express their opinion that the work merited an English translation, and no one else showing any inclination to make it, I undertook the task. I have added to the translation,—the Chinese text of which I regret that I have not been able to obtain permission to reprint,—a Glossary, and a monograph on Tone and Accent in Pekinese, both of which I somewhat faintly hope may be found of assistance at least to those who are entering on the study of this unhappy language.

My sincere thanks are due to Messrs. BULLOCK and JORDAN, of H.B.M. Legation, Peking, and to the Revd. G. OWEN, of that city, for their ungrudging and valuable assistance upon many doubtful points that came to light in the compilation of the Glossary. Finally, I am deeply indebted to Mr. W. H. WILKINSON, of H.B.M. Consulate, Swatow, for seeing the whole work through the press, a labour which, at all times irksome, must have been with the Glossary almost as revolting as its preparation.

L. C. HOPKINS.

CONTENTS.

	PAGE.
Part I.	1
„ II.	10
„ III.	70
„ IV.	96
Essay on Tone and Accent in Pekinese	130
Glossary of Phrases	138

THE GUIDE TO KUAN HUA

A TRANSLATION OF THE "KUAN HUA CHIH NAN."

PART I.

No. 1   *a.* What is your honoured surname?

b. My poor surname is Wu.

a. May I ask your eminent Style?

b. My humble Style is Tzŭ-ching.

a. How many distinguished brothers have you?

b. There are three of us.

a. And what province do you come from, Sir?

b. My lowly home is in the capital of Honan.

a. Is your residence situated inside the city?

b. Yes, inside the city.

a. I am delighted to make your acquaintance, and I must apologise for not having done so before.

No. 2   *a.* What is your venerable age now, Sir?

b. I have wasted some sixty years.

a. The world has gone well with you; you are quite robust, and neither your hair nor beard are very grey.

b. Many thanks! But my hair and beard have turned half white already.

a. Well I am just fifty this year, and most of my beard has turned before this.

No. 3   *a.* What is your distinguished surname, and your noted name?

b. My poor surname is Chang, my official name is Shou Hsien.

a. What is your distinguished place in the family?

b. I am the eldest.

a. And the honoured year of your birth?

b. Oh, I am still very young, twenty-four this year.

a. What position do you hold, Sir?

b. I am in business at T'ungchow and a friend of your esteemed uncle, and for that reason I made a point of coming to present my compliments to you.

a. You are very kind! May I inquire the name of your Firm?

b. My little business is styled Hsin Ch'ang.

No. 4 *a.* I'm delighted to meet you again for I've been longing to see you. * I heard early this morning you had arrived, so I came on purpose to inquire after you.

b. Thank you, I'm very much obliged. I should have come to call upon you, but I only got here late yesterday evening and, as none of my baggage is ready nor my boxes unpacked and I haven't changed the clothes I was wearing, you'll excuse my not returning your call till to-morrow.

a. Don't mention it!

No. 5 *a.* How do you do! I haven't seen you about these last few days, and you've been a great deal in my thoughts. You must have been ill again I'm afraid.

b. Yes indeed I have.

a. You had just recovered the day I saw you, but you are not looking yourself yet. I suspect you must have gone out and had another attack.

b. I have caught a chill, and I feel headachy and sore all over.

a. Well, the only way is to send for a doctor and be properly attended to.

No. 6 *a.* You really and truly cannot believe that man. Everything he utters is a gross exaggeration.

b. You will have your trouble for nothing if you depend on what he says. Haven't you found out the sort of man he is yet? Why, he has a perfect passion for exaggeration and brags and boasts to any extent; if you put any faith in what he tells you, you'll infallibly be let in.

No. 7 *a.* Have you quite recovered from your recent indisposition?

b. Thank you, quite. My cough is not so troublesome.

a. You've had a long attack this time, and though you are well again now, you must ask your doctor to give you a tonic, and keep quiet and take care of yourself.

b. Yes; thank you very much for your kind attention.

NOTE.—The Chinese text here requires some alteration.

No. 8 *a.* While you're here you should make yourself at home,—don't stand on ceremony.

    b. Thank you, you are very kind! I'm not doing so.

    a. That's all right then! And after this, if I want anything I shan't hesitate to apply to you.

    b. Anything you will let me do, I shall take as a favour.

No. 9 *a.* Thank you very much for the tea you were so kind as to send me yesterday. Its flavour is excellent.

    b. Don't mention it. During my last visit to Ch'ung An, I spent two days in the Bohea Hills, and just bought a little tea there. You must excuse my sending such a trifling quantity.

    a. Not at all! Friendship is essentially a matter of feeling, not one of £. s. d.

No. 10 *a.* Where are you off to?

    b. I want to make a call on Chang *lao shih*.

    a. Oh! well I wish you would remember me to him and say I don't forget him; tell him, when he's got time, I wish he would drop in.

    b. Some days ago, when I was with him, he was asking me to remember him to yourself. He has not been able to go out on account of his wife's being out of sorts.

No. 11 *a.* Everybody must be truthful in what they say.

    b. There is no doubt about that. Anything like lying and cheating, when people find it out, brings disgrace to a man.

    a. Your view exactly coincides with my own opinion.

No. 12 *a.* Do you think this thing is real or imitation?

    b. An imitation, I think.

    a. I think so too, but as I can't tell for certain whether it is or not, I don't like to say so.

    b. No, you haven't examined how coarse the carving is, and the want of lustre in the colouring.

No. 13 *a.* We are both out of employment at present; what's to be done?

    b. What do you think there is to be done?

    a. I think we are very hard up; neither you nor I have any capital to start a business on our own account, and we don't know any trade to earn wages by as shopmen.

b. Well, if that's the case, we must starve then!

a. But after all, Providence doesn't bring anybody into the world to be quite destitute. We shall think of something by-and-by.

No. 14 *a.* I should like to walk out there but I don't feel inclined to go by myself.

b. I'd like a walk too, but it's dull without a companion, so what do you say to our going together?

a. Oh, if you would join me it would be very convenient to *me*.

No. 15 *a.* You speak in such a low tone that a great deal that you say people don't hear distinctly.

b. I have by nature not a strong voice, and besides I don't like bawling out loud at people, and so the sounds uttered are low.

a. But the pitch of the voice matters considerably in talking, for if the pitch is right, it will be audible naturally, and if the enunciation is distinct, it follows that there will be nothing lost.

No. 16 *a.* Did you hear what I said to him behind the screen just now?

b. No, I didn't. I've been rather deaf lately.

a. Well anyhow, please don't on any account divulge it, as it's a secret.

b. Then I certainly won't go and do harm by talking.

No. 17 *a.* Do you understand Chinese?

b. A little, but the Amoy language is not much understood elsewhere.

a. Chinese no doubt is difficult; each place has its own dialect, though Mandarin passes current throughout.

b. I am told that Mandarin itself has two pronunciations,—a northern and a southern.

a. The accent in northern and southern Mandarin is different, the pronunciation of the words is much the same.

No. 18 *a.* How do you do once more! Do you remember me?

b. Your face seems quite familiar, but I don't recollect where we met. I must really apologise, but I don't like to address you by name quite at random.

a. What, have you forgotten our having taken wine together at the same table, the year before last, at Chang Erh's place?

b. Now you mention it I *do* remember you; you are Mr. Ho Erh.

No. 19 *a.* How do you do! I hope you are well. I want you to do something for me.

　b. Pray tell me what it is.

　　a. I recollect seeing in a newspaper two days ago mention of a Mr. Chu, an admirable scroll-writer, whom I hear you know. Might I ask you to introduce me to him.

　　b. Oh that will be easy enough; I will not fail to oblige you, don't trouble but leave it to me.

No. 20 *a.* Of all the celebrated spots we have visited, the scenery on the hill we came to at noon to-day was best.

　b. Yes, and I liked most the mile or so of path through the bamboos outside the Halfway Lodge.

　a. And best of all when, after following that path, we turned a corner and sat on that big rock. How refreshing it was to listen to the brook.

NOTE.—The Chinese text here requires some alteration.

No. 21 *a.* Did you return early or late from your trip on the lake yesterday?

　b. It was after midnight when we got back.

　a. I should think the moon last night was beautiful, and the scene on the lake must have been especially fine.

　b. The view by night is even better than by day,—quite twice as fine.

No. 22 *a.* This temple is very large.

　b. Very; it is supposed to be the largest about here, and behind there is a very high pagoda.

　a. Can one go up it?

　b. It had a staircase to one storey which has been taken away now, so one can't go up.

　a. Why did they take away the stairs?

　b. Because so many people went up and were continually doing wanton damage.

No. 23 *a.* The moon was so beautiful last night before midnight that I lay on the *kang* looking at the moonbeams shining on the window, and couldn't bring myself to go to sleep.

　b. However, when it grew late, the wind suddenly sprang up, the sky was full of dark, scudding clouds, and there was very heavy thunder.

No. 24   *a.* I suppose that was after I had gone to sleep, though I know it was raining last night.

a. How can you go out just now in this fierce sun and dreadful heat?

b. But I have important business; I *must* go out.

a. Well, even if you have, you ought to hold on a while, and wait till the sun goes down a bit and it is a little cooler, before starting.

b. Very well.

No. 25   *a.* At daylight this morning, when I got up and went out to the rear, I saw a very thick frost on the roof.

b. Then there *was* a heavy frost last night! That accounts for my waking up about 4 in the morning, feeling very cold, and wishing my cotton coverlet was not so thin.

No. 26   *a.* It is late; I think it must be 3 o'clock by now.

b. Just now I heard the clock go *ding dong*,—it seemed to strike two.

a. I'm afraid that clock is not right; I'll look at my watch. The watch makes it three.

b. Then the clock is certainly slow.

No. 27   *a.* Which of the Four Seasons do you prefer?

b. They each of them have their advantages.

a. Which do you like best?

b. You needn't ask *that!* Who does not delight in the flowers and fragrance of balmy Spring, and who not does not fear the heats of Summer and the chills of Autumn, and worst of all the great cold of Winter?

a. I like both Spring and Autumn.

No. 28   *a.* Where is the school I hear you go to?

b. It's at that corner,—the doorway with the poster.

a. Who is the Master?

b. His name is Mr. Chin.

a. How many school-fellows have you?

b. Not many.

No. 29   *a.* Have you read the Dynastic Histories?

b. No, I have not.

a. Educated people should not fail to read them; it is by them that one understands the rise and fall of dynasties, and the virtues and vices of mankind.

b. What are you doing in caligraphy?

a. Wang Yu-chin's writing copies.

b. Capital!

No. 30 *a.* What sort of a *teacher* is your Master?

b. Very good; he explains passages most carefully, he writes a very pretty hand, takes a great deal of pains in correcting our compositions, doesn't ignore the least merits we have, he's correct in his own habits and strict about discipline.

a. With such a good Master as that, if you choose to take pains, there's no fear of your not making progress in your studies.

No. 31 *a.* Mr. Priest!

b. In the name of Amita!

a. Is the head priest in?

b. The head priest went out yesterday.

a. May I ask your name in religion?

b. I am called Liao K'ung.

a. What is your lay name?

b. My lay name is Ku.

a. You've a large piece of land here; what a pity no one has laid it out in grounds.

b. This land is no good; the soil is so salt that nothing that's planted will grow.

No. 32 *a.* To-day being your honoured father's birthday, I have come for the purpose of offering my congratulations, and I've prepared a small present which I beg you will do me the honour of accepting. Pray don't decline it on any account. Would you also kindly take me and present me to your father, to convey my congratulations.

b. You are too kind! I am really very much obliged to you for your trouble.

No. 33 *a.* Oh dear, what a good-for-nothing child this is! All day long idling his time away, and doing nothing that's right.

b. Don't his father and mother look after him?

a. If he's allowed to go on in this way, doing exactly as he pleases, why he'll never stop at all.

b. I should advise them to bury him alive and have done with him.

No. 34 *a.* Whatever you do, in order to come to the front, you must work hard to get on, and not be your own enemy.

b. That's all very well; but I am satisfied if I don't neglect my duties. I cannot do as some people do, and simply make sudden displays of zeal, or cringe to people and do their dirty work for them. I can't bring myself to do such miserable tricks.

No. 35 *a.* The Emperor is certain to be pleased with good public servants, and as certain to be angry with the incompetent; and it rests with each individual what his own character shall be.

b. That goes without saying. It is beyond all doubt that strict integrity brings understanding of public business, while if a man has only ordinary abilities, and is in the habit of taking money besides, he will soon have to go home and nurse the baby.

No. 36 *a.* The present members of the Central Government are men of character and talents, and zealous in the discharge of their duties; the consequence is, that the provincial authorities follow their good example.

b. An example is always required to be set and to be followed respectively. If those in the higher ranks are not venal, their subordinates dare not be extortionate.

No. 37 *a.* He came several times and I never took much notice of him, but still he has the shameless effrontery to be always coming here. He really is perfectly dead to all sense of right or wrong.

b. He's a bullying, cowardly blusterer,—I don't call him a *man*. Don't ever take any notice of him, and then of course he won't come.

No. 38 *a.* I wonder what family that girl belongs to that passed just now; she is elegant and dignified too. To-morrow I shall make a proposal on behalf of my relative. Yes, that is a really nice girl.

b. I recognise her as one of Mr. Chang Erh's children. It would be a suitable match, were you to speak on behalf of your relative.

No. 39 *a.* That's a good child, that! Up to working at night, and able to make a living; persevering, too, and trustworthy. One can't help liking him.

b. You think so? I consider him very idle. He's asleep as soon as it's dark. That's a question like the beancurd strung on a horsehair,—not to be raised, as the saying goes. Quite puts me out of temper.

No. 40 *a.* I have always had so many benefits from you that I could never, in any case, cease to be thankful, and now I've received this further favour, I don't know how I am to repay your kindness in being so good to me as you have been.

b. Oh, not at all! There is no need for you to be so grateful for this slight service.

No. 41 *a.* When one's teeth are gone, one cannot chew one's food, and it has to be stewed to a pulp. Don't have food done so fearfully hard and tough that you can't eat it.

b. My teeth are better than yours. I can eat anything; tough or brittle it makes no difference. I can even crack melon-seeds with my teeth.

No. 42 *a.* I want to ask your advice as to what should be done about this. I am inclined, if he won't do as he's wanted, to speak out fairly and squarely. What do you think?

b. I tell you what it is. Your temper is too unyielding. It would be better if you were more conciliatory. It *never* does to be too hard upon people. When a man has confessed he is in the wrong, that's enough. What *is* the use of never letting the matter drop.

No. 43 *a.* Why is this cat always so lazy? The place swarms with rats, but she never catches one. Better not feed her to-morrow.

b. The rats are the most terrible nuisance. One can't get to sleep for their noise, and they gnaw everything to pieces. I don't know what's to be done.

No. 44 *a.* There were two dogs over there coupled, and a girl with her hand before her eyes who wouldn't look, but all the same she *did* have a stealthy glance through her fingers. Rather amusing, eh?

b. After coming to a certain age the passions must be excited. Modest as she may *seem*, do you suppose she *feels* no emotions? There is nothing to be surprised at her for.

No. 45 *a.* I was standing on the steps when all of a sudden he pushed me backwards, and I nearly had a very bad fall.

b. What a mean brute! He won't play any more such tricks with me. If he provokes me I'll give him one unawares with my whole strength, and send him away with something more than he wants.

PART II.

No. 1 *a.* May I ask you your name?
  b. With pleasure. My name is Wang.
  a. Where is your residence situated?
  b. My house is in the Tsung pu Hutung at the East Tan P'ailou.
  a. At which Yamên are you employed?
  b. I have a post in the Board of War.
  a. To what do I owe the honour of your visit?
  b. I have come in order to make certain inquiries from you. I am told the house in your western compound is to let. Is that the case?
  a. Certainly, it is. Why, do you wish to take it?
  b. Yes, I was thinking of doing so.
  a. You are too late; I've already let the house.
  b. Let it! To whom?
  a. To a connection of my own.
  b. Oh, very good. Well, have you any houses elsewhere?
  a. I have none, but a friend of mine has a house that he wants to let.
  b. Where is it?
  a. In the An fu Hutung, to the north of us.
  b. How many rooms are there?
  a. Some thirty or more.
  b. Thirty or more would be too many. I couldn't occupy such a number.
  a. But supposing you couldn't, you might *take* them all; and all that you didn't use yourself you might sublet to other tenants.
  b. I being responsible for the rent?
  a. Quite so; you being responsible for the rent.
  b. But then I'm afraid I couldn't let the rooms at once; and I should have to pay the landlord his full rent every month.
  a. Oh, I don't think you need be under any apprehension about that. At present, houses let easily enough.

b. Well, when I have finally taken the house, I hope you will procure tenants for me for the rooms I don't use.

a. That is quite feasible. If you will let me know, as soon as you have finally taken the house, how many rooms you have portioned off for letting, I can find tenants for you.

b. Very good then. But now, do you know how much the rent is a month?

a. Yes, my friend has told me it is 70 *tiao* a month.

b. Oh, that is too high.

a. It does *sound* as if it were too high. But you should know that the house is really a very fine one indeed; the compound is large, the site very good, close to a main street, and very convenient for shopping.

b. Well, if I take it, have I to pay tea-money?

a. Yes, tea-money of course.

b. What, if I take it through you, must I still pay tea-money?

a. Why, though you do take the house through me, and there's no other Agent, you will have to pay tea-money all the same. I'll tell you how it is. The tea-money you give doesn't come to me, nor does my friend get it; it is divided among all my friend's servants.

b. Then how many payments are there for tea-money?

a. One for tea-money, and one for rent.

b. Very well. Now I suppose I must have substantial security?

a. You must, of course. Can you find one?

b. Yes, I can.

a. What would your security be?

b. Whatever is required.

a. Very good. And when would you like to go and look at the house.?

b. I should like to go with you and look at it in a day or two.

a. Very well then; we will meet in a day or two.

b. Yes.

No. 2 *a.* May I inquire your name?

b. With pleasure. My name is Li. I have not the pleasure of knowing yours.

a. My name is Chao.

b. May I ask what part you come from?

a. From Kalgan.

b. And what is your object in visiting Peking?

a. I have come to sell goods.

b. What goods have you brought to dispose of?

a. They are furs.

b. Where are you lodging?

a. At an inn in the Chinese city.

b. At which inn?

a. The Ta Ch'êng inn on the West Brook.

b. How are prices ruling this year in the fur market?

a. They are rather moderate this year.

b. I was told prices ruled very high some years ago.

a. Yes, some years ago the market rates were very high.

b. What was the reason of it?

a. Simply that stocks were short.

b. Have you sold out all the stock you brought?

a. No, not yet.

b. When you have sold out, do you take back cash, or a return stock for sale?

a. A return stock of goods.

b. Of what sort?

a. Always Foreign and Canton Assorted.

b. Have you a shop in Kalgan?

a. Yes, I have.

b. What name?

a. The name is I T'ai.

b. At what house have you bought your stock for your previous return journeys?

a. That would all depend. I buy whosever goods suit best.

b. Very well now. I have a friend who has lately opened a Foreign and Canton Assorted Goods house outside the Hata Mên. The stock has been laid in by himself from Canton, and the prices are altogether lower than in the other houses; so any goods you buy in future you might get there.

a. What is the name of your friend's establishment?

b. Tê Fa is the name.

a. Then it would be all right if I go to his place some day to purchase, and mention your name?

b. Yes, or I could go *with* you some day.

a. That would be even better. May I ask, were you in business once?

b. Yes, I was.

a. What was your business?

b. I kept a druggist's store.

a. In the Chinese city?

b. In the Chinese city.

a. Do you still keep it?

b. Oh no. I closed it seven or eight years ago.

a. Indeed, and what is your present occupation?

b. I practise medicine at present.

a. In your practice do you merely receive patients, or do you visit them as well?

b. In the morning I receive, after noon I pay visits.

a. No doubt you find medicine better than trade.

b. Well no. There's no other advantage beyond that it has not the same anxieties as trade.

a. Where is your residence, sir?

b. I live in the Paofang Hutung, East Ssŭ Pailou.

a. I shall come and call upon you soon at your house.

b. Thank you! In a day or two I shall call also on you at your hotel.

a. You are very kind. Any time you are disengaged you might come to my inn for a chat.

b. Yes; then *au revoir!*

No. 3 *a.* Have you come from home, sir?

b. Yes, from home.

a. You haven't yet fixed when you start, have you?

b. Well, it will be in four or five days time, and I came to-day on purpose to take leave of you.

a. It is exceedingly polite of you. Are you taking your family too this time?

b. Oh yes, I intend to take my family too.

a. Are you travelling in company or alone?

b. In company.

a. Is your fellow traveller also in the Government service?

b. He is. He's a recently nominated Assistant Sub-Prefect by purchase, leaving the capital to serve his Expectancy.

a. And I suppose, as soon as you reach the provincial capital you will take up your post?

b. Probably.

a. Is your appointment an Arduous Post?

b. No, an Easy Post.

a. And what is the name of the man who is now acting there?

b. It is a man named Chou.

a. Does he hold a substantive appointment?

b. Yes. He has quite recently been appointed to a post too; so when I reach mine, he will hand over charge and go and take up his new appointment.

a. Well, I suppose for these few days you remain at home, don't you?

b. I do, yes.

a. Then during the next day or two I shall call at your house to bid you good-bye.

b. You are very good. And now I must be getting back.

a. When you are home again, please give my kind inquiries to your people.

b. I will do so.

No. 4 *Servant.*—If you please, Sir, Mr. Li has come to pay you a New Year call.

a. Oh, ask him to come in, and show him into the library.

b. A Happy New Year to you!

a. The same to you.

b. Please take the seat of honour and I will make my New Year's salute to you.

a. Oh, you are very good but let me take the will for the deed; sit down and drink some tea.

b. After you.

a. Is to-day the first day you have gone out?

b. No, I began going out yesterday.

a. How many days calls shall you make?

b. Oh, I shall have finished them all in five or six days.

a. And when do you mean to go into town?

b. On the 8th.

a. And when do you come back?

b. After the holidays.

a. I suppose you haven't been to the Yamên at all since closing last year.

b. Yes, I've been twice since then, to do one or two little things.

a. You must be busy, I presume, as soon as you open again?

b. Yes indeed! We don't have a moment's spare time then.

a. No; won't you have another cup of tea?

b. No more thank you, I must be going.

a. Oh, there's no hurry, it is quite early yet.

b. Well, but I have a good number of places to go to, and it wouldn't do to be late.

a. Well then, thank you for your visit. When you get home, please give my compliments and wish them a Happy New Year.

b. I will do so on my return.

No. 5 *a.* I heard yesterday that you have been promoted to a Prefectship, and consequently I've come to-day to offer my congratulations.

b. You are very kind, and I'm sure I am very much obliged to you.

a. When are you likely to proceed to your new post?

b. I can't fix beforehand, because I have to wait for the Chiefs to send a deputy to take over my duties before I can hand over charge.

a. And after handing over charge, do you then go to your new post, or must you first go to the provincial capital?

b. I go first to the capital.

a. What year did you take your Degree?

b. I graduated in the year Hsin Yu.

a. And when did you take your Doctor's degree?

b. In the Jên Hsü year.

a. Really, you have carried all before you,—most talented, upon my word.

b. You flatter me; it is merely a piece of temporary good luck, that's all.

a. Oh, you are too modest. May I ask where you have held office?

b. I was District Magistrate of Shang Yüan hsien for a period; afterwards, when my term was up, I had the honour to be recommended for promotion to my present post by the late Governor, but for some years, I am ashamed to say, I have rendered no service whatever.

a. Oh, don't say that! With such great talents no wonder that you are so fully appreciated in the higher circles. What is more, it is very fortunate for the locality that you, who are like a father to the people, have now been promoted to be Prefect.

b. You are quite too good!

a. Well, so soon as the day of your departure is fixed, I shall come again to bid you good-bye.

b. Oh, I could not hear of such a thing. I am very much obliged to you now, and I shall come to your office shortly to return your call.

a. Thank you, thank you.

No. 6   *a.* I hear there was a robbery committed by a number of men at the Bank at the East end of the street some nights ago; is it true?

b. It wasn't a robbery, it was a fight.

a. What about?

b. Why, some common fellow had picked up a Bank Note and went to the Bank to cash it, but the Bank people said, "This is a lost Note, it has been advertised for already. Wait a bit and we will send for the person who lost it, and you two can settle it between yourselves personally; he won't give you your trouble for nothing, he is sure to pay you some Taels reward." But the fellow wouldn't agree. "The Note's mine," he said, "and all I know is that I've brought the Note to be cashed; what you say about somebody else having lost it is no business of mine, I'm not going to have anything to do with all that; just you give me the money and let's have no more about it." But the Bank wouldn't do it. Well, he was going to take back the Note itself, but they wouldn't give him that either, and detained it. So he goes away, and in the evening this fellow, with four others he had got, goes to the Bank to have a row. No sooner had they got there than they began to use bad language, got hold of one of the attendants at the counter, pulled him out and thrashed him, and knocked down the counting-boards lying on the counter. Well, just then the Police officials heard about it, and thinking it was a Bank robbery, they took their men, carried off these five fellows and sent them to the Magistracy. Afterwards, when they found it was a case of fighting they cangued all five of them on the East end of the street, and they are to have half a month of it before they're set free.

No. 7 *a.* What's that man sitting in the compound with the bundle want?

Servant.—He sells cloisonné.

a. Do you know him?

Servant.—No, I don't know him.

a. Then how do you know he sells cloisonné?

Servant.—I was asking him just now, and he said he came from a cloisonné makers.

a. Then is it cloisonné that he has wrapped up in his bundle?

Servant.—That's it, I expect.

a. Well go and call him in.

Servant.—Come in, Mr. Manager.

a. You sell cloisonné, do you?

b. Yes.

a. And what cloisonné is it that you have in your bundle?

b. It's a pair of cloisonné vases.

a. Open the bundle and let me have a look.

b. There, Sir! what do you think of that pair of vases?

a. Too large. Have you any rather smaller than that?

b. We have in our place of business a smaller pair,—models, not for sale,—but you can have ones made of any size you want.

a. I was merely asking, that's all. How many dollars would a pair like that be?

b. They would be over $100.

a. Have you any small things?

b. What kind of small things do you mean?

a. Such as small pen-vases, scaling-oil cases, candlesticks,—small knicknacks like that.

b. All the different articles you mention are now being made but they are not finished off yet.

a. Well, how long will it be before they are?

b. Another four or five days.

a. Well, when they are finished, you might bring me several kinds, and the pair of vases you keep for models in your place, for me to look at, and if they suit me, I can order a pair of the same pattern.

b. Yes, I will bring them in a few days.

a. Where is your place of business?

b. In High Street, Hou Mên.

a. What name?

b. Kuang Ch'êng.

a. Have you ever sold anything at this house before?

b. No, we never have.

a. Well, this pair of vases is too large for my liking, you can take them away again.

b. Yes; excuse my leaving you, Sir.

a. Good-day to you.

No. 8   *a.* Is your master at home?

Servant.—Yes, Sir.

a. Go in and tell your master that my name is Hsü, and I live at the Hou Mên, and that I have something I wish to speak to him about.

Servant.—Yes, Sir......My master begs you will step in to the library, Sir.

b. How do you do, Sir; glad to see you again.

a. The pleasure is mutual; and how have you been?

b. Quite well, thank you; have you?

a. Yes, thank you very much.

b. Have you been anywhere since we last met?

a. Indeed I have; I've been away for some time.

b. Where did you go?

a. Beyond the Wall, to receive my rents.

b. Ah!

a. I have called on you to-day, Sir, because I have something to consult you about.

b. What is it?

a. A friend of mine, who lives to the west of the city, owns a few hundred acres, with an orchard and a vegetable garden, and having at present occasion for ready money, he has asked me to mortgage this land for him, and so I have come to ask you about it. If you care to take it on mortgage, I can arrange it for you.

b. Is he at present farming the land himself or has he a tenant?

a. He farms it himself.

b. And how much does he want to raise on it?

a. A thousand taels.

b. Then I'm afraid I couldn't find so much as that.

a. How much could you manage?

b. Well I *might* manage some five or six hundred taels.

a. On that point let me go back and speak to him, will you?

b. But now—for how many years does he want to mortgage?

a. I was asking him about that, and he said there was no occasion to specify in writing the length of the mortgage in years, but the best way would be to provide that receipt of the money shall redeem the mortgage.

b. There are objections to not stating the length of the term of years, because if in the course of the next few years I am given a provincial appointment, I shall require this sum, and consequently the length of the mortgage *must* be expressed.

a. Ah, then I would see him about that. How long should you think it will probably be before you get a provincial appointment?

b. I should *think* about five or six years.

a. I fancy if I consulted him about inserting five or six years he would be pretty certain to agree.

b. Then there are the Title Deeds; have you seen them?

a. I have.

b. How many stamped Deeds are there and how many unstamped?

a. Two stamped and two unstamped.

b. Very well, will you go back and talk the matter over with him, and if he's willing to deal at that figure and also to say for five or six years in writing, we will settle the matter.

a. When the matter has been finally arranged, you will want to go and look at the land?

b. Well it's this way: if you will agree to give first-rate security guaranteeing that the transaction is perfectly in order, why then I needn't view the land first.

a. The transaction is perfectly in order, for that I can produce first-rate security.

b. In that case then I will take your word for it, and after we have completed all the arrangements I will go to the place with him and have a look at it.

No. 9 *Servant.*—If you please, Sir, Mr. Hsü, the Manager of the Ta Hêng piece goods shop, has come and says he wishes to see you on business.

   a. Go and ask him to come in; show him into the drawing-room.

   Servant.—Yes, Sir......My master begs you will step into the drawing-room, Sir.

   a. Well, Mr. Hsü, how do you come to be disengaged like this?

   b. I came to see if I could see you and have a few words with you.

   a. Yes; won't you sit down?

   b. After you, Sir. You haven't been out, have you, Sir, these few days?

   a. No I have not, because I haven't been very well.

   b. But you are all right now, I hope.

   a. Yes, quite.

   b. I came to borrow some money from you, Sir.

   a. How much do you want?

   b. Not less than Tls. 500, it would have to be.

   a. Are you getting some more great bargains?

   b. No, Sir, it is a shop that I am buying the goodwill of.

   a. What sort of shop?

   b. A cash bank.

   a. How many frontages has it?

   b. Two.

   a. Whereabouts is it?

   b. In the Chinese city here,—west end of Pa Pao Street.

   a. Whose was it before?

   b. It belonged to a southern man before.

   a. Was it closed before the goodwill was sold, or how?

   b. No, it isn't closed, but the proprietor is an Expectant District Magistrate who has lately been selected for a post, and as he must go off on service and has no brothers or relations to look after the business, he is obliged to sell the goodwill.

   a. And what did you pay for it?

   b. The price was 1,000 taels.

   a. Does that include fittings as well?

   b. Yes, fittings and all are included.

a. Have you paid over the amount?

b. Yes.

a. Then what you want now is money for the business?

b. Exactly. I have 500 taels in hand at present, but that's not enough for my requirements, and I must have 500 more.

a. Ah! well I will lend you 500 taels.

b. I am very much obliged to you; and you will name your own figure for what the rate of interest is to be.

NOTE.—Notice *Tsü'-ch'ing*, written incorrectly here and in No. 24 *Tsü'-hsiang*.

a. What are you talking of? How can you mention such a thing as interest between such friends as ourselves because you require this small sum; if you pay interest I won't lend it you!

b. Well, I will do as you wish.

a. Thank you; and what was the name of this shop?

b. Its name *was* Tê Ho.

a. After taking it over, do you change the name?

b. Yes.

a. What do you mean to change it to?

b. I was going to make it Su Ch'êng; what do you think of it?

a. A very good one. Are you acquainted with cash-banking business?

b. No, I don't understand about it, but my nephew has learnt cash-banking, and I mean to set him up in this shop to carry on the business.

a. Capital! And when do you intend to start the concern?

b. It won't be before early next month.

a. When you do I shall come and offer my good wishes.

b. You are too good! But I must be going back.

a. Why should you hurry; sit down again for a while.

b. No, I can't, for I've work to do in the shop.

a. Well, I will send the money to your shop to-morrow evening.

b. Yes, yes.

a. Then you are off home now?

b. Yes, pray go indoors again.

No. 10 *Servant.*—If you please, Sir, Liu, the carpenter, is here and would like to see you.

    a. Tell him to come in.

    Servant.—Mr. Liu, my master bids you come in.

    b. Are you quite well, Sir?

    a. Quite well; are you?

    b. Quite well, thank you, Sir.

    a. How is it I haven't seen you at all for some time?

    b. I've been home on a visit.

    a. On what business?

    b. I went home to get in the harvest.

    a. And what sort of a harvest is it in your part of the world?

    b. Very near a full crop.

    a. How much land do you farm?

    b. I farm something over a *ch'ing* of land.

    a. How many piculs of grain was your yield this year?

    b. A hundred piculs.

    a. Now that you've come back, have you undertaken any works?

    b. Not yet. I came to see you to-day because there's a job I want to undertake, but I've no one to recommend me, and so I thought I would beg you to give me a recommendation.

    a. Where is the place?

    b. Why, you know Mr. Chiang, in the Western city, is going to build a house, and I should like to undertake the job.

    a. I've been told Mr. Chiang has had a number of people to look at it, but I don't know if anyone has decided to do the work.

    b. Quite right, Sir. I hear three men have been shown it; two of them wanted 8,000 taels, and one 7,500, which Mr. Chiang wasn't willing to give, so the matter is still open.

    a. Very well, if you take the contract, of course you must offer better terms than the others.

    b. Of course; if I took the contract I would not only do the work several hundred taels cheaper, but the workmanship would certainly be substantial,—no scamping whatever.

    a. Well, look here, I can easily *mention* you, but there's one thing, and that is, that I'm told Mr. Chiang's intention is, after he has finally decided, and signs the Agreement, to pay down half the amount at once, and to wait until the work is done before giving the other half,—now can you find that amount in the meantime?

b. Yes, I know half the sum will be received in the first instance, and I find on reckoning up that I can find the amount, because I've a friend who keeps a brickkiln, and he will willingly let me have bricks and tiles on credit till the works are finished. Besides that, my wife's younger brother keeps a timber-yard with a very large stock of timber which I may use as I like, also on credit. The half of the money, which I should receive, would only be to provide stone and lime and pay all the workmen's wages. I reckon I shan't be far out.

a. Very good then, to-morrow I will go and see Mr. Chiang and tell him about you.

b. If you will, Sir, I shall be very much obliged to you. When shall I come and hear from you, Sir?

a. Come the day after to-morrow and hear my message.

b. Yes, Sir; then I'll be going back now.

a. Very good.

No. 11 *a.* When did you come?

b. I came once before, and hearing you weren't in I went off somewhere else again, and when I came back just now, they told me you hadn't returned yet, so I just waited here until you did.

a. Then I've kept you waiting.

b. Oh, don't mention it. Where is it you've been to?

a. I've been out of the city to have a look at the crops on the country.

b. The present crop is well forward, I suppose.

a. Yes, it is.

b. This autumn's harvest promises well then?

a. From what one can see at present, this year's harvest will certainly be a fine one.

b. Did you watch the farm-labourers at work?

a. Yes; when I went they were all hoeing away, but at noon they all went home for their midday meal, so I found a big tree, and took it easy under its shade for a while, watched the drovers and shepherds a bit, and then, when I had got cool enough, I strolled back home.

b. Upon my word you know how to enjoy yourself.

a. Enjoy myself! It is simply this, that it's very dull sitting indoors, and if I take a siesta, I'm uncomfortable when I wake, so the best thing to do is to go out for a stroll.

b. Quite a constitutional exercise, really!

a. Nonsense!......Did you call to-day because you had something to speak to me about?

b. Yes, I did; I'm in a difficulty and I want you to help me out of it.

a. What is it?

b. Well it is this,—my brother wants all of a sudden to set up a separate establishment.

a. Why, have not you and your brother always been very good friends? What has made him suddenly take up this notion?

b. I really don't know what the reason is. I think most likely he has been prompted to it by other people, or he wouldn't have wanted to set up for himself.

a. Amongst us relations and friends it is impossible that anyone would cause an estrangement between you and your brother.

b. Of course none of our relatives and friends could have urged him to set up for himself, but I know he has made some new friends lately, and not particularly desirable ones, and I think it must be they who have egged him on.

a. Then how do you want me to act?

b. I came because you have always got on well with my brother, and I thought I would ask you to bring him into your house one of these days and remonstrate with him,—the thing is to succeed in preventing him.

a. Oh, there would be no difficulty about getting him in and remonstrating with him, but the thing is *this*, although we *have* generally got on well together, unfortunately your brother has such a queer temper that I can't answer for his listening to me. What is to be done if he won't?

b. If he positively *will* not listen to advice, why there is no help for it, and he must have his own way and set up for himself.

a. And supposing he insists on doing so, what division do you propose to make?

b. Well, our house-property consists of two dwelling-houses and two shop-premises. The Title Deeds of the dwelling-house in the Western city, and the shop-premises in the Chinese city, are both held as securities elsewhere, but the Deeds of the house we are living in and of our shop, are not. I will give him these two properties, and besides, he can take away what he desires of the household effects and movables,—I shan't make any objection whatever.

a. Well, that is exceedingly fair; none of your friends and relations can possibly have any criticism to pass upon you.

No. 12 *a.* How is it I haven't seen you at all for some time?

b. I went home for the harvest.

a. And what sort of a harvest is it this year?

b. Well, pretty fair.

a. How much land do you farm?

b. Oh, I haven't much, just over one *ch'ing*.

a. How many piculs of grain was your yield this year?

b. Over 100.

a. That's more than last year then.

b. Yes, last year it was just 60, so the yield is over 40 piculs more this year.

a. You were away a good long time, weren't you?

b. Why yes, two months and more.

a. What, all that time at home!

b. I had a lawsuit, and I sold some land.

a. With whom did you have your suit?

b It was with a neighbour of ours.

a. What was it about?

b. Well, I have some acres of lowlying land, which are under water every summer during the heavy rains, and so I haven't farmed them for the last few years, but just let them lie fallow. Now this land of mine abuts on the land of a man called Yü, and, as I said, I haven't cultivated it for the last few years, and bit by bit several *mou* of it have been encroached on by him. Being always away, I didn't know of it until this time when I went back and heard from an old farm-hand of ours. Then I went to the place and looked for myself, and sure enough he had appropriated my land. Well, I went to see this man Yü, and asked him about the matter. He denied it altogether. So then I went to the Yamên and lodged a complaint against him, and when the Magistrate had gone into the case, he ordered him to restore me the land he had appropriated, and then I sold it.

a. Ah! Now do you keep the grain you get in every year for your own consumption, or do you sell it?

b. We don't keep it all,—say some 30 or 40 piculs,—the rest we sell.

a. And where do you sell it?

b. A few *li* from where we live there's a large market-town with a market every five days, and we load beasts with the grain and send it to be sold there.

a. And when it is at this place, do you sell it at a corn-dealer's, or to individual buyers in the market?

b. To the latter as a rule.

a. Do you sell it them yourself?

b. No, it is sold by the salesmen.

a. Are they licensed by the Government?

b. Yes, they must all have a License given by Government before they can be salesmen.

a. And the measures they use, are they all fixed by the Government too?

b. Yes, they are.

a. Then where does the salesman's profit come from?

b. He gets his Salesman's Fee.

a. Does the salesman fix the market-price?

b. Oh no.

a. Who does?

b. No one does. Speaking broadly it is like this: if on a particular day there is much grain brought, the market-rate naturally drops, if there's *not* much, it naturally rises. The thing is a matter of course, a market-rate isn't decided beforehand by anybody.

a. Yes, I see now.

No. 13   *a.* I came to ask you about something.

b. What is it?

a. You have an orchard, haven't you, in the Western Hills?

b. Yes, I have one.

a. What sized one is it?

b. Over 50 *mou*.

a. Do you gather the fruit every year and sell it yourself, or do you make over the trees to some other person on contract?

b. Some years ago I gathered and sold the fruit myself; the last few years I have made it over on contract.

a. To whom?

b. To a General Dealer's called Shun I, at Hai Tien.

a. Well, the reason I came to see you to-day is that a friend of mine has opened a Dried Fruit Shop in the Western City, and he has several times asked me if I would arrange this matter of a Fruit contract for him, so knowing you had an orchard, I came to ask you. Should you be willing to make over the trees to him next year on a contract, I would bring you together.

b. I have no objection to it if he wishes for one.

a. He also told me to inquire as to what the conditions of the contract would be.

b. Then your friend is not in the business?

a. You are right; he *has* not been before. This is his first venture in that line.

b. Well, the conditions of a Fruit contract are not many. When the fruit is ripe, I go with him to look at the orchard, and afterwards we come to an agreement as to the price of the contract, and after we have settled that, and the money is paid, the fruit for the year is his.

a. And after the contract is concluded, there has to be a watcher, hasn't there?

b. Of course; you must get a man to be in the orchard day and night watching.

a. Do you and I get this watcher for him, or does he do that himself?

b. Just as he likes; if he asks us to get him, why we can; if he prefers to get a man himself, there's no difficulty.

a. Isn't the watcher likely to steal the fruit and sell it?

b. Well, it is like this; in case it's a man that I get, I have to give a guarantee of course, and if there is any stealing and selling of fruit, then I am solely responsible.

a. And the watcher is given his monthly wages and nothing else?

b. Just his wages. Only the contractor for the fruit has to buy the matting, planks, ropes, poles, etc. for putting up a matshed for him, but when the matshed is taken down he can take them all back again.

a. And what ought to be done with any fruit that may drop from the tree?

b. Well, if it is not much and falls in the ordinary way, it is put on the ground, and the contractor is told of it any time that he goes there, but if by any chance there should happen to be a gale or a hailstorm, and the windfall should be very large, the watcher must at once go and inform the contractor, so that he can go and collect it.

a. Yes; well I will return and let my friend know all you have told me, and if he has any message I will come and see you again.

b. Very good.

No. 14 *a.* Liu Ts'ai!

b. Sir!

a. The clock in the study won't go. Go presently to the Hsiang Shêng Watchmakers' shop, and ask Mr. Hsü, the Manager, to come round and repair it.

b. Yes, Sir.

* * * * *

b. Excuse my troubling you, gentlemen!

c. Ah, it's you,—please to take a seat.

b. My master has sent me to ask Mr. Hsü, the manager, to go to his place and repair a clock of his.

c. Whose house are you in?

b. Mr. Fu's.

c. Of Mien hua Lane?

b. That's it.

c. May I ask your name?

b. Mine is Liu; what is yours, please?

c. Hsü.

b. Ah, you are Mr. Hsü, the manager, then! I hope you will befriend me now and then.

c. And the same with yourself. Is Mr. Chu still the butler at your place?

b. No, they have changed.

c. Who have they taken on?

b. It's a Mr. Fan.

c. How was that then; did Mr. Chu give up his place?

b. That's it, he left.

c. What was the reason of that?

b. On account of his health.

c. What was his complaint?

b. Well, he never *was* strong, and then he smoked opium. This year he suddenly left it off, but before he had given it up altogether he fell ill, and got worse and worse every day until at last it became a downright consumption, and he wasn't able to do anything, so he left his situation and went home to try and get cured.

c. Ah! And can you tell me whether it is only to repair a clock, or are there watches to repair too.

b. Master said, to mend a clock, but he didn't mention any watches to be repaired. All the same, if you take my advice, you'll take your watch-mending things along with you, there *might* possibly be one to repair perhaps.

c. Very well, then let us be going.

*　　　*　　　*　　　*　　　*

b. Please to take a seat in the study, Mr. Manager, while I go in and tell Master.

c. Certainly.

a. How do you do Mr. Hsü?

c. Quite well, thank you; and you, Mr. Fu, how have you been?

a. Thank you, quite well. How is business?

c. Well, pretty fair, I'm much obliged to you.

a. Are you working at night now?

c. Yes, Sir, we are.

a. And how many assistants have you in your shop now?

c. Just at present, four.

a. And how many apprentices?

c. Two apprentices.

a. All advanced enough to work at the table?

c. One is, but the others are new-comers and can't yet.

a. And are you working every day in the shop?

c. No, I can't be working in the shop all the time; mostly I'm out attending to business.

a. What amount of money does the work you do at present every month represent?

c. Just now in a month,—Well, it's about 400 *tiaos* worth or so.

a. More than 400 *tiaos* worth! Why that's a good deal.

c. Pretty fair, that is all; but very different from what it used to be.

a. How much then used you to do in a month formerly?

c. In former days we did quite 700 *tiaos* worth.

a. Really, so much as that!

c. Yes, at that time fully as much as that.

a. Well, I sent for you to-day to have a look at this clock and see what is the reason it won't go.

c. I will look and see. The chain is broken.

a. It will have to be replaced by a new one then, won't it?

c. No, there's no need for that; I will take the chain away to the shop and rejoin it, and bring it back afterwards and put it in.

a. Ah, that will be better. Will you have some tea?

c. After you, Sir.

a. Tell me, in your business how many years are you learning?

c. We are six years learning our business.

a. Do you have to sign a written Agreement?

c. Yes, we do.

a. And does an apprentice sign his Agreement as soon as ever he begins to work at the table?

c. No, Sir, he must be tried for a year first, and if he is a good apprentice, *then* he signs an Agreement.

a. And after he has finished serving his apprenticeship, does he remain and practice his trade in the same shop, or does he then go elsewhere to do so?

c. He can do as he like about that; if he wishes to remain working in the same shop, his wages are paid him at the same rate as an Assistant; if he doesn't, and wants to go elsewhere as an Assistant, he can.

a. I see, yes. Oh, and have you bought me the Alarum I asked you to get me last time?

c. Yes. I made inquiries for you at all the shops in the city here, and there were none, but a man in our trade has gone to Tientsin lately, and I have asked him to try and find one at the Foreign stores there, and if there is one, I will bring it for you on his return.

a. I'm really very much obliged to you.

c. Not at all. And now I must be going back. Good-day to **you,** Sir.

PART II   THE GUIDÉ TO KUAN-HUA.   31

    a. You are off home again then; much obliged to you for your trouble in coming.
    c. Thank you, thank you!

No. 15 *a*. Have you come from your house, Sir?
    b. Yes.
    a. How is it I haven't seen you these last few days?
    b. I've been away shooting.
    a. With whom?
    b. With a neighbour of ours.
    a. Where did you go to shoot?
    b. To the Eastern Hills.
    a. When did you come back?
    b. Last night.
    a. What sort of bag did you make?
    b. We shot some pheasants and hares, and also a wild boar.
    a. Why then, you had good shooting this time.
    b. Yes, the shooting was good enough, but still we had a pretty hard time of it.
    a. In what way?
    b. Well, we were each of us riding our own horse, and when we got to within a mile or two of the Eastern Hills, there was a market-town, so we found an inn in the place, where we put up. Next day, after we had finished our meal, we baited our two horses at the inn, and then shouldered our guns and strolled off to the hills. When we got there we only shot some pheasants and hares at first, but towards sundown a wild boar suddenly broke cover. We both fired and killed him. Where we were, there was nobody to be hired to carry the beast on a pole, so we dragged him back to the inn, and when we had reached it, we slung him on to one of the horses, and we ourselves took it in turns to ride the other. When we got home we were so tired we couldn't move. Pretty hard work, wasn't it?
    a. Well, you had hard work, but still you had some shooting. Now a connection of ours went out shooting some days ago, and not only shot nothing, but he lost his horse.
    b. How did he come to lose his horse, out shooting?
    a. Well, he told me he rode a horse to the Northern Hills to shoot, and tied it up to a tree at the foot of the hill, while he shouldered his gun and went up it in search of game. He searched for a long time but not a single thing could he see, so

down he came, and when he got to the bottom and looked, his horse was gone. Just then it suddenly began to snow, and he searched for a time, snowing as it was, all about the place, but it was nowhere to be seen. Well, by this time it had got dark, so he found a ruined temple, and there he made shift to spend the night. Next morning he felt very unwell, but there was no help for it, and he managed to get as far as the Yamên and reported the thing to the authorities. The official there asked him about the way he lost his horse, and then said, "I will send a man to make a thorough search for your horse, and if he has been stolen by any of the people of the place, he is sure to be found sooner or later; but if he's been stolen by some passer-by, then he *won't* be recovered; meantime you had better go home." So he hired a donkey and came back, and after reaching home he grew worse and hasn't recovered yet. *Wasn't* that wretched luck?

No. 16 *a.* Haven't you heard that our friend Feng Tzŭ-yüan is dead?
    b. No I've not; when did he die?
    a. I was told this morning he died last night.
    b. Do you know from what illness?
    a. I'm told it wasn't a natural death.
    b. How did it happen?
    a. It is said he took opium.
    b. What did he do that for?
    a. The story I've heard is this. A friend of his in the country came to Peking last year with several thousand taels, which he gave into his care, and then went home. Well, this year he came up to town again and asked for this money, whereupon Tzŭ-yüan denied having got it. So the man went to the Yamên and entered a charge against him. When Tzŭ-yüan was summoned to the Yamên and interrogated, he denied the whole story, and said, "If I had kept his money, there must have been some evidence of it in writing; now he has none whatever. It is an attempt to extort money from me on his part." The Magistrate then asked this man whether or no he had any written evidence. "No," he said, "we were on such good terms that none was drawn up at the time." "Well," said the Magistrate, "since there is no evidence in writing,—merely your verbal statement,—I can do nothing for you in the matter," and so the parties left the Court. The other man was so angry at this that he went home and, not very many days after, hanged himself. On the District Magistrate coming to hold the inquest, they shook out from the dead man's leggings a Dying Declaration, which was an accusation of Tzŭ-yüan; and when Tzŭ-yüan heard of the scandal this had caused, he got alarmed and took opium.

b. What you mention reminds me that this Spring I heard vaguely of his having gone to law with some one; I suspect it was about this.

a. Probably it was that.

b. There is something else too which very likely you don't know of. Before we were acquainted with him he had already been guilty of a piece of rascality.

a. What was that?

b. Why, you know he used to keep a cash-bank.

a. Certainly, he did.

b. During that time a friend of his, from one of the provinces, lived by his leave in these premises, where he afterwards was taken very ill, and before his death he said to him, "In that box there are more than a thousand taels. You and I have been friends all this time, and I hope after my death you will send all my money and things back to my family for me." He promised to do so at the time. However, after the man's death, he changed his mind about it, and only sent back the man's effects to his family, but secreted these thousand and odd taels, and when the man's family afterwards wrote and asked him whether the deceased had left any money, he wrote back and said he had not. Later on *he* fell ill, and while he was at home nursing himself, one of his assistants in the shop bolted with several hundred taels, and on his recovery he closed his business.

a. From whom did you hear that?

b. I heard it from an apprentice who had learnt his trade in his bank.

a. Well, having committed such a rascally thing as he had previously done, he should have reformed instead of committing another one, and now he has brought his own death on himself.

b. But don't you know, all these unscrupulous people are generally like that: as soon as they see money, they immediately throw all thoughts of retribution to the winds. The fact is, that his death by taking opium simply serves him right.

No. 17 *a.* What did that man Ma come in just now to see you about?

b. He said he wanted to take something out of pawn, and asked me to lend him a few dozen *tiao*, and besides that he asked me if I could find him a place in the service of some official.

a. And did you promise to do so?

b. Yes, I did. I told him this,—I said, "I've no ready money by me just now; wait until I go and borrow some for you, and if I succeed in getting it, you take it, and if I can't, then you had better find some other means. With regard to getting you a place with an official, I will certainly recommend you as soon as one offers."

a. If you will take my advice, you won't interest yourself for him about either of these things.

b. What?

a. He certainly won't pay you back if you borrow money for him.

b. How do you know that?

a. I know he won't repay you in the future money you lend him now, because before he hasn't paid other people money he has borrowed from them.

b. He is hardly likely to fail to pay these few dozen *tiao*, I think.

a. He wouldn't pay a few *tiao*, let alone a few dozen. And besides, he doesn't really borrow this money to take a thing out of pawn with.

b. What *is* it for then if it's not for that?

a. It's to gamble with.

b. What, does he gamble?

a. He's very fond of it indeed, he is in gambling-houses all day long.

b. Who are there at his home?

a. His mother is dead long ago, but his father is still living.

b. Has he no brothers and sisters?

a. He has no brothers older or younger than himself, he has one elder sister, who married long ago.

b. Hasn't he married yet?

a. No, not yet.

b. What age is his father?

a. He must be over seventy now.

b. What is he?

a. He's a carpenter by trade. He used to keep a small timber yard, which he gave up afterwards; now, he depends altogether on working for other people to make enough money to get along with.

b. And this man himself, what can he do?

a. He can't do anything whatever, except spend money.

b. Has he learnt no trade then?

a. Yes, he learnt for a time.

b. What did he learn?

a. He was in a druggist's store learning the business, but after he had been there a month the manager discharged him.

b. What for?

a. For being gluttonous and lazy, and for not keeping the rules of the establishment.

b. Well, and afterwards did he do nothing else?

a. Yes, afterwards he went for a time into service with an official?

b. What official?

a. Someone holding a provincial appointment some years ago, who came to Peking for Audience and stayed in a Club in the Chinese city, to whom he was recommended as a servant. This gentleman used to send him out every day to buy all sorts of curios and objects of art, and he made no end of money; in two months he had made a good many hundred taels. The gentleman found out this failing of his afterwards and dismissed him. Now, I suppose, these hundreds of taels are all spent, and so he comes to you to borrow money for him, but if you take my advice, you will neither borrow money nor find a place for him. If you do the one, he won't pay you, and if you do the other, he will certainly do you no credit; far better make up your mind to do nothing for him.

b. Well, from what you say, he will come to grief when his father dies.

a. I prophesied it of him long ago, that after his father's death he was certain to take to begging.

b. Well, what reply am I to give him about these two applications of his to me?

a. Just tell him that you are not able to borrow the money, and that there's no situation to be had.

b. Very well, I will speak to him as you say, and prevent him from expecting them.

No. 18 *a.* Li Ch'i!

b. Sir?

a. Take this set of volumes to the Pao Wên T'ang, the booksellers in the Liu Li Ch'ang, and tell Mr. Yü, the manager, to have it fitted in boards; and also give him this list, and tell him to take one set of volumes of each of the works mentioned in it, and to give them you for the time to bring back for me to look at.

b. Yes, Sir; if you have nothing else for me I could go at once, then?

a. I've nothing else, you had better go now.

* * * * *

b. Excuse my troubling you, gentlemen; is Mr. Yü, the manager, in the shop?

c. Yes; please come in and take a seat.

b. Excuse me, Mr. Yü, for troubling you.

d. Ah! Mr. Li, are you come from your place?

b. Yes, I am.

d. Have you come on business?

b. Why yes; my master told me to bring this set of volumes and get you to fit it in boards: and then, you see this list here, I was to tell you to take one set of volumes from each of the works mentioned in it and give them me to take back for the time for him to look at.

d. Then I'll just put this set of volumes into boards. We have two of the books in this list in the shop; all the others I must go elsewhere to get.

b. Very well, if you'll give me the two you have now in the shop first to take back and go and procure all the rest elsewhere, I will come back again here in a few days and fetch them, eh?

d. There's no occasion, I think, for you to come here and fetch them; in a few days, if I can procure them, I will bring them myself to your place.

b. Yes, that will be better still.

d. Here are these two sets wrapped up for you.

b. Well, I will say good-bye to you.

d. Good-day.

* * * * *

b. Please, Sir, I gave Mr. Yü that set of volumes and told him to fit them in boards,—and they're only got two of the books you wanted in the shop, and they have given me two sets from them to bring back for you to see, and the rest Mr. Yü must go elsewhere for, and in a few days, if he can procure them, he will bring them himself.

a. Very good; put those two sets in the bookshelves for the present.

  * * * * *

d. Excuse my troubling you, Mr. Li.

b. Ah, Mr. Yü, have you just come into the city?

d. Yes, I've just come in.

b. What are these books you've brought?

d. They are those books your master ordered to be got the other day, which I have got and brought here.

b. Master has gone to Tientsin.

d. When did he go?

b. He started yesterday morning.

d. Has he gone on duty?

b. No, on private business of his own.

d. How many days will he be away?

b. He'll have to be ten days, including the journey there and back.

d. Then how about these books I've brought?

b. Master left word to say you were to leave the books here for the present, if you brought them.

d. Well, you see, here are six sets of volumes. There were eight books mentioned in the original list, you brought back two sets the other day, and to-day I've brought one set from each book,—eight sets of books brought altogether, first and last. And here is the list too which I should be obliged by your giving to your master; it has the cost of all these books written on it.

b. Yes; and the set to be fitted in boards, have you finished them?

d. They are finished; I forget to bring them with me to-day, I'll bring them some other day when I come again, eh?

b. Very well.

d. When do you think I'd better come?

b. Well, I should think master won't come back before the end of the month. I'll tell you what, when he's back, I'll come out of the city for you, eh?

d. Oh there is no occasion to put you to the trouble. At the end of this month or the beginning of next, I shall be coming into the city on other business, and I can come here on my way and inquire.

b. Yes, *that* would do.

d. Then I will wish you good-day.

b. Good-day to you.

d. We shall meet again soon.

No. 19 *a.* How is it you've been not at home every time I've come to see you; what has kept you so busy?

b. I have been arranging a dispute.

a. And what was the dispute you have been arranging? Is it anything I may be told or not?

b. Oh, there's nothing in it that mustn't be told. A friend of a relative of mine has been litigating with somebody, and my relative asked me to come forward and reconcile them.

a. Some question of accounts?

b. No, about a purchase of some goods.

a. How did that come to lead to litigation?

b. Well, it was this. My relative's friend is named Shên, and keeps a large Foreign Goods store in Pao Ting Fu called Hsin I. He came here this summer, and stayed at the Fu Shêng Inn, in the eastern suburbs, and ordered sixty bales of piece goods at the T'ai Ho Foreign Goods warehouse in Main East Street here. It was stated in writing in the Note of Contract of Sale that delivery of the goods was to be made in two months. When the time came last month, Mr. Shên went to T'ai Ho, and asked if the goods had arrived: "No," they said, "not yet." So Mr. Shên waited some days longer and then went and inquired again,—still the goods had not come. Well, a few days ago Mr. Shên went to a warehouse in the west end of the suburb on other business, and there he heard that a dealer had lately bought sixty bales of piece goods from the T'ai Ho Firm through a broker called Wang, and that the price paid by this dealer was higher than the one agreed upon by himself, Shên, but that the money had not been paid yet, nor the goods taken delivery of. It struck Mr. Shên that these were no doubt the sixty bales he had bargained for, and that T'ai Ho now wanted to make a larger profit by reselling them to another man, and he was very angry indeed. So the other afternoon he want to T'ai Ho and asked them about it, and they denied that there was anything of the sort; but afterwards, on his mentioning Wang, the broker, by name, they were obliged to admit it. But, they said, next month there were sixty more bales of piece goods coming, and they told him to wait for these. Mr. Shên wouldn't wait,—he said he *would* have the sixty bales they had got now. T'ai Ho refused to give them him; if he really could not wait for those other sixty bales, they said, the only course was to return the original Deposit, burn the Note of Contract of Sale, and consider the whole transaction cancelled. No, Mr. Shên wouldn't agree. It wouldn't do to return the Deposit merely, they must also undertake to make good the profit made. But T'ai Ho positively refused to admit their liability to do this. So Mr. Shên drew up a formal charge, to which he appended the Note of Contract of Sale, and brought his case against the T'ai Ho Firm in the District Magistracy. The case came on before the Court the day before yesterday, and the Magistrate, after hearing a general statement of their case from both parties, directed them to go out of Court and get someone, before going farther, to try and effect an arrangement. If none was possible, further pleas to be put in, and another hearing to be held. So my relative applied to me to assist him in coming forward and reconciling them, which we only finally managed to do yesterday evening.

a. And how?

b. We did it in this way; we *did* make T'ai Ho give Mr. Shên the sixty bales actually in their hands first of all, and they are to tell the other dealer to wait till the other lot of sixty bales arrives next month, and he will be given those. Well, all parties have agreed to this. Yesterday evening delivery of the goods was made, the money was paid down, and to-morrow Mr. Shên is to present a Declaration of Reconciliation at the District Magistrate's and terminate the matter.

No. 20 *a.* Have you come from the shop?

b. No, I'm just back from the T'ien Shêng Pawnbrokers', where I've been making tenders.

a. Have you dined?

b. Yes, I've had my dinner.

a. If you've not, I can tell the cook to get you something to eat at once.

b. No, really I've had dinner; I had it away from home with a friend of mine.

a. Oh, very well. Were there many things to-day at T'ien Shêng's?

b. Not many curios and works of art, but a lot of clothing, and copper and tin ware.

a. What did you tender for?

b. For two watches, nothing else.

a. I think tendering seldom pays, one nearly always loses.

b. Well *that* depends on one's luck. If a lucky man goes and makes tenders, he is sure to come across great bargains; when he tenders, the pawnbroker lets him have things dirt cheap, so that he is able to make a heap of money. If an unlucky man makes a tender for a thing, he's let in at once,—the pawnshop having been let in, when it was pledged, he is too, when he tenders for it, and not only doesn't make money, but actually loses a lot by it.

a. It's perfectly true, what you say. Some years ago our shop made a number of tenders and lost money in every case, so now, no matter what pawnbrokers we are asked by, we never go and tender.

b. But I tell you, last year there was an instance of a man making a good thing by tendering. He was a distant connection of ours, and in the tenth moon last year he was invited to tender by the Hêng Shun pawnbroker's in the Western City. He bid for a copper watch, four taels, and the pawnbrokers sold it him. When he got home and examined it, blessed if it wasn't a *gold* watch, and he polished it up properly and sold it for more than forty taels,—a thousand per cent profit. Now that was coming across a good bargain, and a paying one too.

No. 21 *a.* Oh, I've just been to your hotel for you, but the assistants said you had gone to the west end, so I came to try and *meet* you on your way back, and I have done so by a lucky chance. How came you to go to the west end so early?

b. Why, a steamer came in this morning, and the people in our hotel had hired a wheel-barrow for a visitor, to carry his baggage; the barrowman carried two boxes wrong, and the visitor was angry about it, so the shopmen, not knowing what to do, sent somebody to my house for me. I was just up, and when I heard of this I made haste and washed my face and went off to the hotel and saw the visitor. He told me in reply to my question, that his name was Ch'ên, and he was a Fuhkien man, in the Kiangsu public service. He was now on his way to Peking. His steamer arrived this morning, and he came ashore and stopped at our hotel, where he told our people to hire two wheel-barrows for him. He ordered his servant to go with these to the steamer and bring off his baggage, but when it was brought to the hotel, and he looked at it, two red leather trunks were missing, and besides this, amongst the luggage there were two white leather trunks, that weren't his, with the three words "Hsü Tzŭ-Ch'in" written on them. Then he asked his two servants how it was that two boxes had been taken wrong. It wasn't their fault, they said, they had both been on board getting together the small odds and ends; the two wheel-barrow men came on board themselves and removed the boxes, and that was why they had been taken wrong. So the visitor told our people to tell the wheel-barrow men to go at once and recover his two red leather trunks. They went and searched for some time, but couldn't find them, and as he was thoroughly angry, and insisted on getting his boxes, our people got rather bothered and sent off in a hurry for me.

a. And you have recovered your visitor's boxes?

b. Yes, I have now found this Mr. Hsü. Mr. Ch'ên's two red leather trunks are with *him*, and I'm now going back to the hotel to hire a wheel-barrow first to wheel off Mr. Hsü's two white trunks, and bring back the two red ones instead.

a. How did you discover this Mr. Hsü?

b. I inquired at all the hotels in our street first, and there being no such person there, I went westwards and asked at each hotel, one after another. When I reached the Yung Li they told me that a visitor of the name of Hsü had just arrived, so I went into his room, and asked him his style, which he told me was Tzŭ-ch'in. Then I told him about the luggage that had been mis-sent. "Oh," he said, "my luggage has just been brought,— I haven't counted it over yet. Just let me go over it and make sure." When he had done so, he said, "Two of the trunks are wrong. Two white leather trunks of my own are missing, and there are two red ones too many." As what he said just corresponded, I said to him, "I'll send a wheel-barrow in a minute to bring your boxes, and you can give them these two red trunks to take back," and then I came away. And what pressing business have you on hand, that you are hurrying off for me so early?

a. Why, we have rather a pressing call upon us to-day and want to apply to you to let us have temporary accommodation for a few hundred dollars.

b. I can; come with me to the hotel and fetch them.

No. 22 *a*. Is it true, what I hear, that your relative Wang Tzŭ-ch'üan has been denounced?

b. Yes, it is.

a. Do you know on what charge?

b. Well, during last year I heard he was going to be denounced, but without much believing it. Now, however, he has actually been denounced. A few days ago I saw Tzŭ-ch'üan's eldest brother, and according to him, he has been disgraced on account of two cases. One of these was that, in the autumn of the year before last there was a cash-bank robbery in the District City, and several hundred taels plunder were carried off, and not a single one of the thieves was caught. Then the Governor denounced him, took away his button, and gave him so many months time to remain at his post, telling him to capture the thieves as quickly as possible. When the limit of time expired, he still hadn't caught a single thief. Well, they gave him several extensions of time, right up to last winter, but the gang were *never* caught at all. This spring, as luck would have it, a man in the District City went into someone's house in the middle of the night and murdered two persons, the murderer making his escape. So when there was this further case of "flight after after murder," the Governor denounced him to the Throne for dismissal.

a. Then he has already left his post?

b. Yes, he is living in the provincial capital.

a. What sort of a fortune has he made?

b. Fortune! he hasn't a penny in the world.

a. Then why should he remain living in the provincial capital, if he's in such straitened circumstances?

b. Oh, he would like to come back, but he can't do so all at once.

a. Why not? Can't find money for travelling expenses?

b. No, it isn't that. After cashiering him, the Governor sent a Deputy to his Yamên, to examine the Treasury, and it was found that there was a deficit in his Land Tax receipts of over 4,000 taels. When the Deputy asked how he came to have such a deficit as that, he confessed that he had misappropriated the money; and so, on the Deputy's reporting this to the Governor, he sent and had the things in his residence sealed up, and transferred Wang Tzŭ-ch'üan himself to the provincial capital, giving him two months time in which to refund the amount of his deficit to Government on the Land Tax account, and if he didn't refund within the limit of time, he would apply for Imperial sanction to seize his house in Peking. So Wang, in his extremity, sent one of his domestics with a letter to Peking to see his brother, to tell him to find some way or other of raising 5,000 taels for him at once, and to give them to the man to bring back. His brother was in a great state on reading this letter, and came to me, and asked me to sell his shop-premises in the Chinese city, which I did at once, fortunately enough I must say, for 5,000 taels, and his brother gave the amount to the domestic, that had come, to take back.

a. And how about the things in his residence, that were put under seal, if he refunds this deficit in full?

b. Oh, after he has refunded the money, of course his Chiefs will send some officer to his place to remove the seals, and give him back his things again; and *then* he can come back.

No. 23 *a.* Tell me, why has your friend Ch'ien Fu-ch'ên's pawnshop commenced winding up its pawnbroking business?

b. He's about to close; the business doesn't pay.

a. Why, isn't it said that line of business is a capital one? How comes it not to pay?

b. Ah, you judge by appearances only. When he first started pawnbroking it wasn't with his own money only. He had a relation in the public service, who lent him more than 10,000 taels to use free and without interest,—he himself having only a few thousand,—and with this he started. The business for some years was very good indeed, and his profits were pretty large. But the year before last his relation was appointed to a prefecture, and wanted his 10,000 taels back. However, in spite of this money being withdrawn, his business might have struggled along, when he suddenly took a whim into his head to go into the opium trade. He began by only buying a chest or two for sale, on which he made a profit, as it so happened, and this encouraged him, and he bought seven or eight chests more, and again sold them at a profit. The consequence was he grew bolder still, and just before the river closed last year, a hundred chests of drug arrived for a Cantonese dealer, and hearing there were no more steamers coming, he thought if he bought up these hundred chests, and kept them for sale during the winter, he must make a good thing of it. So off he went to this Cantonese dealer's and talked it over with the Manager, he wanting to take these hundred chests on two months' credit, and the Cantonese agreeing. Two or three days after his purchase another steamer suddenly came in, bringing five or six hundred chests of drug, and down went the market-price with a jump, so all he could do was to dispose of all his at once, at a loss of several thousand taels, which brought down his pawnbroking business too, in the crash. And the whole of his misfortune is the result of his giving up a safe business through this over-eagerness to get rich.

a. Well, you know, the only people who never remain rich for long are those who go in for the opium business; even if they make a fortune by it, it is only a short-lived pleasure; naturally not many years pass before they are ruined.

b. That's a matter of course. How can a man long enjoy wealth made in a trade which benefits himself by injuring others?

a. In my native place there was a wholesale opium-house called Hêng Yüan, which had a very large and widely-known business. The proprietor, a man named Hao, used to go himself to Tientsin and buy drug from a Foreign hong,—as much as several hundred chests at a time,—and there must have been quite several dozen assistants in the shop. For several years he made a *lot* of money, had a house with ever so many buildings, and more than a hundred persons of all ranks in his household, and a large stud of horses and mules, and was a wealthy man of that sort. Last year he became absolutely beggared.

At first I didn't understand how it came about so quickly, but afterwards, on making particular inquiries, I found that actually for several years, whilst his business was making money, the proprietor never went to the shop at all, but stayed at home all the time enjoying himself, and for a long time he had not even struck a general balance of his books.

Every day at dark the shop assistants used to secretly remove opium, he knowing nothing whatever about it. Last year, however, two friends of Hao, who knew that things were wrong in his shop, told him to go there, and make up his accounts and take stock. So then he went, made up his accounts, and found a Debit Balance of many tens of thousands of taels. And besides, on taking stock, only a few chests of drug remained. When he asked the assistants how it was the books showed a Debit Balance, and the stock was short, they all said they didn't know. So he had nothing for it but to sell his house and his stud, and just managed to pay what he owed the Foreign Hong, and after that closed his shop. But from the vexation all this caused him, he fell ill and died; all his dependents left, and there only remained the members of his own family, and now they are in such poverty that if they get one meal they go without the next. So you see what comes of selling opium.

No. 24   *a.* When did you come back?

b. A short time ago.

a. From Kiangsi, was it not?

b. No, from Kiangsu.

a. Didn't you go to Kiangsi originally; how is it you are returning now from Kiangsu?

b. I went to Kiangsi first, and then afterwards to Soochow.

a. And how have things gone with you since you've been away?

b. Capitally, for the few years I was in Kiangsi; but after my arrival at Soochow nothing has gone right.

a. Why did you go to Soochow, then, if you were so well off in Kiangsi?

b. Why, my patron was appointed last year to a post in Yünnan, and proposed to invite me to accompany him, but I objected to the distance and was unwilling to go, and proposed to return to Peking. He dissuaded me from that, and said there was a chüjên of his year, a man named Ho, who was an Expectant Taotai at Soochow, and he wanted to give me an introduction to go there, and undertake the drafting of his official reports. I was willing enough, and so he despatched me with a letter of introduction from himself to Soochow. On reaching there I found this gentleman had two secretaries, both of them Chehkiang men, who, as soon as they found me there, imposed so much on my ignorance that I was obstructed in everything. When they began to talk in their own patois, I couldn't understand a single word; if by any chance I asked them any question, they would pretend not to know and wouldn't tell me. Even when out walking they used to leave me by myself. Finding their manner so extremely unsociable, I thought, "If we are to go *on* like that, why we shall have an open quarrel," so I threw up my engagement and came back.

a. How did this gentleman, Mr. Ho, treat you?

b. Oh, *he* treated me well enough. But when I gave up my engagement he asked me what my reason was for doing so, and as I couldn't well mention that I didn't get on with my companions, I said I had a matter of importance in Peking which required me to return there for a time. However, he said he hoped when I had finished with it in Peking I would go back.

a. Well, now you are back, do you mean to go away again or not?

b. Now that I'm back, my first intention was to be examined for an Official Writership, and *supposing* I passed, I should have liked to serve in Peking, and not go away, but on my arrival I found the examination was over, and now my idea is this,— if there is anything suitable to be had I will go, if there is nothing that suits, then to remain in Peking for the present.

a. Well, there is a place to be had away from Peking,—I don't know whether you would accept it.

b. What sort of place?

a. A very great friend of mine has lately been appointed to the Prefecture of T'ai Yuan in Shansi, vacated on promotion. Two days ago he asked me to engage some one as Despatch Writer for him. I have no one at present in my eye whom I can recommend, and now you have returned, if you care to accept it, I would give you the recommendation.

b. What is this gentleman's name?

a. His surname is Ch'ang, and Ch'un-fu is his style.
b. A Bannerman?
a. Yes, a Bannerman.
b. What is he like?
a. An exceedingly honourable, and an exceedingly kind man.
b. In that case you might speak to him on my behalf.
a. As to salary, now what would you propose?
b. That's easily arranged; I'll leave it to you. Provided the person is agreeable, what does it matter how much or how little pay there is?
a. I can assure you that you will be certain to get on well together. Then to-morrow I'll see him and speak to him about you.
b. Thank you, thank you.
a. Not at all.
b. Now you yourself, have you no duties at present?
a. No, how could I? Ever since my return on sick-leave my old complaint has been chronic.
b. What do you do at home every day then?
a. Oh, on fine days I can go and look up my friends and talk, and when it blows or rains I just stay at home and read.
b. Why, then you are quite a man of elegant leisure.
a. Elegant leisure! Wasting away my time, that's all!

No. 25 *a.* I'll tell you an amusing thing.
b. What's that?
a. One night towards the end of last month, some time after midnight, I had just gone to sleep, when I heard in the back court a man jump in with a heavy thud. It startled me out of my sleep, and supposing it was thieves, I called at once to the servants to get up and be quick and take lanterns and show a light. So the servants, hearing there was a man, at once got up, lit lanterns and got sticks, and went to the back court. Meanwhile I got up too, opened the room-door and went to the back court to look. When I got there I heard the servants saying they had caught a man; that he was very well dressed, and didn't look like a thief. Then I heard the man say, "Don't haul at me, my ankle is sprained and hurts me very much. I'm not a thief. I'm making my escape." When I heard him say he was making his escape, I went forward and looked, and saw a very nice-looking young man, and on looking at him

closely I recognized him as an educated man named Chiang, living in the Chinese city, where we had twice met in a curio-shop, and had mutually taken to each other.

So then I made two of the servants give him an arm each and walk him about for a while, and he got all right. After that I invited him into my study, and when he was in there and saw it was me, he looked very sheepish. I asked what had happened to him, and he said he had been playing in a gambling saloon behind our house, when suddenly an official with a number of police had gone there and made a seizure. He had ran out meanwhile, but finding no place to hide in, he had climbed up on to the top of the wall and jumped down into this courtyard. And so, after giving him some advice to give up gambling any more, I made him stay the night, till daylight, when he went back.

Yesterday he came to thank me, and he told me he had now taken an oath never to gamble again after this.

b. He has a strong will, then, to be able to reform at once like that, as soon as you gave him your advice. I used to have a friend who was an opium-smoker, but when I advised him to give up the habit, why he was so angry with me that he will have nothing more to do with me.

a. A very curious person, then, your friend! Why should he be angry with you for advising him to give up smoking?

b. He really was a perfect fool. He *used* not to smoke, but afterwards, from being much with a friend who did, he gradually got to acquire the craving. At first he didn't smoke much, but then he took more and more, until last year his face had the regular "opium complexion," and he lost all energy. Thinking him in a very bad way, I said to him, "Take my advice and give up smoking; for if you go *on* doing so, I'm afraid it will go badly with you. I will buy you some anti-opium medicine from Shanghai, and if you take some every day according to the directions, no doubt you will gradually break off smoking." Well, he heard what I said, and agreed; and so I got a friend of mine to buy some anti-opium medicine in Shanghai, costing a good many dollars, and sent it to him. A few days after, meeting one of his servants, I inquired whether he had stopped smoking, but his man told me that he hadn't taken any of the anti-opium medicine and was smoking more than ever. That wouldn't have mattered, but I afterwards heard that he said at a friend's house that I was officious; that without any occasion I had advised him to leave off smoking, and that he didn't at all like it; that he daren't take the anti-opium medicine I had sent him, because, as he said, he was afraid it had poison in it, intended for him. Well, my friend couldn't allow this to pass, and told him, "You've no right to say that. A man means well, doesn't he, when he advises you to give up smoking. And why should a person poison you, who has no grudge against you? What you say is most unjust!" From that time he was angry with this friend of his also. And this year, he didn't come and pay me a New Year's call, so I know he has broken off acquaintance with me. Did you ever hear of a man with such a disposition as that?

No. 26 *a.* I'll tell you an irritating thing.

b. What is it?

a. That man Chiang, whom I know very well, the other day conspired with some other people, and they swindled me out of a good many thousand *tiao*.

b. Why, how did he succeed in swindling so much out of you?

a. He came to my house the other day, and said an acquaintance of his was now having a private gambling club at his house, and he invited me to go and play. So I went. When I got there and looked, I found seven or eight people there seated and playing. I didn't know one of them, and so he introduced me, and told me there were no strangers, and that he knew them all. So I sat down and began to play, and won a score or so of *tiao*, and then we broke up. Last night I *had* meant not to go, but as he insisted on my doing so, I couldn't help myself, and went again, and I then lost a good many hundred *tiao*. "Oh, it doesn't matter," he said to me, "go again a few times and you'll win several thousand *tiao* from them." Well, I believed what he said, and went with him again five or six times, and lost over 4,000 *tiao* more, and they closed their club.

Every day there were always two or three men coming to my house wanting the amount of my gambling debt. I went to see Chiang, but he was invisible and wouldn't see me. So I pawned two boxes of clothes to enable me to pay this debt. Yesterday a friend of mine told me that it was all a conspiracy against me, deliberately got up by Chiang with these other men. Most aggravating, is it not.

b. Certainly, it is detestable on Chiang's part. However, you yourself are to blame too, for if you had not gone with him to gamble he couldn't have swindled you.

a. That's perfectly true. Still the man's nothing less than a brute, to be on good terms with me and yet help other people to cheat me.

b. Speaking of conspiracies to defraud people, I'll tell you of a case. In my part of the world, one year, some of the bad characters of the place opened a gambling saloon, simply with the intention of swindling people, and lots of people did get let in. Another thing was, that they were a desperate set of blackguards, and so if anybody that lost money to them couldn't pay, he had to settle accounts by giving them his house or land property. Well, where we lived there was a rich man, who was very clever, and very kind to the people about there too, and when he heard of this he was very angry. So one evening he drove in his own cart to the gambling house. When had gone in and found these fellows, he gave his name, and said he'd come on purpose to play; and hearing this, and knowing him as a local magnate, they were all highly delighted. So they had a private consultation. "As this is his first visit," they said, "we'll let him win a few times to begin with, so that he will be willing to come again, and then one fine day we'll make him lose to the tune of ten thousand *tiao* or so, and we shall make our fortunes." Having made their plans they sat down and began playing, and sure enough he did win, and they paid up there and then. After this he went again twice and again won, and again they paid cash. Well, one evening he went again, and they played from watch-setting right on till close on daylight, and he had lost more than 10,000 *tiao*; so when it had got to be broad daylight he said to them, "I'll go home first and get the money ready for you, and at noon you can come to my house and get it," which they agreed to do. Back he went, and at midday two of them went to his house to get the money, and were announced by the servants. He called them into his library and asked them who they were and what they had come for. "Why," they said, "how is it you don't know us? We have a gambling saloon at so-and-so. You've forgotten, but last night didn't you play at our place and lose over 10,000 *tiao*, and tell us to come for the money at this time?" Directly he heard this, the moneyed man said, in a rage, "Don't talk nonsense! I, a man of property, play with rascals like you! You must be out of your senses. If you want to do me, you've mistaken your man; be off directly both of you, and think yourselves lucky, otherwise I'll send you both to the Yamèn and have you punished for extorting money!" They were so frightened at hearing this, that they didn't dare say a word, and made off as quick as they could.

No. 27 *a.* Why, what's made you look so deadly pale in the face?

b. I have been unwell for some days.

a. How's that?

b. I interfered in another person's affairs, and I have rather given offence, and it has brought on an attack of the spleen.

a. In whose affairs was it, and how did you give offence?

b. Well, last month our friend Wên Tzŭ-shan commissioned me to buy some land for him. I knew a man named Sun, living to the East of the city, who had a property of over a *ch'ing* that he wanted to sell, and so I took him to see Wên Tzŭ-shan. Later on they both went to the East of the city, and viewed the land, and afterwards asked my good offices in arranging the price for them. A thousand taels was decided on, and agreed to on both sides, and three days ago was fixed for the Agreement to be signed and the money to be paid over. Well, three days ago Sun and I went to Wên Tzŭ-shan's, but when we got there, he hadn't got up, and we waited for him some time in his study till he did. When he saw us, he said he couldn't buy that land, and when we asked him why not, he said he had been raising money for some time, but the amount was short of a thousand taels. We asked him how much he had raised, and he told us 950 taels. "Very well," said Sun, when he heard this, "let it be 950 taels then!" and accordingly the Agreement was signed and the money was paid. He put me in a very disagreeable position with Sun, for if he really and truly hadn't been able to raise this fifty taels there would be some excuse for him, but with means like his, he can put his hand on fifty thousand taels, let alone fifty. I hate him. He deliberately takes advantage of a man and puts *me* into the false position with him. So when I got home again that day, the more I thought over it the more angry I felt, and owing to this my old complaint came back and I fell ill.

a. Well, do you know Wên Tzŭ-shan's younger brother is worse than he is. He was once my partner in business, and with all the stock that was sold by him, when it came to the division of profits, he always paid me my share short by two or three strings of cash, knowing I shouldn't like to ask him for them, but he used always to say, "Oh, this time I owe you two or three *tiao*; in a day or two I'll make it up to you in some way." However, he never mentioned it again, and after a good long time *I* used to forget too, and then I thought no more about the matter. By this meanness I must have lost several hundred *tiao* in a few years. Then again, if you take the way he treats his friends, and the terms he is on with his relatives, he absolutely understands nothing about it. It is always "Take care of Number One;" that's the sort of fellow he is! Last year there was a death in his family, and he begged me over and over again to ask two friends to help him at home by sitting up all night with him. So I asked two very good friends of mine, who sat up with him five or six nights, and did all they possibly could for him. And when it was all over he never even went and thanked them for all their trouble, and one day afterwards meeting one of them in the street, he bent his head down and passed on. The fact is, he is quite unprincipled. Such a disposition as *his* is *too* hateful you know! And I've heard recently he's doing still worse. He is lending money at high rates; whoever borrows money from him pays 8 per cent per month. He's become notorious for his exorbitant rates of interest. I knew how it would be long ago. He's a rich man, but it won't be long before he's ruined. The ancients said, and it's a certain truth, "Ill-gotten gains don't prosper long."

No. 28 *a.* So I hear your brother has returned. How is it I haven't seen him out?

b. He has been ill since he came back.

a. How's that? Did he get fever on the journey?

b. Well no, not fever, but a shock.

a. What sort of a shock?

b. He met pirates when on board his boat.

a. Tell me how it was?

b. He was on his boat in company with a friend. There was one servant and one boat. One evening, while the boat was anchored at a place, some ten or more pirates came on board from the shore, armed with torches, swords, and spears, and came into the cabin, after cutting open the boarding. They presented their swords at my brother and asked him, "What have you got?" "Oh," said my brother, "our things are all lying about in this cabin; there's nothing anywhere else." So the gang took the boxes, bundles and cash, and went off with them, leaving them the bedding. Luckily, my brother had a money-belt on, in which there were some ten ounces of gold or more, and they also saved a few dozen taels. At daylight they went to a landing-place, and my brother and his friend, after talking it over, thought of disembarking and travelling by land. His friend being quite willing, they removed their bedding, and at the landing-place they hired two carts, and came on by land. When he got home he felt ill, and the doctor whom he called in said he had received a shock which was accompanied by a touch of the prevailing sickness.

He is taking medicine now, but he's not well.

No. 29 *a.* Your speaking of your brother's encounter with pirates on his journey, reminds me of an incident I'll tell you about. My father's elder brother, now dead, was once going with a friend to Kansuh. They hired two carts and took two servants, each going in one cart, and so they started. One day they came to a place where their carters didn't know the road, and they missed their way.

They went on until it was nearly dark, but not a town could they find. They were all in a great state of mind, but there was nothing to be done, and so they wandered blindly on. They travelled along till close upon the watch-setting, and then they reached a large wood, from the further side of which a little gleam of lamp-light was visible. So their two carts made for this light, and on coming close up they saw it was an inn. Outside there were two meal-sellers' sign-boards hanging; the inn-door was shut, and looking out on the street was a window with a lighted lamp inside. Well, they called out to open the door, and drove in. When they got inside and looked round, the place was quite lonely and deserted, without a single visitor. So they selected three rooms and brought in their luggage, and then told the people of the inn to get some water for washing, make tea,' and get some food ready. My uncle saw the inn-people were such a dubious-looking set that his suspicions were rather aroused. When they had finished their meal, and while his friend was on the $k'ang$ arranging the baggage, in came one of the inn-servants to make some tea. My uncle noticed that all the time he kept on looking at the baggage on the $k'ang$, and, seeing this sort of thing, my uncle's doubts increased. However, he didn't like to say anything for fear of alarming his friend. After drinking his tea he went to the back yard to relieve himself. When he got there, he saw three rooms, one was a w.-c. and the other two were rooms for stacking provender. After my uncle had entered the w.-c. and while he was relieving himself, he heard two men come from the front court, push open the door of the room with the provender, and go in to get some fodder. He then heard one say to the other, "What did the Master arrange with you when he called you away just now?" Then he heard the other man say, "It was arranged like this: at dead of night, you and I are to go and kill the two carters, and they three will go and kill the two visitors. I have agreed with the Master that after the job is done, the two carts shall be given us for our share, one cart apiece, and that never mind how much money the two visitors have got, that's to be no concern of ours at all. What I mean to do is this: when you and I have got hold of our share, early to-morrow we'll give up our business here, and go back home, one of us in each cart. After this we'll both reform and not do any mischief to people any more. What do you think of that?" The other man said, "You're right, that's a first-rate plan." When they had finished talking, he heard them go off to the front side. "Well," said my uncle to himself, "no wonder I thought the inn-people such a rascally-looking lot. No doubt about it, this is a 'flash' inn." Well, after this he came out of the w.-c., went to his own room, and told his friend all he'd heard. His friend on hearing this was terribly frightened. So while they were both in their room in great trouble, and not knowing what to do, they suddenly heard a large number of carts coming along, until there was a knocking at the gate, and when that was opened, they saw six Government Treasure carts enter, with two visitors and four Treasure Escort men. "There's no fear *now*," said my uncle, " we can go to sleep directly in security." And then they sent one of their servants across and asked the Treasure carts, and were told the latter were going to start next morning at the fifth watch. My uncle's party slept till the fifth watch, then rose, told their carters to put to the carts, and went off in company with the Treasure carts. In that way they just managed to avoid this great danger. A narrow escape, wasn't it?

No. 30 *a*. I say, I'll tell you a story.

In our village there lives a man who is pretty well off, and who has always been very stingy. He has never helped anyone, nor given any money in charity. Well, some days ago a married younger sister of his came to his house, in spite of the rain, and said that her husband had now got employment as accountant on board a sea-going ship, which had put to sea two days ago, and that now, having nothing to eat in the house, she had come through the rain to try and borrow a picul of rice and a few taels until her husband's return, when they should be paid back without fail. When the man had heard this, he told his sister he had no rice and no money, and he couldn't possibly provide her with them, and said she must go and borrow elsewhere. So the sister, finding he wouldn't do anything, broke out crying, and he seeing her do so went off out of her way in the sulks. Now there was a neighbour of his living in the same compound, a cheery sort of fellow, who was very angry at hearing that he wouldn't do anything for his sister, and so he asked her in, lent her a picul of rice and several taels besides, and hired a donkey for her into the bargain, and then sent her back.

When the man returned and heard from his people of his neighbour lending his sister rice and money to take back with her, not a word of any kind did he say, but pretended not to know. Now that night, as it happened, a thief came, who bored a hole in the back wall of the house, got into his room and stole some dozens of taels and some clothes from him. Next morning, when he found there had been a robbery and he had lost things, being afraid that his sister, when she heard of his losing his money and clothes, would be sure to exult over it and come to ask about it, instead of going to the Yamên and giving notice of the robbery in his house, he even asked his neighbour, living in the same compound, not to tell people he had been robbed. But do you know, the same night this thief had stolen his things, as luck would have it, when he reached the main street he got arrested by the night-patrol and sent to the Yamên. The official asked the fellow from whose house the money and clothes were stolen, and he then confessed they were stolen from so-and-so's house in such-and-such a village. Thereupon the official sent a runner to tell the person concerned to receive back the stolen property. When this man heard this he was much disturbed, for it wouldn't do not to go and receive his things from the Yamên. while if he did go he was afraid of his sister hearing of it. So he thought of a way by which he asked this neighbour of his to assume his name and go and receive his property at the Yamên for him. His friend agreed, and went instead; but he despised the man for his former refusal to help his sister and determined to pay him out. So after receiving over the money and the clothes from the Yamên, he sent them all to the sister, and on reaching the house and seeing him, he told him a lie, and said, "After coming from the Yamên just now, when I got into the the street I came right on your sister. She asked me where I had been to, and I said I had been to the Yamên to receive your money and clothes for you. Then she told me to give them to *her*, and as she is your own sister I couldn't well refuse to, and so I did give them to her."

The man, on hearing this, not only didn't venture to get angry but he had, on the contrary, to express his thanks. And now everybody who hears about it says it was a smart thing and done by a smart man.

No. 31 *a*. Speaking of that miserly fellow meeting with his deserts, I'll tell you another story. One year when I was lodging at an inn in the South, there was a Shansi merchant stopping in the same house. One day there suddenly appeared a poor fellow, also a Shansi man, who was all in rags, and who wanted to see this merchant. The inn-servants showed him in, and when he saw the merchant he said, "I've wandered to this place. I can't go home because I've no money for the journey, and am in the greatest distress. Yesterday a fellow-countryman of ours told me you had come here on business, and were staying at this inn. I was very glad to hear it, and so I've come to see you and to beg you, for the sake of Auld Lang Syne, to lend me a hundred taels to pay my expenses to get home. When I get there I will find some means of repaying you." "Oh," the other man replied, "I've already laid out all my money in stock; just now I haven't got a single tael in hand. Think of some other plan, for really I can't give you any help." The poor man, when he heard him say he couldn't give any help, wept, and the merchant then went into an inner room and sat down. Now there happened to be a Ssŭ-chuan man staying in the same inn who went to the room to have a chat with this merchant, and seeing this poor man sitting in a chair weeping, he asked him for what reason he was in such grief. The man replied: "This merchant used to be a near neighbour of mine in my native place. In years gone by, while he was poor, I have often helped him with money and food; afterwards too I lent him money to start in business, and now he has grown rich. I have lost money in my business in this part of the country and have none to pay for my journey home. I come to him to borrow a hundred taels in order to go back, and he refuses to lend it me. That is why I am in such deep grief." When the Ssŭ-chuan man had heard to the end of the story, he went into the inner room and asked the merchant, "This story of your fellow-countryman's, that he has given you help in former years, is it true?" "Yes," said the merchant, "it's true enough. Unfortunately I have no money at present to lend him." "Well," said the Ssŭ-chuan man, "supposing, for instance, I lent you a hundred taels, which you gave him for travelling-expenses home, and you repaid me in a month from this, giving me an I.O.U.— no interest charged either,—would you be willing or not?" Well, he was obliged to say he was willing, whereupon the Ssŭ-chuan man brought a hundred taels from his own room to lend him, and made him give it to the poor man to take away with him, got the merchant to write him an I.O.U., which he kept, and after a day or two the Ssŭ-chuan man moved from the house also. After a few more days the merchant opened his box and saw at once that a hundred taels were missing, and the I.O.U. was lying there.

Then he discovered that the Ssŭ-chuan man was a conjuror and knew the art of spiriting things away; that he had spirited away his hundred taels, and given them to the poor man to take with him. Some time afterwards one of the merchant's servants let out the story, and everybody said, who heard it, that it served him quite right.

No. 32 *a*. I hear your brother has been engaged in a lawsuit; is it true?

    b. Yes, quite true.

    a. With whom?

    b. With a rascal living in our town.

    a. And what about?

    b. It happened like this. One day my brother went pigeon-shooting in a wood to the north of the town. Well, he fired, and without his knowing it, there happened to be someone standing outside the wood, who was leading a horse. All of a sudden the horse, hearing the report of the gun, was startled and bolted away. The man, in his annoyance, caught hold of my brother, and told him to make good the value of the horse. "Don't get excited," said my brother, "which way did the beast gallop?" "North-west," said the man. "What colour is he?" "Chestnut," said the man. "Well," said my brother, "this business is easily managed. I'll go at once with you into the town, and get myself secured in your presence by a substantial guarantor. Then you go and look for the horse first, and if afterwards you can't find him, and he's really lost, I'll pay up for him, that's all." The man was very well pleased at this. So my brother and he went along together to the town, and my brother got secured to him by Ch'uan Shun, the grain-dealers, and then he went to look for the horse, while my brother came home. After a bit the man comes back to Ch'uan Shun's and says, "The horse is lost, and I haven't been able to find him," and wants to see my brother. Well, the grain-dealers sent one of their apprentices to our house to fetch my brother. As soon as the man saw him, he said, "I looked for him a long time, but I can't find my horse *anywhere*. I gave sixty taels for that animal. Now, as a favour to you, I'll take fifty taels." "Oh," said my brother, "I don't call that making quite sure he's lost, merely looking about in a general sort of way, as you've been doing, and not finding him. Let me go and have another thorough search for you. If after a day or two he doesn't turn up, then he will really be lost. Plenty of time if I pay for him by that time." But the man wouldn't have it; he must be paid at once. Then my brother began disputing with him about it, but the other people intervened ; whereupon, what did the man do but go to the Deputy Magistrate's and lay a charge against my brother, and he was summoned by the people from the Yamên. When he came before the Court he gave the true account of the matter. The Deputy Magistrate then allowed my brother a limit of five days, and told him to go and try to find the horse. Accordingly he went inquiring in every village, and afterwards heard news of it. North-west of our town there is a village, where a man of the name of Chao lives. Two days before this man had bought a chestnut horse. Well, away went my brother to find out this man Chao, and questioned him. Actually, the other fellow, some days before, had sold his horse to Chao, agreed on eight taels as the price, and arranged what day to bring the horse to him and get the money, That day, when the horse heard the report of the gun, as I told you, he bolted, and the fellow went after him and caught him, took him to Chao's place, got the money, came back and told my brother the beast was lost, and he must pay him fifty taels for him. My brother persuaded Chao to bring the horse and go with him to the Yamên as a witness. As soon as the other man saw that there was a witness, he had nothing to say, and he himself acknowledged it was a swindle. The Deputy Magistrate then gave him forty blows for utter rascality, and let him go.

No. 33   *a.* When I was at the Yung Fa Godown yesterday, I heard you had sent them a hundred bales of cotton from your godown one bale short; how did it happen?

b. Oh, it's rather amusing, what you mention. Yesterday, before sending them the cotton, we got out a hundred tally-sticks, and afterwards gave one tally to each man that carried a bale. When we had sent the whole of the hundred bales, and a good long while after, Mr. Wang, the Manager of the Yung Fa Godown, sent a man to our godown to ask why we sent them a bale short. We told him, "We have sent a hundred bales of cotton; what do you mean by 'sending a bale short'?" The man said they had received in their godown ninety-nine bales— one bale short. I was very much surprised at hearing this, and so I went with the man to their place. As soon as Mr. Wang saw me, he seemed annoyed and said, "Your godown-men are really too careless! How is it they've sent us a bale of cotton short?" I asked him, "How do you know they have?" "Oh," he said, "when the cotton had all been delivered, the tally-keeper had ninety-nine tallies,—isn't that one bale short?" Then I asked them, "Which of you was it just now in the godown that took the tallies?" One of the assistants standing by said *he* had. I asked him, "When you were taking the tallies just now, didn't you go anywhere else?" "No," he said, "I didn't go anywhere, except that I had a sudden stomachache and I went to the w.-c. to relieve myself for a short time." So I said to him, "First of all, let you and me go and have a look in the w.-c." When we went there together and looked, there was a tally lying on the ground. I picked it up and took it along with me to Mr. Wang. "Now then," I said, "whose are the careless godown-men now? Your assistant drops a tally in the w.-c. and then you say we have sent you a bale short! It's true it is of no great importance, but still you can't deny you have been a good deal too hasty." This made him look very sheepish, and he didn't utter a single word. Then I went on, "Although we have found the tally, let us go through the goods again all the same, and see if they are short or not, and then we shall both be more satisfied." So I told their assistants to pass the bales from the godown into the yard, and counted them up carefully, and right enough there were one hundred bales. "Well," I said, "you see plainly there's no mistake." "Yes," they replied, they saw it was all right, and so I came back. Rather amusing, wasn't it?

a. I told you once before, this Mr. Wang is a stupid fellow, though you didn't quite believe me. The idea of his simply taking the tallies and without checking the goods, saying you had sent him a bale short!

b. Well, do you know, this is what happened last year. We bought a hundred taels worth of goods from their godown, and gave them a bank-note for that sum. Two days afterwards he brought back the note and said it was forged. I looked at the note, and it had no mark showing it was forged, so I asked him, "If it's a forgery, why has it no mark to show it?" He said it had none because he hadn't gone to the House concerned. "How do you know then it is a forgery if you haven't been to the House itself?" I asked him. "Oh," he said, "their accountant thought it looked like a forged note." At such a wild remark as this I said, "We'll take the note together and get it cashed at the bank, and see whether it's forged or not." So we went, and actually it wasn't a forgery at all, and we cashed it.

He couldn't hide his embarrassment, and took away the money, looking very much confused.

No. 34 *a.* Mr. Manager, I've got a bad note here that I have brought back to you.

b. Let me have a look at it. This isn't one of ours.

a. Why not?

b. Because it hasn't got our endorsement on it.

a. But indeed it *was* got from you, I remember. Why do you say now it wasn't?

b. I'll tell you. If it was a note coming from us, it would certainly have our endorsement, and our chop. As this had got neither the one nor the other, why it can't be ours.

a. You say it hasn't your endorsement, but this note of mine *has* an endorsement as being received from you.

b. It isn't enough merely to have *your* endorsement as being received from us; it requires to have our endorsement showing the person we received it from.

a. Oh, well! if it has your endorsement, and you won't acknowledge it, why I'm helpless.

b. There's no reason why we shouldn't acknowledge it. If it had been got from us, *we* should return it back to the other person, we should lose nothing, so why shouldn't we recognize it?

a. But it's possible you may have forgotten to endorse *this* note.

b. That's out of the question! We *couldn't* forget to do so. Besides there's another reason, which I'll tell you. This note is issued by one of the "sly" banks, and we have never used the notes of these "sly" banks in our shop, so we are still more certain it didn't come from us.

a. Well, if you insist on saying it didn't come from you, why then I can't help myself, and I must grin and bear it, that's all.

b. I should advise you to take it back, and think it over again from whom you got it.

a. Will you change this 10-*tiao* note for me into five 1-*tiao* notes and one 5-*tiao*?

b. We haven't got any of our own notes for 1 *tiao*. Will it do if we change it for the notes of another house?

a. Yes, that will do.

b. Just count them and see that they're right.

a. Quite right! Have these all got your endorsement?

b. Yes, all.

No. 35 *a.* I say, I've just seen a bit of an excitement in the market-town.

b. What was it?

a. A Southern man had got hold of one of the natives and was going to the Sub-District Deputy Magistrate's Yamên with him to have him up, and a whole lot of people were following, so not knowing what it was about, I went with them to the Yamên to see what it all meant. Then I saw the pair of them reach the Yamên, and the Southerner told the Yamên-runners, that they two had a case to settle, whereupon they took them in. I went in too, and saw the Deputy Magistrate take his seat in Court, and both of them came up before him and knelt down. The Magistrate first questioned the Southern man. "What's your name? Where do you come from? What is it you have come to have decided?" Then the Southern man made a kotow and said, "My name is Yü-p'ei; I come from Lin-Chiang-fu in Kiangsi, and I keep a ready-made clothes shop in this place. Last year I bought a concubine, so I rented a two-roomed dwelling-house in Têng-Lung Lane, in the market-town here. Just now I was at work in my shop, and sent an apprentice to fetch something from my house. When he came back he said there was a young man sitting in my house, but he didn't know who he was. This made me feel very suspicious, and I hurried home to see. When I got there I saw the street-door was closed. I pushed it open, went into the room and looked, and saw this man sitting there drinking tea, talking and laughing with my concubine. Then I asked him, "Who are you and what have come to my house for?" He answered that he had come there as a knocking-shop. I was very angry indeed on hearing that, and gave him a slap in the face, and in return he scratched mine, so then I dragged him here for the case to be heard. Please Your Honour to ask him what he really did go to my house for."

Then the Deputy Magistrate asked the other man, "What's your name? Where do you live? What are you? and why did you go to Yü-p'ei's house?" The man answered, "My name is Wang An; I live in Hung Chu Lane in this town: my usual business is making short loans of money. Yü-p'ei's concubine used to live in the same compound as I did. Two months ago she borrowed from me ten taels at interest, and every month I go to her house to get the interest on it. To-day the date had come round again, and I took my stamp and went to her house. The concubine asked me to step inside and have some tea, and I went in. She gave me the interest, and after that she made tea in the tea-pot. While I was sitting there, drinking my tea, Yü-p'ei came back. When he saw me he glowered all over, and with his eyes staring at me he asked me, "Who are you? and what have you come to my house for?" When I heard him speak so rudely to me, why I *did* get angry and said I came to his house as a knocking-shop. At that he slapped me in the face, and I was provoked and scratched his face back. Then he dragged me here to have the case heard."

When he had finished, he took out a folded parcel of interest-money, and showed it to the Magistrate. Then the Magistrate said, "As Yü-p'ei doesn't like your going to his house, after this you must go every month to his shop for the interest on your loan. You are forbidden to go again to his house. If you *do*, and Yü-p'ei comes and informs against you, I shall certainly punish you for it," and with that he told them both to go back again.

No. 36 *a.* I say, I've got something to tell you.

b. What's that?

a. I came back from the country a short time ago. One day, when I was stopping at an inn in a large market-town, I heard the landlord say, that some days before a man had gone with a bangle to sell to a cash-bank in the town, called the Tĕ Ch'êng Bank. Well, the people in the shop had just fetched a pair of scales to weigh the bangle, when another man came in, who said to the one who was selling the bangle, "I've just been to your house to take you a Letter of Advice. Your servants said you had gone into the street, so I went to try and find you, and I happened to see you come in here." As he was speaking, he pulled out from his breast a letter and a packet of silver, and said,

"This is a Letter of Advice from Chehkiang." The man who was selling the bangle took the Letter of Advice, gave the man who brought it a hundred cash, and he went away. The man with the bangle then said to the people of the shop, "My brother has sent me some money from Chehkiang, so I won't sell the bangle. Shall I sell you the silver? There's another thing, I'm no scholar, would you open the letter and read it out to me?" So they gave him the bangle again, opened the letter and read it out to him. It began by simply saying that things were going on well there, and that his brother was not to be anxious; then it continued, "I'm sending you ten taels now, which please use, and when there's another opportunity I will send you a further remittance." The man then said, "Will you take the silver away and weigh it, and change it for me into *cash*?" The bank-people did take it away and weigh it, and found there were eleven taels. They were delighted at this, and thought they would do him out of a tael, so they changed it into cash as ten taels, and gave it to him, and off he went with it. After a little while another man came in with a note to cash, who said to them, "You've been done; the man who sold you the silver just now is a swindler. It's bad silver, what he sold you. How did you come to let him cheat you?" As soon as they heard this they at once got the sycee-shears and cut open the silver, and saw at a glance the silver *was* bad, sure enough. So the bank-people asked the man, "Do you know the swindler's house?" He replied, "I will take you to see him, if you will pay me for it." Well, the manager gave the man a *tiao*, and told him to take them to see this other man. The fellow took the *tiao*, and went off with the two men from the bank. When they had reached the door of a confectioner's shop, he said to the two men. "Look, there's the swindler, eating pastry inside the shop. Go in and see him for yourselves." So in went the two with the bad packet of silver, and when they found him they said, "This packet you sold us is bad silver." "Well," he said, "*I* didn't know whether it was bad or not; it was brought me, you know, from my brother in the provinces. As it's bad I'll give you back the cash." Thereupon he asked the manager of the confectioner's shop to see whether the silver weighed ten taels or not.

When the manager had taken the silver and put it in the balance scales and weighed it, he said, "This is eleven taels." On hearing this the man said to the two men from the bank, "What I just sold you was ten taels; this packet is eleven; how can it be mine? You have brought some other bad silver and want to cheat me!" The two men from the bank made no reply, and some other people who were there eating refreshments were so indignant at hearing this, that they all wanted to lay hands on the men from the bank, who had nothing for it but to take the packet of bad silver as quick as they could and run away back.

No. 37 *a.* Your story of the swindler reminds me of a thing I will tell you about. Some years ago, in my part of the country, there used to live a celebrated doctor named Fang. He possessed a title and had a small fortune of his own, and used to receive several dozens of patients every forenoon. One morning a man came to him, who seemed by his dress to be a servant in some large establishment. On seeing Dr. Fang he said, "I belong to such-and-such a house. My master and mistress are both ill, and wish to come and consult you; and they would be glad if you will be at home to-morrow morning," which Dr. Fang said he would be. Next morning the same servant again appeared, accompanied by another man carrying a bundle in his hand. The servant entered and said to Dr. Fang, "I beg your pardon, Sir : Master first, or Mistress first?" "Your mistress first, of course," Dr. Fang answered. The servant then took the bundle from the other man's hand, and went out with it, while the latter sat down on a seat and waited. After the consultations were over and all the people gone, Dr. Fang asked the man, "Have you come to consult me?" "No," he said, "I come from a second-hand clothes shop; I'm only waiting here for your servant to bring me out the clothes." This surprised Dr. Fang very much, so he asked, "What servant of mine? What clothes have you brought?" "Why," the man replied, "the servant that came in along with me just now, didn't you tell him the Mistress was to see first, and then he took the clothes inside?" "What did that man tell you?" asked Dr. Fang again, "that he was my servant? And what piece of clothing did you bring anyhow?" The shopman said, "This morning that man came to our shop, and said he was your servant, and that you wanted to buy a lady's fur-cloak, and that we were to bring one for you to look at, and if it suited you would keep it. He told one of us to come with him, so I came." "Now, look here," said Dr. Fang, "that man is no servant of mine, and I don't know who he is. He came here yesterday and said he belonged to the so-and-so's, that his master and mistress were ill and wished to come and consult me, and told me to remain at home for them this morning. When he came in just now and asked me, 'Master first, or Mistress first?' I thought his master and mistress had come, and that's why I said, 'Your mistress first, of course.' I meant I would see his mistress first. I know nothing whatever about any clothes. You be quick and go and try and find him." When he had heard this, the man from the second-hand clothes shop understood that the other fellow was a swindler and had made off with the clothes.

THE GUIDE TO KUAN-HUA.

No. 38 *a.* Huo Fu!

b. Yes, Sir!

a. Go and ask the teacher to come to me.

b. The teacher has come, Sir; he is sitting in the outer room.

a. (*to c*). Ah! have you rested yourself, Sir?

c. Yes, I have; I hope you have too.

a. Well, I don't feel very tired. There's something I want to consult you about.

c. What is that?

a. It's about the diary I kept while we were on our trip; it wants putting in order; and to find someone to copy it out.

c. Well, if you will get me out the rough draft, I will look over it first.

a. And there's one thing in it I have forgotten; I wish you would think of it for me.

c. What is it?

a. It was when we were having breakfast in the inn at San Ho Chên, I heard one of the visitors say that some man stopping at a temple somewhere had hanged himself, which got the priest of the temple into trouble, and also that there had been some legal proceedings; but I don't recollect exactly how it all was. Do you remember?

c. Ah! Yes, I remember that.

a. Then tell it me again please.

c. The visitor who was breakfasting said that there was a temple where he lived called the Shui Hsien Miao, in which a man was stopping who hanged himself one night. Next day, as soon as it was light, the priest gave notice to the authorities, and the District Magistrate with his examiners held an inquest. The examiners, without making a thorough inspection, said the man seemed to have been strangled. On this the magistrate took the priest to his Yamên and asked him why he had strangled his visitor. The priest answered, "I have neither any old grudge or recent grievance with the man; how could I have strangled him?" The magistrate, not believing this, applied corporal punishment to make him confess, but it was all in vain,—he would not confess, so the magistrate then imprisoned him. Now the priest had a novice, who was so disturbed by this that he went to the provincial capital and laid a charge at the Governor's Yamên, whereupon the Governor deputed the magistrate of the adjoining district, and he took skilled examiners with him and held a second inquest at the temple, when it turned out that the dead man had died by hanging. The magistrate of the adjoining district having finished an accurate report of the facts to the governor, then degraded the magistrate who held the original inquiry, and punished the examiners who made the original inspection, and released the priest. That was the story.

a. Yes, you're quite right; that was it. I wish you would insert it in the diary,—what do you say?

c. Yes, certainly. When I have put it in proper order, who is to transcribe it?

a. I was going to engage someone to copy it.

c. If it is transcribed there would probably be some clerical errors in it.

a. Then what had I better do?

c. Well, if you're not in a hurry, I should think I might transcribe it when I have time.

a. Oh, if you would take the trouble, I should be very much obliged indeed.

c. No trouble at all.

No. 39 *a.* It is dull drinking our wine and doing nothing, as we are doing to-day. Why shouldn't we fill up and play a few rounds at morra?

b. All right. Let you and I have a round first.

a. Why, that will be giving away the game to me for nothing, won't it?

b. Don't begin boasting yet. It's not certain who wins and who loses, you know.

a. Here you are. Four seasons making money.

b. Sixes!

a. Quits!

b. *Five* golden prizemen.

a. Look! how's that?

b. Oh, you're losing. This time you only won by a perfect fluke.

a. Drink your wine first, and we'll compare notes afterwards.

b. I've drunk it already.

a. When? I didn't see it.

b. Ask the others whether I've drunk it or not.

a. Gentlemen, did you see him drink?

c. We didn't notice.

a. The others haven't seen you; it is evident you're shirking it. Be quick and drink.

b. I've drunk already; I can't drink again.

a. If you don't, we'll all pour it down your throat.

b. This is awful! Well now, look here, I can't stand much liquor, let my forfeit be a funny story.

a. Yes, that will do; and if you don't tell a good one, you'll still have to pay the forfeit.

b. Well, listen; it is really a good one.

a. Out with it then.

b. The story is against the Censorate, so it's a good thing there are no Censors in the company.

a. Just you tell your story. There's no one here who won't take your side.

b. Well, listen. There was once a countryman who was very poor and quite without means. So after turning the matter over in his mind, he thought he would go to Peking and be a eunuch, and have a fine position and make plenty of money. So he went to Peking and entered himself as a pupil under an Imperial eunuch.

a. But wait a bit. Your story needs explanation. There would be no difficulty, of course, even for such a raw countryman, in coming to Peking and going straight into the Palace, would there?

b. Well, I'm going to tell you. He got someone to introduce him.

a. Well, why didn't you tell us that clearly at first?

b. Don't be so excessively critical, and let me go on at once.

a. Go on. What happened next?

b. Well, having got the eunuch to be his tutor, he begged him to instruct him in all matters and look after him. So the eunuch sent him into the Imperial Palace as a domestic servant. One day His Majesty's orders were given that refreshments were to be served, so the countryman said, "The Everlasting Lord wants luncheon!" The eunuch cried out at him with, "Don't speak in that stupid way! You must say, 'The Everlasting Lord desires to be served with Imperial Refreshments.'" So he made a note of this in his mind. One day commands were given for a grand Court banquet, and the countryman again said, "The Everlasting Lord wishes to give a dinner-party." Again the eunuch scolded him: "You've used the wrong words; you ought to have said, 'The Everlasting Lord desires to give an Imperial banquet.' In future recollect well. For example, the Palace Gardens are called the 'Imperial Gardens;' the soldiers of the escort are called the 'Imperial Guard.'"

The countryman heard this, and all of a sudden it all flashed upon him, and he said to himself, "Why, of course! You put on the word 'Imperial' to everything that's in sight of the Emperor. I understand it *now*. From this time I shall be an old hand at it." One day, as he was passing the gate of the Palace Gardens, he trod in a lump of excrement, which made him very angry, and he was just going to swear when he thought, "I suppose it's been left by His Majesty," whereupon he pointed with his finger at the lump and said, "If I didn't think you were an *Imperial Privy Counsellor*, I would give you a good cursing and no mistake!"

a. It's lucky there are none of those gentlemen among the company, or your mouth would have been swollen with twisting by this time.

b. Well, my mouth isn't twisted. Now you should tell us something.

a. My joke is against District Police Masters.

b. That's fun. We must all listen.

a. It's called the Ten Orders of a District Police Master.

b. Let's hear what you call the Ten Orders.

a. Listen. He is addressed with honour for *one* whole lifetime: he has *two* pieces of bamboo borne before him: he receives *three* times ten taels of salary: he summons the ti-paos of *four* quarters: he inflicts *five* blows on the face: he sends circulars to the *six* directions: he depends on the District Officers of the *seventh* rank: he builds a figure of *eight* shaped wall: he tacks on his uniform a badge of the *ninth* rank: and he doesn't get his ten shares of enjoyment.

b. Good. The other nine sentences are all right, but the last one is too bad.

a. If there were a District Police Master here to-day, wouldn't you just have to make your peace with him!

No. 40 *a.* Have you kept at home this last day or two for the New Year, and not gone out at all?

b. I go out every evening.

a. Then why don't you come to me here?

b. The last few days I and some friends of mine have been guessing riddles in the evening at the entrance of the Ts'un Ku Chai curio-shop.

a. Who set them?

b. They were set by a chüjên.

a. Were they well written?

b. Not bad at all.

a. Did you succeed in guessing any?

b. Yes, I took off some.[1]

a. What were they?

b. One that I guessed was, "The character *yen* (word) without the top dot: four passages from the Four Books."

a. Tell me, what were the passages?

b. One was, "What words are those?"; one was, "Without giving it the dot;" another was, "The last words were but in jest;" and the other, "How true these words!"[2]

a. That was a hard one to guess.

b. I guessed another, which was three passages to be solved by a single word.

a. Tell me, what were they?

b. Listen: "Tzŭ-lu said, 'It is that,' Yen-hui said, 'It is like that,' Confucius said, 'It is not that; in *that* lies a right line.'" The word *mieh* (乜) solves it.[3] And another of four sentences to be solved by one word: "With ten its mouth is filled, but say not it is *field*, having nought for its head or its tail, it worried a hsiu-ts'ai to death." I took this off by guessing the word Fish (魚).[4]

a. Those two were very ingenious.

b. Yesterday evening I guessed two more. One was: "The course of history passing the Dragon Gate;" to be solved by a man's name in the Four Books. Answer: Fish the Chronicler.[5] The other was: "The sacrificial meats in shrines to the Virtuous Dead;" to be solved by a passage from the Four Books. Answer: "Few there be that eat of them."[6]

a. Very neat, those two.

b. There was another, guessed by a friend of mine: "Playing chess on a *wei-ch'i* board;" a sentence from the Four Books to solve it. Answer: "Tzŭ-lu answered not."[7]

a. That is even neater. Do you know, some years ago I guessed a conundrum: "At the east end of the street clearing the drains, and at the west end unclean;" to be guessed by a couple of nursery rhymes. Answer: "Puddles on this side, devils on that."[8]

b. Better than ever. I consider that will quite bear comparison, in point of cleverness, with those composed by this chüjĕn.

a. And I'll tell you one more. Last year a friend of mine, who is a Chief Clerk in a public office, asked me to write him a pair of New Year Scrolls. I wrote for the first, "Wishing you the compliments of the season for the despatch of last year, I have the honour to acknowledge the receipt of, etc., etc., etc." For the second I put, "A Happy New Year from one who is with great truth and regard, Your Excellency's most obedient humble servant."[9]

b. Too bad of you, really. How could you use their shop-phrases? I've no doubt he would never hang that pair of New Year Scrolls.

a. No, of course he wouldn't hang them up. "Very well," he said, "I can't hang these up, but I shall keep them because they are quite in our line, and hereafter they will be an heirloom."

b. Don't you talk such nonsense! Put on your things and let's go for a bit of a stroll.

a. Wait a moment while I change my things, and I'll go with you.

Notes to No. 40.

[1] The slip of paper on which a riddle is written is attached to the lighted lantern, which thus renders it legible in the surrounding darkness. When guessed, the riddle is removed from the lantern.

[2] This and the following acrostics require explanation, especially as in English translation the word-play must be lost. The four passages of the first are respectively, *Mencius*, Ch. 2, Part 1; *Analects*, Ch. 6, Part 1; *ibid.*, Ch. 9, Part 1; and *ibid.*, Ch. 7, Part 1. I have translated them as they are in the original classical text, except the second, which has here been purposely changed by the substitution of 無 *wu* (not) for the 吾 *wu* (I) of the *Analects*. The clue being the character 言 *yen* (=word or words), maimed by the absence of the top dot, the first passage is made to read, "What 'word' is that?" *q.d.* thus imperfectly written the character is not *yen* (word) at all. The meaning of the second passage, as properly written, is, "I hold with Tien," the latter being a man's name. But a forced application is given by a double pun and the use of a different sense for the second character. Thus *wu* (I) is changed to *wu* (not), *yü* takes the sense of giving, in place of that of holding or agreeing with, and by a second pun *tien* has its ordinary rendering of a dot or stroke, instead of being used as a proper name. The third and fourth passages require no explanation beyond this, that in both "words" must be changed to "word." I think this is quite enough elucidation for an acrostic of which the character of the point turns on the point of a character.

³ This riddle hinges on the likeness in form between the characters 世 *yeh* and 也 *mieh*, and involves also the use of the former as a final particle in the written language. Thus, the three speakers may be supposed to say either "It is so, or that," etc., or "It is (the word) *yeh*," etc. The passage translated "In that lies the right line" (直在其中) is from the *Analects*, Ch. 7, Part 1. In the Classic, CONFUCIUS refers to the right line of conduct to be followed by a son in the embarrassing, indeed painful, position, where his parent having permitted himself an indulgence in the uncertain joys of sheepstealing, the son afterwards becomes cognizant of the fact. But here, the "right line" is a physical not a moral one, being the vertical middle downstroke which distinguishes 世 *yeh* from 也 *mieh*.

⁴ The character 魚 *yü* (fish), thus solves this riddle. The numeral 十 *shih* (ten) within 口 *k'ou* (mouth), forms the character 田 *t'ien* (field), two strokes above and four dots below which, convert it into *yü* (fish) while they are also the upper and lower parts, or the head and tail, of the character 無 *wu* (nought or not).

⁵ He is mentioned in the *Analects*, Ch. 6, Part 1. "The course of history" corresponds to 史 *shih*, meaning both history or a historian; "passing the Dragon Gate" corresponds to 魚 *yü* (fish), standing here for the *li yü* or carp, which, according to an old saying, is transformed into a Dragon after passing the Dragon Gate, for which see MAYERS' *Manual*, p. 282. The phrase is used of successful graduation for degrees.

⁶ *Ta Hsio*, Section 10.

⁷ *Analects*, Ch. 4, Part 1. Tzŭ-lu is the name of one of CONFUCIUS' disciples, but the two words are very neatly applied in this case to solve the riddle by taking *tzŭ lu* as "the moves of the pieces" which *pu tui* "do not correspond," namely in the two games of chess and *wei-ch'i*.

⁸ *Pu kan-ching* has not only the meaning of physical uncleanliness, but of that more dreaded infection caused by the presence of "the spirit that walks in shadow."

It is worth noting that the syllables *shui* and *kuei* are considered to rhyme, though in the orthography of Sir T. WADE this is disguised by a slight difference of spelling.

⁹ "I have the honour," etc., and "Who is with great truth," etc. These formal expressions best convey the spirit of the equally formal and official phrases in the text.

PART III.

No. 1 *a.* Who's there?

b. It is me?

a. Come in.

b. I've brought the lad you told me to find for you the other day, Sir. If you've time just now I'll bring him in for you to see, and if you like him you can keep him.

a. Of course, yes.

b. This gentleman is Mr. Chêng; make your duty to him.

a. Where does he come from, and what's his name; how old is he, and what's his place in the family?

c. I am a Shantung man; my name is Chang; I am eighteen years old and the eldest son.

b. He has been many years in Peking; he doesn't speak like an outsider. He used to be a neighbour of ours and very sharp, but he has never been a servant before, so he must be trained by degrees.

a. That is all right. I've only recently come here and haven't yet engaged anybody; and I don't quite know whether it's necessary to have a guarantee or not.

b. That's as you wish, Sir.

a. Very well, let it be this way then,—as he comes on your recommendation, will *you* be guarantee?

b. Yes, I will. And from when shall he begin to attend on you, Sir?

a. H'm. To-day is the 28th: two days more to the end of the month. Oh, the best way will be just to tell him to come on the 1st of next month.

b. Yes.

a. And there's his bedding and so on, tell him to bring that with him *too*.

b. Yes, Sir; and we must fix on a room for him to live in.

a. Well, I think that empty room facing south, and next the bath-room, on the west, behind the white wall right at the end of the court, would do for him, wouldn't it?

b. To be sure, that would be a capital place.

　　　　◦　　　＊　　　◦　　　＊　　　＊

b. Mr. C. has sent a man with a note for you, Sir.

a. Oh! Mr. C. asks me to see him. I'll go now at once. Then let the matter be settled in that way.

No. 2　*a.* Boy!

b. Yes, Sir!

a. Make some tea for the teacher.

b. What tea do you want, Sir, coffee or black tea?

a. Neither, make some Japanese tea.

b. There's no more tea left, Sir, in the pewter canister.

a. Very well, you know the tin canister on the second shelf of the cupboard in the inner room,—well take that; and after this, whenever you see the tea in the canister is coming to an end, even if I don't tell you, just replenish it.

b. Yes, Sir.

a. Make haste and get the tea, I'll make it myself.

a. Ask the teacher to have whichever cup of tea he likes best. And yesterday you never looked what you were about, and put in ever so much tea. It was made so strong that it was altogether too bitter to drink. Didn't you see what faces Master Wu kept pulling when he was drinking it yesterday?

b. Yes, another time I will take more care when I'm making the tea.

a. And the teapot, and cups and saucers, that are in the tray on the tea-poy, bring them all here, and then see whether there's any fire in the chafing-dish.

b. Yes; Sir. It's nearly out.

a. Then look sharp and bring some boiling water, and while you're about it bring some live charcoal with you.

b. What do you call "live charcoal," Sir?

a. Oh, what a fool you are! Don't you even know what "live charcoal" is? Well, I'll tell you: charcoal that hasn't been lighted is "fresh charcoal," and red-hot charcoal is "live charcoal."

b. Yes, Sir. Here's the hot water; will you make tea, Sir?

a. H'm, this spittoon is quite full. Take it away and rinse it out and then bring it back.

b. Yes, Sir!

No. 3   *a.* Who's there?

b. It's getting late, Sir; get up at once.

a. H'm. Get some water for washing.

b. The water for washing is brought, the water for your teeth is poured out, and the soap-dish is on the washhand-stand.

a. Where's the tooth-powder?

b. It's in the drawer of the table, with the tooth-brush.

a. Bring a towel.

b. Yes, Sir.

a. What are you in such a hurry for? You needn't wash the floor yet; do that when you've folded up the bedding. You'll have to change the pillow-cases and sheets to-day.

b. Yes, Sir. Will you have breakfast now, Sir?

a. H'm, well yes, bring it. I don't want the eggs boiled so hard as they were yesterday; the softer the better.

b. Yes, Sir. Will you have hot buttered toast to-day?

a. No; and look here, don't burn it.

b. Yes, Sir.

a. There's no spoon, nor salt-cellar.

b. Here they are, Sir! Have you enough white sugar?

a. Yes! Ah, this egg is boiled just right.

a. Oh, there's a thing I want to ask you about,—I'm told the milk sold here in Peking is always more than half water. Is that so?

b. Perhaps it *may* be so with the milk bought by ordinary households, but they wouldn't dare to adulterate what we use in this establishment.

a. In buying milk here, do you buy it by the catty or by the bottle?

b. By the bottle or by the bowl. As a rule the price is not less than nine *pai* a bottle, and two *pai* a bowl. Any more coffee, Sir?

a. No, take away. I'm going to Mr. C's rooms. If anybody wants to see me, let me know.

b. Yes, Sir.

No. 4   *a.* Sir, your boy has come to say your dinner is ready, and will you go and have it.

b. All right, I'm coming.

*   *   *   *   *

a. Here!

c. Yes, Sir!

b. You ask me to come to dinner; then why have you dawdled so and not served it? What have you been about?

c. Why, the coalman has just sent the coal-balls, and I weighed them, and then the bill he had made out was wrong, and I went over the memo. slip to see how many times he had sent. *That's* what made me late in getting dinner on the table.

b. Very well. And how much *are* the coal-balls a picul?

c. Four *tiao* and more a picul.

b. Well, now get dinner.

c. Yes, Sir.

b. Tell the cook the chicken-broth he made for tiffin yesterday was bad. Tell him to be more careful in skimming off all the grease when he makes it to-morrow.

c. Yes, Sir.

b. Give me a helping.

c. Yes, Sir.

b. This isn't my rice-bowl; it is your young master's.

c. Ah, I've brought the wrong one; I'll change it for your's, Sir.

b. Never mind about changing it. There's still a very necessary thing wanting,—just think a bit.

c. Yes, yes, Sir;—knives, forks, spoons, cruet-stand, plates, dishes, chop-sticks, are all there,—I really can't think of anything still wanting. Please to remind me, Sir.

b. No wine-glasses!

c. Why, of course! I clean forgot them.

b. What is this?

c. It's broth made of taros and chicken.

b. This is just to my taste. I think the cook must have put in some Japanese Fish sauce.[1]

c. Yes, Sir, I think very likely.

b. This is very good beef. Give me some mustard and salt.

c. Yes, Sir.

b. Now then! Look here, you've knocked over this bowl with your sleeve; get a duster at once and wipe it.

c. Yes, Sir.

---

[1] This is the term for some fish the Japanese name of which the author told me, but I have unfortunately mislaid it.

b. You're always in such a hurry-scurry in what you do. Just look how you have made this brand-new table-cloth all over dirty stains.

c. Please to overlook it, Sir, for after this I will really be careful about things.

b. Give me some salt vegetables.

c. There's no pickled cabbage to-day. I've got some soured beancurd and some pickled cucumber. There *is* soy in the cucumber already. Shall I add some more vinegar?

b. No, I've finished now; take away everything.

c. Toothpicks, Sir!

b. H'm. Bring the tea, and go and have your dinner.

No. 5 *a.* To-day is the 9th; aren't you going to the Lụng Fu Ssŭ, Sir?

b. H'm. I have asked Mr. Wu to go with me. Go and ask if Master Chêng is in or not.

a. I saw them just now go out; most likely he isn't in.

b. Very well, get out my clothes.

a. Which clothes do you want?

b. European.

a. Will you wear the woollen cloth ones or the linen ones?

b. Well, it is rather cool to-day, so get out the black cloth coat and that pair of striped grey linen trousers.

a. Look, Sir, it is this waistcoat and shirt you want, isn't it?

b. Oh, I can't bear this set of studs, get those crystal ones instead. How limp this collar has been starched! Besides, the dirt on it hasn't been washed off; and it has been ironed down the wrong way. When the washerman comes to-morrow, just tell him he must take more care in his washing, and he must use more washing-powder in starching. And when he's spirting the water over a thing, tell him to take an iron and iron it thoroughly, so as to do the thing properly. Take out that pair of half-shoes.

a. Yes, Sir.

b. These socks rather want mending; tell the maid to get a piece of patching and put it in.

a. Yes, Sir.

b. Don't go away yet; stay and help me to dress. Where do you want to go?

a. To get a cart for you, Sir.

b. No need for that; it's not far; I can walk.

a. It looks better to drive.

b. Well, there's plenty of time to get one when I've finished dressing.

a. Yes, Sir.

b. Give me the shoe-horn, and pull the bottom of my trowsers down; and bring me a handkerchief, and the gold watch.

a. Do you want your cigar-case, Sir?

b. Yes; and fold up the Japanese clothes I've taken off, and mind you brush them.

a. Yes. One moment, Sir, there's a bit creased here that wants pulling out.

b. Is it smoothed out now?

a. Quite smooth, Sir.

b. Well, I shall go and sit in Mr. Blank's room until you've got a cart.

a. Yes, Sir.

No. 6 *a.* Please, Sir, the cart's here.

b. Tell him to go first to Legation Street, and from there to the Liu Li Ch'ang. I want to buy some curios.

a. Yes, Sir; if you are going to be there some time, Sir, I think it would be best to hire it for the single journey.

b. No, *there and back*; it will save all further bother. Is the cart you've engaged clean? Is the body of it large or small? And is the mule a good one?

a. All very good; this one to-day isn't a cart from a stand.

b. Then it's a cart that will go anywhere, eh?

a. No, not one of those either; it's a private cart.

b. A private cart! Then how can it ply for hire?

a. Well, their master has no employment just now, so for fear the beast should get troublesome from want of work, he has told the carter to put it to, and take it out for a day's hire. If you don't believe me, Sir, you can see in a minute. It isn't only that the mule is so fat, and that the cover and cushions of the cart are suited to the weather and the time of year, but there are curtains too.

b. Oh! Then no doubt it's a very good one. But there's another thing; if the driver is a raw hand, when he gets to the stone road at the Ch'ien Mên, he's sure to drive into all the ruts and make one giddy and dizzy by the bumping,—even the backside of the person in the cart gets swollen by the jolting.

a. Oh, this one here is a clever driver; he will never do like that.

b. What's the charge?

a. I've settled with him for six *tiao*; that includes the money for his food too. If it's very late when you've driven back, why you could give him a little extra for something to drink. Do you want me to go with you, Sir?

b. H'm. Well, yes; you can ride on the shafts and come with me.

a. Yes, Sir.

b. Put in that coloured rug first, and spread it out. And haven't you got two official hats? You can lend one to the carter to wear.

a. Yes, Sir. Do you want a stool to get in with?

b. H'm, yes. Keep that end of the stool steady with your foot. Oh, quick! fetch my stick.

a. I've brought it; here it is, Sir. Better stick it in under the rug.

b. H'm. Now look sharp and get up.

a. *(to the mule)* Get up!

No. 7

a. Boy!

b. Sir!

a. I don't feel very well to-day. When the teacher comes, tell him I shan't work to-day, as I am unwell, and so you needn't show him in.

b. Yes, Sir.

a. Bring me that stool, and put the pipe-tray on it. I won't take any breakfast this morning, but just bring me some coffee, and then tell the cook he needn't get a meal ready, but to make me a little rice congee, quite soft, but not to break the grains of rice, not too thick and not too thin,—about the consistency of treacle.

b. Yes, Sir.

a. Just pull the counterpane farther up.

b. Yes, Sir. Do you feel better just now, Sir? The flowers you ordered, just now have come: shall I put them in the Juchow porcelain vase?

a. Yes, that will do. Just now my head still seems heavy, and I feel nausea. Be quick and get my card, and go to the Legation, and ask Dr. Yung Chi to come.

b. Does Dr. Yung Chi visit patients?

a. No, but this is a matter of friendship; and besides, his medical attainments are very high. He hasn't been here long, but he has become quite famous in Peking.

b. That's true; I've heard Chinese gentlemen say Dr. Yung Chi's treatment and medicines are wonderfully effective.

a. The only thing is though, that Chinese who are friends of his are always asking him to go and see their cases, so that he's not often at home, and I'm afraid this time yours will be a fruitless errand.

b. It's a good thing that your illness is not serious, Sir. Supposing he's not at home, shall I ask some other doctor to see you, Sir?

a. In that case, yes, you might call in a Chinese doctor.

b. Our doctors all follow the native practice of medicine, which is not the same as the foreign methods of treatment. Wouldn't it be better to ask Dr. Dudgeon, of the Shih I Yuan, to attend you, Sir?

a. Well, yes, it *would* be as well.

b. If you please, Sir, just the very thing, Dr. Yung Chi has called to see you.

a. Well, that *is* fortunate; ask him in at once, and get some wine and refreshments ready.

b. What wine shall I open, Sir?

a. Oh, open some champagne, and bring some claret if there is any. See what there is, in the way of fruit and refreshments, and bring whatever there is.

b. Yes, Sir. You have the corkscrew locked up, haven't you, Sir?

a. Yes; it's on the top shelf of the cupboard, with the screwdriver. Get some tea.

b. Yes, Sir.

a. Pour out some wine.

b. Yes, Sir.

a. Bring some cigars.

a. Show this gentleman out for me.

* * * * *

b. Yes, Sir. The Doctor has gone; he told me to tell you that the powder was to be taken in three doses, and you were to be sure to take it just before sleeping; and he said, too, that you were to avoid eating anything cold and uncooked.

a. Why didn't he tell me that just now?

b. I suppose he only just thought of it.

a. Well, in the evening serve it up to me.

b. Yes, Sir. Will you take some gruel now, Sir?

a. Bring it in if it's ready, and bring me some pears too.

b. But didn't the doctor tell you to avoid eating cold and uncooked things?

a. H'm; well, I won't have them then.

b. No, Sir.

No. 8   *a.* In a day or two I want to go to the Nankou Pass, and on my way back, round by the Western Hills, so as to visit any pretty scenery in the neighbourhood, and then come home. Would you like to come with me?

b. Of course I would, Sir. If you were to go through fire and water, I would go with you, Sir.

a. Have you ever been there before?

b. Yes, I went once last year with another gentleman. Do you mean to go in a chair or to ride, Sir?

a. Oh, anyway will do for *me;* but I'm going to take your Mistress, so tell me beforehand all the different articles we shall need.

b. Well, as Mistress is going too, there's no doubt we must take some extra things. Because you see, Sir, from the time we will leave here, and as soon as we stop at an inn, there is one thing you wouldn't think of, Sir, and that will be wanted, for it is very important for Mistress, because if she were to want to relieve nature, I'm afraid there would be no convenient place for her.

a. Then how shall we manage?

b. Our own women always take their own close-stools when they travel, so we must take the same thing too this time; or else take along a very long and broad piece of cloth, besides getting four bamboo poles; then after we get into the inn, and have settled down, we can put up a screened-off place as a w.-c. *That* might be done.

a. Oh, now I shouldn't wonder if there were some other inconvenience of the kind, eh?

b. Well, Sir, I'll tell you; not to speak of having to take bedding and other articles, we must carry with us some extra stores for Mistress' food too. And supposing you want to go and bathe at T'ang Shan, you will have to spend several more days, and of course you will want still more things for the time you stay there.

a. Well then, to-morrow first engage a chair, and a mule, and then carefully think over what food we must take, get it all ready and pack it in a hamper, for convenience of carrying it.

b. Yes, Sir; you need not give yourself any trouble about taking the things, as you've got *me.* As soon as the traps and the provisions are all put up properly, I will hire a cart, and put them all in it, and then I can look after the things and ride at the same time very nicely.

No. 9 *a.* Oh! I have had such a job! But to-day at last I've managed to rent a house. It used to be a small temple; the rooms are *beautifully* clean, and the rent isn't high.

b. Where is it; and how many rooms are there?

a. Outside the Ch'i-hua Mên, west of the temple of the Sun. I don't know what the name of the place is. The house has three rooms in the main-building, with four side-rooms, besides two rooms facing the main range. In the East angle there's a kitchen and a room for you. I must find a place to put up a w.-c. after I've moved in.

b. And when do you mean to move, Sir?

a. I want to move over to-day as soon as possible, so as to be able to reckon from the beginning of the month, when paying the rent there.

b. Then I must make haste and put all the things together to-day.

a. H'm. Well, first move all the small things into the court-yard. Sweep the carpet first with tea-leaves, roll it up and cord it. Then take the bookshelves and the cupboard, and the rest of the heavy things, pick out the strong ones and pack them in the big cart that Liu Erh has hired.

b. Yes; and I think, Sir, it will be safer if all your small articles outside are put in a large packing case, and the coolie carried them on a pole.

a. Very good, but all the crockery must be carefully wrapped in paper. If the bedstead can't be carried, it must be unshipped and put together after it has been taken across, and then the curtains can be put up as before.

b. Must the nails that the scrolls and the inscription tablet used to hang from be pulled out, Sir?

a. H'm. Hi! hi! Do take care and not knock all the dust on the wall down! Why don't you pull them out with pincers instead of knocking them out with a hammer?

b. Yes, Sir.

a. Hi! Tell the coolie to be careful, when he's going through the front gate, not to spoil the table by knocking it about.

b. Yes, Sir. I'd better go along with the things, and arrange them beforehand as they were before, hadn't I?

a. No, you needn't do that yet. When the place has been swept, and the carpet put down; the tables and chairs can be put anywhere for the time, until I go over and arrange them properly in their places; and if you can't do it all by yourself you can get someone to help you. But everything must be taken over within the day, mind that!

b. Yes, Sir.

No. 10 *a.* It's a fine day to-day, and there's no wind; you must air the clothes.

b. Yes, and shall I air the bedding too?

a. H'm. Bring a piece of cord first, and tie it from this post to the tree; when you've done that, hang the clothes on the line to dry.

b. Yes, Sir. Then perhaps I had best carry out the leather trunk and the box into the court.

a. H'm. Here are the keys, open the boxes yourself. The fur-cloak, the fur-coat, and the long cloak without sleeves, that are hanging on the clothes-horse, must be aired in a shady place.

b. Yes, Sir. * * I've shaken out the clothes, and put them to air in the sun. Will you go and have a look, Sir?

a. H'm. Well, I'll go and see * * What's this? Didn't I tell you the skin-clothes must be aired in the shade? What have you hung them up with the other clothes for? Surely you know if you ever put skin things in the sun, the fur turns yellow.

b. Yes, Sir. Then shall I get a stick and put it through them and hang it on the nail?

a. That will do; and presently you must shake them out thoroughly.

b. Yes, Sir.

a. And those clothes there must be sorted into double things and wadded ones.

b. These ones are wadded.

a. Begin hanging them on a line from this end and go straight on to the other end.

b. Yes, Sir. I think at midday they should be turned the other side about, and the ones that have been in the sun change places, and make those that are in the shade get the sun, don't you think so, Sir?

a. Yes, that will do very well. And now finish doing this, and then take the boxes and knock them out.

b. Yes, Sir; and till what time would you like the things aired before I put them away?

a. Wait till the sun is just over the hills about, but mind, you must fasten the cord up into the room, and let them be exposed to the draught, otherwise if the woollen things are put into the boxes with the heat still in them, their gloss will go off them and they will be spoilt.

b. Yes, Sir; and what about the silk and satin things?

a. They are just the same, so this evening put them by as they are, for the time, and to-morrow morning put them away as they were before in the boxes, in layers and with paper in between; put in some camphor, cover them over with a wrapper and stuff it in tightly all round on each side, and put on the lid, or else the the camphor will evaporate.

b. Yes, Sir.

a. Here, wind up the string as it was before and hang it on the beam in the store-room.

b. Yes, Sir. Please, Sir, I can't remember at the moment how you fold the Japanese clothes.

a. Oh, what a useless creature you are! I took such pains to show you, and you've forgotten it again. You've no memory at all. Look here, they are folded like this. First fold over the left-hand lower edge, then take the right-hand lower edge and fold it over on to the top of that, after that take the dress and give it a pull out, double the collar over on top, smooth it out flat, fold over the two sleeves outside each side, give another double over, and there you are.

b. Thank you kindly for showing me, Sir.

No. 11 *a.* Boy!

b. Yes, Sir!

a. I'm going to invite some people to dinner to-morrow; go into the Chinese city and engage a place.

b. How many guests do you intend to ask, Sir?

a. About ten, I think, there will be.

b. Oh, then a dining-saloon will be better than a restaurant.

a. What's the difference between the two?

b. In a dining-saloon the dinners are ready laid; in a restaurant the dinners are either ready laid or you can order things separately. But when there are many guests a dining-saloon is best.

a. What are "dinners ready laid"?

b. A "dinner ready laid" means one with eight principal dishes and four sorts of cold vegetables, and any "extras" wanted besides can be had at will.

a. And when you order separately?

b. Then you tell them to do for you on the spot whatever you have a fancy for.

a. Oh, then the dinner ready laid will be more comfortable; but mind, the dishes ordered must be plain, not rich.

b. Which dishes, Sir, do you think would be most to liking of your guests?

a. Oh, I can't call to mind the names of the dishes; you must choose some that are not too rich, and decide as you think best after consideration. You had better give 100 *tiao* a head. I want *huang chiu* not *shao chiu*, for wine.

b. Will you go to the theatre?

a. Well, I understand at Chinese dinners they generally go to the theatre, so I will do the same.

b. If you want to engage them immediately, I'm afraid there won't be any boxes to be had; if there aren't, will ordinary seats do?

a. Yes, they will do; if you take boxes, mind and find ones that are not behind a column.

b. It's of no consequence, I suppose, whether they are on the left or the right side of the stage.

a. The right side is best; on the other the gongs are such a nuisance. Another thing,—the last two days when I was at the theatre, I saw a man eating in the box opposite; is that all right?

b. Why yes, Sir, quite. It is mostly done when there are *hsiang kung* invited to meet the guests.

a. Who do you call *hsiang kung*?

b. Haven't you seen very good-looking young actors often standing at the side of the stage, Sir?

a. Oh, I remember. Yes, certainly, there are people like that. What do they do?

b. Sometimes they sing on the stage, sometimes they come in with the wine. If you would like to see, Sir, to-morrow when I go to the dining-saloon, I can send a slip of paper, and tell one or two to come in with the wine; it adds very much to the exhilaration of drinking.

a. Why, it would be very jolly.

b. If you would like a Military Piece, Sir, you will have a castanet accompaniment. If you like a piece from civil history, you have a flute accompaniment.

a. I should like flutes best.

b. Then will you hear the San Ch'ing or the Ssŭ Hsi?

a. The Ssŭ Hsi, I think.

b. Then I will go now and make arrangements.

a. Oh, and the tips for the waiters, and the theatre-money,— I will pay them to-morrow through you.

b. Yes, Sir.

No. 12 *a.* Have you changed those ten dollars yet?

b. Yes, Sir, I have.

a. What did you get for them?

b. 114 *tiao* 4 *pai* 4.

a. What rate for the dollar?

b. 11 *tiao* 4 *pai* 4.

a. How's that? That's a better exchange than yesterday.

b. Yes, Sir, the value of silver has risen.

a. How is it, it has risen again?

b. Because of the heavy fall in the market-rate.

a. Who fixes the market-rate then?

b. You don't understand, Sir. At the Chu Pao Shih, outside the Ch'ien Mên, there is a Silver-Market. Very early every day people from all the cash-banks in Peking go to the market to buy and sell silver. If there is much silver on the market on a particular day, the rate falls; if there is little, the rate rises. When the buying and selling is all arranged, the amount of cash for which a tael exchanges becomes the rate of that day, and all the cash-shops in the Tartar City go by this rate. There can't be any certainty about the buying and selling of silver; each day has its own rate.

a. Then how much does a dollar exchange for in taels?

b. The general rate is reckoned as seven mace to the dollar, and the trade-dollar and the Mexican dollar are supposed to be the same value, and the Japanese dollar to exchange for a little less; but practically there is no difference. Here are the notes, Sir; they're all issued by Ho Fêng.

a. I simply can't read the amounts written on the notes; what do they have such writing as *that* on them for?

b. This is a large 50-*tiao* note, this is for 10 *tiao*, these are small notes for 5 *tiao*, 4 *tiao*, 3 *tiao*, and 2 *tiao*. This is the small change for the 4 *pai* 4.

a. Yes, I will count over the notes myself.

b. Do you make them right?

a. Yes, quite right; but this 50-*tiao* note will be of no use: take it away and get 5 *tiao's* worth of cash, and change the rest into small notes.

b. Yes; do you want them from the same bank?

a. If the same bank has no small notes, you may exchange it for some from another, but mind, the bank's name must be a reliable one.

b. Of course. I'll change it at the Ssŭ Hêng, that will be quite safe.

a. Well, go and do so.

No. 13 *a.* Where have you been?

b. Just now my own elder brother came in from the country to see me, and told me my mother was very ill. He took me outside to speak to for a time; that's why I have been all this time, and wasn't able to tell you, Sir.

a. That's all nonsense. Never mind how long you go out for, yor ought to let me know.

b. Yes, I shan't venture to be so thoughtless in future, Sir. Oh, and another thing, I want to ask a few days' leave to go home and tend my mother while she is sick.

a. Is your mother really sick; aren't you getting leave on false pretences?

b. If I were as bold as bold could be, Sir, I could never dare to bring down a sickness on my mother.

a. Well, as it is true then, how many days' leave do you want to have?

b. If my mother's illness is not serious, I will come back in two or three days, but if by any chance my mother should have something mortal, then I'm afraid I should be some days longer.

  a. When you've gone, have you got a substitute?

  b. There's a friend of mine who has been in service in the French Legation; I can get him to come and take my place for a few days.

  a. What is he like?

  b. Well, there's nothing else against him except that he smokes a little opium.

  a. H'm. No, I don't want an opium-smoker. The best way will be this, you needn't find a substitute, but get Mr. Wu's boy to look after me for you for a few days.

  b. That will be better, yes.

  a. When do you want to go?

  b. If you will let me go, Sir, I will get away from the city this evening.

  a. Well, if you want to get out of the city to-day, as it's getting on now, don't dawdle, but look sharp and put things away.

  b. There's one other thing, Sir,—I hope you will advance me next month's wages.

  a. I haven't got so much money, so I can't advance you the whole of it. I'll give you $3 in advance, and besides that I will make you a present of $1.

  b. Thank you, Sir, for being so kind.

  a. Well, now go and fetch Mr. Wu's boy, and give him over everything that concerns the room, so that he quite understands, and fetch out the lamp-globe you broke yesterday, and give it over to him, and tell him to-morrow to match it with another of the same kind.

  b. Yes, Sir.

No. 14 a. There's a visitor coming to-morrow; take the coolie with you and clean out the guest-room.

  b. Yes, Sir. There's one of the three divisions that has the awning broken and the framework of the awning fallen down, and the paper of the wall has peeled off from the damp.

  a. H'm. Yes, you're right. Well, you must tell a paper-hanger to come and paper it.

  b. Yes, Sir. You have some flowered white paper by you, haven't you, Sir?

a. Yes, ever so many reams of it. You must paper the lower half of the walls with foreign paper, and put a border of the blue-lined paper all round on the awning.

b. Very good, Sir. And we must buy a dozen or so of millet-stalks to lash the framework together.

a. H'm. Well, can you have it all finished in one day?

b. The days are so long now, we can finish it in the day quite well.

a. And the scaffolding,—have we to furnish the man with the poles?

b. No, they bring those themselves.

a. What else is there to be bought?

b. Why, there's the flour to make paste, and some bamboo-slips, and some hemp-cord—three things.

a. Well, first of all go and sweep out thoroughly the two divisions in the outer room, and if there are any cobwebs on the awning you must sweep them away; clean the glass of the windows, too; then take a duster, dip it in water, wring it dry, and scrub the floor; and mind and be careful not to dirty the wall with the duster. Now go and set to work.

b. Yes, Sir.

a. Here!

b. Yes, Sir!

a. I've just got a letter, it's no good; the visitor will be here directly.

b. Why, but the awning hasn't been papered; what had we better do?

a. Well, look here; go at once and clean out the room, and ask the gentleman to put up with it for the time.

b. Yes, Sir.

a. Listen; there's a cart has pulled up outside the front gate; it's probably the visitor.

b. If you please, Sir, it *is* the visitor arrived.

a. I'll go and receive him first; you tell the coolie to be quick and sweep out the room, and you go out and bring in the luggage.

b. The luggage is all brought in; will you ask the gentleman to count over the number, and see if they're all right.

a. Yes, the gentleman says they are quite right.

b. Oh, and the carter says you've forgotten to give him his $2 for the fare.

a. Take out these two dollars to him then, and go and see if the room has been cleaned out; take the luggage and move it into the room and arrange it properly, and then come and make some tea and draw some water to wash with.

b. Yes, Sir.

No. 15 *a.* What! another lamp-globe broken.

b. So there is; that's another one spoilt.

a. I'm always telling you, when the lamp is first lit the flame wants to be low, and then, after a bit, to be turned up higher; but you never pay any attention; you've got no memory at all. Last year you did the same thing,—you never improve. The fact is, you didn't pay any attention to what I told you; what do you mean by it?

b. Well, it was because of my being careless for once.

a. Oh, it isn't only "for once" that you have been careless. You never at any time have been careful. Take last winter for instance,—you never once cleaned the stove. This year, when the fire was left off, you didn't even clear out the coal left inside, and you didn't put any polish on the stove, but just threw it into the lumber-room, and after some time it was all covered with rust. And the coal too, stacked like that in the courtyard, *any day it might catch fire*.

b. I didn't know it was.

a. Then you must be blind!

b. It is the coolie's business, not for me to look after.

a. Don't talk such stupid nonsense! Can't you tell the coolie to put it away?

b. I have told him ever so many times, but he *won't* mind.

a. Don't keep on making excuses. You're always so obstinate.

b. How am I obstinate?

a. Well, tell me then, yesterday when I came back, where had you gone?

b. I hadn't gone anywhere *at all*.

a. Then what do you mean by taking no notice when the things in the room here were all topsy-turvy and had brought ever so many flies in?

b. Why, a friend of mine came and kept me some time, so I couldn't put things to rights.

a. Well, I don't care; but after this, when I go out, you will just have to make the room quite tidy, fold up the clothes, put on some coals in the small stove, bank up the ashes, see what there is that isn't wanted, empty out and throw away whatever has to be emptied or thrown away,—then you'll have eyes in your head; but never to do a thing until you are told of it, is that the way a man should do? Besides that, you are for ever smashing things,—it isn't the way to do at all. Then lately you have got another bad habit,—when your friends come you take out all sorts of things of mine and use them. Do you think that's the right thing?

b. When have I taken your things, Sir?

a. Don't refuse to acknowledge it. Yesterday you took some of my tea, for I came in very quitely and saw you.

b. I didn't take it.

a. As you say you didn't take it, I will go just now to your room and search.

b. You can go and search and welcome.

a. Look here! What's this? Are you still stubborn?

b. I bought that myself.

a. Here it is, the thing stolen and the man that stole it. If you still refuse to confess, go and be d——d to you, *I* don't want you!

b. Don't get angry, Sir. I *did* take your things, Sir; please forgive me.

a. Well, since you've confessed, I'll keep you. But in future, if you continue to have these bad habits you will have to march at once.

b. Yes, Sir; my respects to you, Sir, and thank you for your kindness.

No. 16 *a.* Oh please, Sir, your bridle is broken.

b. Broken, where?

a. The bit is broken.

b. Then take it to the saddler's to be mended.

a. Yes, Sir.

b. And look here, latterly the saddle, stirrups, and the girths, and all that gear, have got fearfully dirty. Why don't you look after them?

a. Not a bit, Sir, *every* day I look after them.

b. Then how could the iron-work on them have got rusted?

a. It's because I haven't rubbed them with brickdust.

b. The last few days I have ridden, the pony has seemed weak in the feet, and kept on stumbling; what's the reason of that?

a. It's true, Sir. *I noticed he had a trick of that, too.*

b. I think very likely he's cast a shoe, or perhaps been badly shod,—it *may* be that possibly.

a. Well, I'll take him to the veterinary surgeon's to-day and have him shod over again.

b. Yes, you might. And another thing,—how is it the beast never makes flesh?

a. What, not make flesh! It's you can't see it, Sir, that's what it is.

b. I can see perfectly well. I know what it is; it is because you don't feed him at night. If the beast goes on not putting on flesh, why I won't let you have the contract for his feed.

a. Don't say that, Sir. Whether it's bran, black pulse, red millet, Indian corn, or hay, there's none of them I don't give him plenty of.

b. This morning I saw a whole lot of water standing outside the stable-door; what water was it?

a. That wasn't my doing; it was the man that looks after the bath-room did it.

b. Tell him to come here then.

a. Yes, Sir, I'll go and find him.

* * * * *

c. Do you want to have a bath now, Sir?

b. I've got a question to ask you first. What did you throw the dirty water from the bath outside the stable for?

c. It wasn't thrown there. It's the mouth of the drain is stopped up, and the water has overflowed.

b. Then you will have to clean the drain out.

c. Yes, Sir; I will go and clean it at once. Isn't to-day the day you have your bath, Sir?

b. Have you heated any bath-water?

c. Yes, it's all ready and poured into the bath.

b. Then take the towels and soap and come with me. Step forward a pace first until I have finished making water.

c. Yes, Sir.

b. Look here, you *must* sweep the bath-room floor clean, and not make it so slippery us this.

c. Yes, Sir. Is the water too hot, Sir?

b. It is rather; put in a little more cold, and give me a scrubbing.

c. Yes, Sir.

b. Is there much dirt on me?

c. Not *very* much.

b. Well, rub me quite clean.

c. Yes, Sir.

No. 17 *a.* I am going to Shanghai, so pack up my things.

b. How soon do you start, Sir?

a. In a day or two.

b. Then shall you take the heavy baggage too?

a. No, no. I mean to ask some friend to sell it by auction. This evening and all night I will separate the things to be sold by auction from those I'm leaving, and then you arrange them.

b. Shall I empty out these boxes first, and stick these small odds and ends inside?

a. All right, but when you have, you must wedge them all tightly in with packing-straw or cotton-wool, so that they shan't shake about.

b. Yes, of course; and what about the clothes?

a. As soon as they are packed in the leather trunk, make them into one bundle with the soft-stuff things.

b. Very good.

a. And the books in the bookshelves, the rubbings, and the scrolls,—wrap them all in paper.

b. I'll just take out the characters from the presentation tablet; the frame can't be taken,—what's to be done with it?

a. Never mind that for the present.

*　　　*　　　*　　　*　　　*　　　**

b. The boxes are packed, Sir; when the lids are put on, I might nail them down at once, I suppose.

a. Yes, certainly. Give me that sheet of red paper, I'll write some labels to stick on the boxes.

b. The lock of the leather trunk must be turned and it must be packed in packing-matting, and after that corded up, and then it will be saved from being knocked about by the cart.

a. Quite right; and the knots in the cord must be tied quite tight, in case after the box is put in the cart it might shake loose. Be quick and send the coolie to buy two sheets of oiled paper, to wrap up the silks in.

b. Yes, Sir; and hadn't I better take down the cloth portière and roll it up?

a. Very well; and put the cover on the sunshade; and then take these writing-materials and pack them in the white box for presents.

b. Shall I roll up your bedding now?

a. Fold up the double coverlet and the wadded quilt, and put them inside the mattress-cover. The mattress I shall want spread in the cart to-morrow.

b. Yes, Sir; and how would it be, do you think, to-morrow, to make the box in matting fast at the back of the cart?

a. All right; and before packing the crockery you must dip some paper in water and stick it on to it to make it safe.

b. Yes, that's a capital plan. If you please, Sir, Mr. C. has sent somebody with a parting present for you.

a. Bring it in. Take out a card and tell him to go back and give my thanks for it.

No. 18 *a.* What have you been doing?

b. I've been watering the flowers in the garden.

a. How are the flowers looking?

b. Just now they are in full bloom; there's a beautiful show of blossoms.

a. What's all that mud on your hands?

b. I have been handling soil in the garden.

a. As soon as you've had your meal, I want to send you with a present.

b. Yes, Sir; for what house is it?

a. For Mr. Hsü, at the Hou Mên.

b. Then I'd better have my head shaved now first.

a. Oh, it's not enough to have your head shaved, you must have your queue dressed.

b. It's all done at one time, shaving and dressing the queue.

a. You must put on some cleaner clothes too. Your common ones you do your dirty work about the house in, they'll never look nice. When you go to another house, if you want to do the proper thing, you must be tidy.

b. The fact is, Sir, I haven't got any boots or hat.

a. You can borrow a hat and a pair of shoes from the other servants. Now look sharp and go and get ready; don't waste time.

* * * * *

b. I'm quite ready now, Sir. Please give me what orders you have for me. And have you sorted out the presents, Sir?

a. Look here, here are four boxes of things, and here's my official card.

b. I must go and hire a cart then?

a. Not at all, the things inside are fragile, and the cart might jolt them, so you will have to tell the coolie to go along with you and carry them.

b. Yes, that will do very well.

a. When you get there say, "These things are special local products brought by my master, who has recently come back from the country, which he has taken the liberty to send for your master's use;" and you must be sure and leave the card; then come back home.

b. Yes, Sir; then I can go now, Sir'?

a. Oh, and besides that, go into the garden and pick a few bunches of flowers and take with you, and leave them at Mr. Wu's house on your way.

* * * * *

b. I've come back, Sir.

a. Was Mr. Hsü at home?

b. Yes, Sir, and he called me in and said, "Your master should have kept these things, that he has brought back from ever so far off, for his own use; why should he have troubled himself to think of me? It makes me feel quite uncomfortable." With that he gave me a card in return, and I was to thank you for your kind attention, Sir.

a. Yes, and what's that red packet you have in your hand?

b. Oh yes, to be sure! I was going to tell you, Sir, it is a present that the gentleman there gave me. I did want not to accept it, but Mr. Hsü said, "You just take it; if you don't accept it, why I shall be angry," and so I felt forced to accept it from him.

a. Well, well, go and rest a bit.

No. 19 *a.* Have you finished washing your face?

b. I have, Sir.

a. I want to send you out to buy some things.

b. What things, Sir?

a. I want to get some mushrooms from outside the Wall, some dried prawns, and some dough-strips.

b. Shall I buy them at the Ssu P'ai-lou?

a. No, *not* from the Ssu P'ai-lou. Those shops there haven't a single good one amongst them.

b. Then shall I go into the Chinese city to get them?

a. The best way will be to get them in the Chinese city, at a salt provisions' store on the east of the Ch'ien Mên Street.

b. Ah, yes; their things are certainly good, but rather dear.

a. They are, but nothing out of the way.

b. How much do you want, Sir?

a. I want one catty of mushrooms, a catty and a-half of dried prawns, and ten strips of dough. Now how much are the mushrooms a catty?

b. Some are 6 *tiao* 4, and some 4 *tiao* 8.

a. The cheaper ones are not so good, no doubt?

b. Of course.

a. Then buy the dearer ones, but make them give you full weight.

b. They wouldn't dare to give short weight.

a. Well, it is the way of these trading people to be in the habit of asking extravagant prices, so don't you simply agree to what they ask, you must bargain back.

b. But you don't know, Sir, the large shops have all fixed prices; they wouldn't think of asking extravagant prices.

a. That's all right then. Also bring some fresh fruit from outside the city, for me.

b. What sort of fruit do you want, Sir?

a. Are there any apricots and plums to be had still?

b. No, there are no more of those two kinds now.

a. Then buy some pears, peaches, apples, *sha-k'uo-tzŭ* [a small variety of apple], some small, red apples [*pin'-tzŭ*], dried dates, and grapes,—those sorts.

b. How much of each?

a. Buy one catty of grapes, and one of dates, and get ten of each sort of all the rest.

b. Yes, Sir.

a. Take this 40-*tiao* note with you; and besides getting these things, mind and buy some sugar-candy and arrow-root with the spare cash.

b. Yes, Sir; then I'll be going now at once.

a. Wait a bit; look here, here is a bad 10-*tiao* note; take it to the Wan Shun Furriers' shop in the Chu Shih K'ourh, and tell them it is a forged note, and they are to change it immediately for another and give you that to bring back.

b. But how do you know it is their bad note, Sir?

a. I marked it; and besides, I went there to buy something some days ago, and they got it for me.

b. After that have you anything more, Sir?

a. Yes, I have. As you come back, just take that tailor's shop on your road, and inquire if the article I ordered is ready or not; if it is, wrap it up in a parcel and bring it home.

No. 20 *a.* Chang Fu!

b. Sir!

a. Come here; I've something to say to you.

b. Yes, Sir, what have you to tell me?

a. There's a gentleman, that has been promoted to be Consul at Canton, who is looking out for a servant, and I'm thinking of recommending you to him. Would you like to go or not?

b. I'm much beholden to you, Sir, for your great kindness, and I should like to go, but then I don't know for how many years it will be.

a. This gentleman would probably have to remain three years at Canton. If he is willing for you to stay with him there for three years, what do you say?

b. Yes, I wouldn't mind that.

a. But there's one thing now; if this gentleman, when the three years are up, should be promoted to another place, he would pay you your passage and send you back here; and if before the end of the three years he discharges you, he will also pay your passage back here. But if, before the three years are up, you yourself leave his service to come back, then you'll have to find the passage-money, and it will be no affair of his whatever.

b. Yes, I understand, Sir.

a. Then about wages; the gentleman offers to give you $10 a month, and he will find you in clothes all the year round. What do you say?

b. I'm quite willing to take $10 a month wages, but there are two things, Sir, I'd be much obliged if you would mention, Sir.

a. What are they?

b. One is, I hope you'll first ask the gentleman to advance me $10 as an allotment to my family. The other is, that five or six dollars a month of my wages should be paid in Peking to my family, so as to save the trouble of their getting the money to Peking from a distance.

a. Yes, I'll speak to him about that; that can be managed. But about advancing you $10 as allotment-money, what sort of deduction a month do you propose?

b. It can be as the gentleman pleases; he could stop a dollar or two dollars every month.

a. Very well.

b. If the gentleman agrees to these two things, I should like to pay the money to my family through your hands, Sir.

a. Very proper. As soon as it is all settled I will write a pay order and give it you. Someone from your family can be sent to me on the first of each month, with the pay order, to fetch the money.

b. I am much obliged to you, Sir. Now, after I'm gone, Sir, you will want another servant, won't you, Sir. What do you think if a relative of mine came into your service, Sir?

a. How old is he?

b. Eighteen this year.

a. Has he been in service before?

b. Yes, Sir, he was in service first in the Russian Legation.

a. Well, let that stand over for a bit, because there's a gentleman that has recommended a servant to me. He is coming in a day or two on trial. If he won't do, then tell *your* relative to come.

b. I'll wait till I hear from you, Sir, then.

a. Within the next day or two put all my things in order, so that you can hand them over to the new man, and reckon up everything outstanding from first to last.

b. Yes, Sir; and supposing everything is decided, when shall I commence work?

a. Well, there are eight days more from now to the end of the month,—then, of course, you'll begin work on the first of next month.

b. Very well.

PART IV.

No 1. *a.* This is His Excellency our newly-appoined Minister. H.E. has called for the purpose of paying his respects to Your Highness and Your Excellencies, the Grand Secretary and the Ministers.

b. Ah, we have been looking forward to this moment, and that we should to-day be so fortunate as to meet shows, I assure you, a predestined connection between us.

a. The Minister begs to inquire after the health of Your Highness and Your Excellencies.

b. Thank you, thank you! Pray beg H.E. the Minister to take the seat of honour.

a. The Minister says that he could not venture to take that seat, which he begs Your Highnsss will take.

b. But that is impossible; this being H.E.'s first visit to our Office, the place of honour is his by right.

a. In that case, the Minister says, he shall bow to your wishes.

b. Quite right, quite right! When did H.E. arrive in Peking?

a. On the 16th of this month.

b. We have long ago heard what an impartial administrator H.E. here is, and what an extreme value he sets upon friendly relations. Now that he has been appointed to represent his Government in this country he will not fail in his conduct of relations to be guided in all things by a spirit of justice and fairness, to the advantage of the people of both countries. Nothing could be more fortunate!

a. The Minister says that Your Highness and Your Excellencies are far too flattering. He is painfully conscious of his own deficiencies and of his unfitness to undertake this responsible position, in which he shall at all times beg Your Highness and Your Excellencies to afford him your advice.

b. His Excellency is really too modest. It is we who will beg advice from H.E.

a. The Minister says that that would be presumption on his part.

b. May I enquire how old H.E. is?

a. The Minister is sixty-one this year.

b. H.E.'s care of his health must be excellent indeed, to have passed his sixth decade and remain so vigorous as he does.

a. Dja!

b. *(to servants)* Some refreshments and fruit, and heat some wine.

a. The Minister says that, this being his first visit to Your Excellencies' Yamèn, he could not think of trespassing on your hospitality.

b. H.E. is punctilious. It is true we have met H.E. to-day for the first time, but we seem like old friends, and besides, there is nothing here but some ordinary refreshments to help us to prolong the interview. I hope H.E. will give us the honour of his company and not decline.

a. The Minister says that he really feels disturbed at having put Your Highness and Your Excellencies to such trouble.

b. Not at all. There is nothing here at all adequate to meet the occasion; I hope H.E. will excuse it.

a. Thank you, thank you; the Minister says this is altogether too sumptous an entertainment.

b. There is nothing here at all; it is quite inadequate.

b. Allow me to offer Y.E. a glass of wine.

a. The Minister says it is really too great an honour.

b. Pray be seated Y.E.

a. The Minister begs Your Highness to accept a glass in return.

b. No, indeed, I could not venture to accept *that*.

a. Then I will return the toast to Your Highness and Your Excellencies on behalf of the Minister.

b. You are our guest, Sir, how could we allow it? Well, let us fill our own glasses then.

a. Very well, since obedience is better than deference.

b. No ceremony, no ceremony. Ask H.E. to try some of this dish.

a. The Minister begs that Your Highness and Y.E.E. will not pass the dishes to him, but allow him to help himself.

b. If H.E. will eat heartily, why we will not help him to the dishes.

a. The Minister says he will on no account make any pretences.

b. That's capital!

b. Pray take a little more Y.E.

a. The Minister says he is fully satisfied.

b. Then ask H.E. to come and sit in the room over there.

* * * * *

a. The Minister begs to inquire of Your Highness and Y.E.E. when he can present his credentials?

b. With regard to that, we will communicate officially with H.E. in a day or two, after we have memorialized His Majesty and requested his commands as to the date.

a. Then he will await word from Your Highness.

b. Very good.

a. The Minister desires to take his leave now and to return home.

b. Why should we not have a little more conversation?

a. The Minister has some other important business which requires him to return and dispose of at once, and prevents him making a long stay here. He begs to express his thanks to Your Highness and Your Excellencies for your trouble.

b. The merest trifle, not worth mentioning, done without any ceremony whatever.

a. Not at all.

b. We shall return this visit shortly at your Legation.

a. You are very kind indeed. Pray Your Highness and Y.E.E. do not come out.

b. Good-day, good-day!

a. Au revoir, au revoir!

No. 2   *a.* I hope Y.E. has been well since we last met.

b. Thank you, Your Highness, quite well; and I hope Your Highness has been in good health lately.

a. Yes, thank you.

b. And Your Excellencies the Grand Secretaries and the others have also been well I hope.

c. You are very kind. Did you return home comfortably the other day?

b. Quite; I am much obliged to Y.E.E. for your kind inquiries.

a. The object of our visit to-day is, in the first place, to offer our congratulations, and, secondly, to return Your Excellency's call.

b. You are too kind. Your Highness and Y.E.E. the Grand Secretaries and the others are more than polite.

d. I hope you will excuse us for coming late.

b. Don't mention it. What is this gentleman's name? for we have not met before.

c. Of course! We had forgotten. Let me introduce you to each other. This gentleman is the newly-appointed Minister H.E. ——; this gentleman is Liu *tajen*, one of our colleagues.

b. I am delighted to make your acquaintance.

d. The pleasure is mutual then. I hope you will forgive my absence the other day, when you were good enough to call, but I was on leave at the time.

b. Don't mention it! May I ask what is Your Excellency's native place?

d. I am a Kiangsu man.

b. Which of the public offices are you a member of?

d. I am at present Vice-President of the Board of Civil Office, and a member of the Tsungli Yamên.

b. Ah! And when did Y.E. take your degree?

d. I took my chü-jên's degree in the *chi mao* year, and my chin-shih degree in the *kuei wei*.

b. What provincial posts have you held?

d. I have never held a provincial appointment. From the *kuei wei* year, after my success I took up my position in the Han Lin Yuan. Later on, I was appointed once to a Literary Chancellorship and once to a Chief Examinership.

b. In which province were you appointed Literary Chancellor?

d. I was appointed Literary Chancellor in Ssŭ-ch'uan, and my subsequent appointment as Chief Examiner was in Shensi.

b. What is Y.E.'s age?

d. I am forty-seven this year.

b. It is easy to perceive that Y.E.'s abilities must be great, when you have held such distinguished posts before reaching your fiftieth year.

d. You flatter me; it is all due to good luck. Indeed I am ashamed of my want of talent,—I am a mere stop-gap, that is all.

b. Y.E. is over modest. I have prepared a few refreshments to-day, and I hope Your Highness and Y.E.E. will stay here and chat for a while.

a. You are very kind, and we ought rightly to take advantage of your hospitality. Unfortunately, to-day a matter has been specially remitted to us by Imperial Decree, which we have to return and attend to at once, so we must beg to be excused.

b. In that case, then, I will not press you to stay.

a. Then we will come and pay our respects to you another day, and take leave of you just now.

b. Thank your Highness and Your Excellencies for your visit.

a. Not at all. Pray do not come out.

b. I must see you off.

a. Thank you, thank you.

No. 3 *a.* Allow me to introduce to Y.E. this gentleman, who is our newly-appointed Minister. H.E. has come to-day in order to pay his respects to Your Excellency.

l. Ah! I am delighted to meet him.

a. The Minister hopes Y.E. is well.

l. Ah! I hope *he* is well.

a. The Minister thanks Y.E.

l. And the health of His Imperial Majesty your Sovereign, has been good?

a. Yes, the Minister says that the health of His Majesty our Emperor has been recently excellent, and he begs to inquire whether H.I. Majesty has been enjoying satisfactory health.

l. Yes, His Imperial Majesty has been enjoying most satisfactory health. I beg H.E. will take the seat of honour.

a. The Minister begs to yield that to Y.E.

l. Impossible! His Excellency having come here is entitled to the seat of honour.

a. The Minister protests that it would be presumption on his part.

l. Pray be seated. May I ask when H.E. left his own country?

a. On the 10th of last month by our calendar.

l. I hope the journey has been a comfortable one.

a. The Minister says that, under Y.E.'s auspices, all has gone very well on the journey.

l. What stay did H.E. make in Shanghai?

a. The Minister remained only two days in Shanghai before coming on here.

l. It is a very long journey to make, to come here overland. I don't know if there is any news that we might learn?

a. The Minister says that there were a number of historic spots on the road, but that there is nothing new so far as the politics of the present day are concerned.

l. Indeed. And what day has H.E. decided to leave for Peking?

a. The Minister intends going North the day after to-morrow.

l. Why should H.E. hasten his departure so?

a. Because the term of his Mission is about to expire, consequently he cannot loiter.

l. Is H.E. going by river or by road?

a. He intends travelling by river, on account of the quantity of baggage he has.

l. Have the boats been hired yet?

a. We have sent a man to-day to hire them; to-morrow, most likely, they will all be ready.

l. Tell H.E. that I will despatch two petty officers with twenty men, to escort him to T'ung-chow.

a. The Minister says he is extremely obliged to Y.E. for being so kind.

l. Not at all. It is my duty to do what I can for H.E. on his arrival here.

a. The Minister says it is a great favour on your part.

l. Then I will send off a despatch this evening, advising the Tsungli Yamên that H.E. the Minister is starting for the North by river the day after to-morrow.

a. That will be excellent. The Minister will also have a despatch for our Legation in Peking.

l. Yes, that will be even better.

a. And now the Minister says he must take leave.

l. Ask H.E. to stay awhile and give me the pleasure of his company for a little longer.

a. The Minister has still some business that he must return and despatch at once.

l. Well, then, I must thank H.E. for coming to see me, and to-morrow I shall return his call.

a. The Minister would not like to put Y.E. to that trouble.

l. I am bound to.

a. Pray do not come out.

l. I must see you off.

a. Thank you very much.

No. 4

l. I come to-day to return Y.E.'s call, in the first place, and in the second, to thank you for your visit.

a. You are very kind, and really too punctilious, Your Excellency.

l. Not at all, it is *de rigueur*. Is your departure fixed for to-morrow?

a. Yes, I start to-morrow for certain.

l. The boats, I suppose, are all ready.

a. Yes, they are all quite ready.

l. Then at what time to-morrow shall you begin your journey?

a. Probably about nine o'clock in the morning.

l. In that case, at eight to-morrow I shall come over and see you off.

a. Oh, I really could not think of putting you to that trouble. Our meeting to-day fulfils everything, and some other time, when I come again or when Y.E. goes up to Peking, we could spend a few more days together.

l. In that case then, as you don't wish it, I won't come over.

a. Thank you. And when does Your Excellency expect to go to Peking?

l. Probably at the end of the eleventh month, when I shall certainly not fail to call on you at your Legation.

a. In the event of your coming to Peking, I hope Y.E. will drop me a line beforehand, so that I may make preparations to receive you.

l. Thank you; before I leave I shall, of course, do myself the honour of informing you first.

a. There is another favour I should like to ask of Y.E.

l. If there is anything, Y.E. has only to mention it.

a. Thank you. Our Consul here is very young, and, moreover, this is his first post, and he is wanting in experience as yet, so I trust Y.E. will be somewhat tolerant. I hope, too, Y.E. will advise him in all matters, so that he may have something to guide him. I shall appreciate it as a kindness done to myself.

l. Your Excellency is too modest. The Consul you mention, though young, is very intelligent. For some months past I have heard by report how satisfactory his treatment of international matters has been. I have a great respect for him. Only, having lived in China but a few years as yet, I suppose he can hardly be perfectly informed as to our Chinese social organisation, and popular manners and customs. If, whenever he finds something that he doesn't quite understand, he will apply to me, I will, in deference to your desire, explain it fully to him.

a. Your Excellency is excessively laudatory ; he is at present only learning the duty of his post.

l. And now I must be saying good-bye, as I have another engagement.

a. Then good-bye until we meet in Peking.

l. Yes, and as soon as you have reached Peking, I hope you will send me word, as a consolation for your absence.

a. Yes, on my arrival there, I will not fail to do myself the honour of letting you know.

l. Very well, to-morrow morning I will send a petty officer here with some men to be at Y.E.'s disposal.

a. Very many thanks. It really is exceedingly kind of Your Excellency.

l. My duty merely! Pray don't move.

a. Good-bye, and *au revoir*.

No. 5 *a.* I hope Your Excellencies the Grand Secretary and the other Ministers are well.

b. Thank you, thank you. And you?

a. Quite well, I thank Your Excellencies.

b. Please be seated.

a. After your Excellencies.

b. Have you had much to do lately?

a. Well, not very much.

b. What business have you called here to-day upon, and what can we do for you?

a. I have been sent to your Yamén to-day by the Minister to speak about a matter of public business.

b. Oh! Please tell us what it is.

a. It is this. Last month, one of our interpreters, who was provided with a passport, visited a certain place. On reaching the place, he put up at an inn; whereupon, what should happen but the people of the place, in their ignorant curiosity, collected every day at the gateway of the inn, in groups of four or five,

and crowded together to stare, some of them using very rude
language. Besides this, the Interpreter heard it rumoured that
the people intended to make trouble, so, as the inn was not far
from the Police Station, he thereupon went there, meaning to
see the Police Official and ask him to take measures to keep
order and prevent disturbance. Strange to say, the Official
actually excused himself from seeing him on the plea of being ill.
Our Interpreter had no other course than to go off again and
call at the District Magistrate's Yamên. When he got there,
he sent in his card, and after he had waited a long time, a door-
keeper came out and said the Magistrate was entertaining visitors,
and couldn't receive him. So the Interpreter came back to the
inn, and the first thing next morning he returned again to the
Magistrate's Yamên and asked to see him. Then a clerk named
Wang came out, and asked him into the Board Office. The
clerk Wang asked him what he came for, and he told him all
about it,—that the people intended to make trouble, and that he
wished to ask the Magistrate to take means to protect him. The
clerk then declared that the Magistrate was engaged officially
and couldn't receive him. The Interpreter said, "Well, since
the Magistrate is so busy, it would be inconvenient for me to
ask to see him. Only I hope you will give my message to the
Magistrate and mention that I have asked him at once to keep
order, so that no catastrophe may occur, and that the matter is
urgent." The clerk Wang made profuse promises to do so, and
our Interpreter then took his leave and returned to the inn. And
it is an actual fact that he waited two days more in the inn,
without a word of news, the people collecting in larger and larger
crowds, and freely using the most outrageous language, so that a
riot seemed inevitable.

Seeing how threatening matters looked, he sent off a letter
reporting affairs to our Minister, and at the same time started
for the Prefecture, with the intention of personally begging the
Prefect to instruct the Magistrate to give proper protection.
However, we don't know what may have been done when he got
to the Prefecture. But the receipt of his Report has greatly
surprised the Minister, because he feels that subjects of the
Powers, when travelling to any place, provided with passports,
have a right to be protected according to Regulation, by the local
authorities; and not only is this mentioned in the Treaties, but
Imperial Commands to the same effect have repeatedly been
received ordering the Provincial Governors-General and Governors
to give orders to the local authorities to conform scrupulously
to the Treaties in the protection of foreigners. It is perfectly
incomprehensible how it is that, while Viceroys and Governors
of Provinces can act up to Treaty provisions, the local officials—
Magistrates of Departments and Districts—still regard the duty

of affording protection as a perfectly immaterial matter. The Minister now begs Your Highness and Your Excellencies the Grand Secretary and the Ministers, to move the Provincial Governments to give orders to their subordinates that it is of importance to observe the Treaties, and that in future, whatever foreigners with passports may travel, it will be the duty of the local authorities to render them all possible protection.

b. Quite so. When you get back, will you tell H.E. the Minister, with regard to this case, that a despatch shall be sent to the place to-morrow, requesting the Governor of the Province to ask the District Magistrate and the Police Official *why* they wouldn't receive the visit, and the reasons for their not maintaining order. If it appears that they have acted with negligence, they shall certainly be denounced by name. We will also again request the Provincial Governments to issue stringent orders to the Department and District Magistrates, that whenever after this a foreigner visits any place, they must not fail to observe the Treaties and give him every possible protection, and that if they refuse to make every possible effort to do so, they shall certainly be impeached to the Throne by name.

a. Yes, if Your Excellencies will take that trouble, our officials and people in general will be most deeply grateful.

b. Not at all. It is a thing we are bound to do our utmost in.

a. Well, I will return and report to the Minister exactly what Your Excellencies have said.

b. And on your return pray give His Excellency our kind inquiries.

a. Yes, I shall certainly tell him.

b. Good-day to you.

a. Au revoir.

No. 6 *a.* I have been deputed to-day by the Minister to call on his Highness and Your Excellencies the Grand Secretary and Ministers to verbally acquaint you with a matter of Public business.

b. Ah! what is it?

a. It is this. Last month, a steamer under our flag, called the "Feng-shun," came to Tientsin from Shanghai. She had got as far as just above Taku, when she came in collision with and damaged a Chinese merchant-vessel at anchor there. After the "Feng-shun's" arrival at Tientsin, the Master reported the matter to our Consul. Moreover, he stated in his report that the place where the Chinese vessel was anchored, was where she obstructed the fairway of steamers; and he asserted that the cause of her being run into and damaged by the steamer was that she had not anchored in accordance with the Harbour Regulations, and therefore he was not liable for such damage. Our Consul afterwards received a despatch from the Taotai, saying that the Chinese junk-master Chou Li-ch'êng complained that while his vessel was under way off Taku, the steamer "Fêngshun" came up astern and collided with her, knocking off her rudder and damaging her side. The Consul then replied to the Taotai's despatch, mentioning that the Master of the "Fêngshun" had declared that the Chinese junk was at anchor in the river, that the collision was occasioned by her having anchored in the fairway of steamers, and that under the Harbour Regulations he was not liable. However, the two Powers should, before taking further steps, each of them depute an officer to proceed together to the scene of the collision and make an inspection, and afterwards decide as to the question of liability. The Taotai accordingly deputed an officer who accompanied our Interpreter to the scene of the collision, and they made their inspection.

The petition of the junk-master Chou Li-ch'êng stated that the junk's rudder had been broken off, and the side of the vessel damaged, but on their making their inspection, only the rudder had been broken off, and no damage had been done to the junk's side. This point therefore disagreed with the original statement. Again, according to the junk-master Chou Li-ch'êng, on the day in question his vessel was run into while under way, but the Master of the steamer said that Chou Li-ch'êng's vessel was *not* under way in the river, but anchored and obstructing the steamer fairway, and it was owing to this that she was run into. The Taotai insisted on disbelieving the account given by the Master of the steamer and on believing that of the Chinese junk-master. Our Consul argued, in discussing the case with the Taotai, that as for believing the story of the Chinese Master, why he had asserted in his original statement that the steamer had knocked off his rudder and also damaged the junk's side, but as soon as she was inspected it was found that only the rudder had been knocked off, and no damage done to the side. From this fact alone it was evident the junk-master's story was not to be believed. But the Taotai, though he had nothing to meet this contention with, all the same urged the Consul to order the Master of the steamer to pay an indemnity for the cost of repairs. The Consul, on the faith of the Master of the steamer, said that as the Chinese junk had been run into through not anchoring in accordance with the Harbour Regulations, there was no legal liability for damages, and if he, the Consul, were to compel the Master to pay for the cost of repairs, he could not prevent him from protesting against the decision. Unfortunately, the Taotai altogether dissents from the Consul's views, and as they have argued the case without result, the Consul has no course open to him but to report fully to the Minister and request instructions how to proceed. The Minister has sent me here to inquire from Your Highness and Your Excellencies what ought to be done in this case, in order to prevent controversy.

b. Although His Highness is not present to-day, our view is that the statements of the two parties in the case being conflicting, cannot be depended upon, and that the Consul should be officially instructed by H.E. the Minister, and the Taotai by us, that they are to call upon the two parties both to bring witnesses, and afterwards to hold a joint investigation, when, no doubt, the true facts will be elicited. If you will inform H.E. of this on your return, and if he sees no objection to it, would he send us word, and we will then write to the Taotai.

a. Yes; then I will return and let the Minister know Y.E.'s proposal, so that he may consider it and send you a note.

b. Yes, then *that* will be the arrangement.

a. Well then, I will bid you good-bye for the present.

b. Good-bye, good-bye.

No. 7 *a.* How do you do?

b. (*Taotai*) Thank you, quite well. And how are you?

a. I am much obliged for your inquiries.

b. Please take a seat.

a. After you, Sir.

b. Have you been busy lately?

a. Well, not *very* busy.

b. To what business do I owe the honour of your visit to-day?

a. It is a matter of business which I have been deputed by the Consul to-day to come and consult you upon.

b. What is it?

a. It is this. There is a native merchant of this place, called Lin Yün-fa, who chartered a sailing vessel flying our flag, at Foochow, and loaded her with a general cargo for this port. He agreed to pay $4,500 as freight, of which he had paid down $1,500 at Foochow, and it was expressly stated that the balance of $3,000 was to be paid over on arrival at this place, to which the Master then agreed. All this was arranged without any broker or mercantile firm as intermediaries, but was simply an understanding come to directly between the two parties. Four days ago the ship arrived here, and early on the following morning Liu Yün-fa, with some lighters, took delivery of the cargo, lightered it, and conveyed it to the Customs' Examination Shed for examination. He then told the Master he was going home to get together the freight, and would be back on board in the evening, when he would hand over the full amount of the balance in cash, and he also wrote his address and gave it to the Master to keep. So the Master, thinking the man to be a respectable merchant, allowed him to go away. When the evening came, Liu Yün-fa didn't return on board, and even up to yesterday night he still hadn't come back to the ship. The Master therefore despatched a man to go and look for him at the place he had written down as his address, but as he couldn't be found, the Master couldn't help becoming suspicious, and in consequence reported the matter to the Consul, who wrote a note to the Commissioner of Customs asking him when Liu Yün-fa paid the duties, to temporarily detain the goods and not release them until the freight had been paid in full. The Consul afterwards received a note from the Commissioner in reply, saying that if Liu Yün-fa paid his duties in full, the Customs had no power to temporarily detain the goods, so that he would be unable to do as requested in the matter. The Consul, fearing Liu Yün-fa might suddenly pay the duties, and the Customs release the boats and their cargoes, and that in this way this money for freight would not be recovered, has sent me here to ask you to write to the Commissioner of Customs, if Liu Yün-fa pays his duties, to temporarily detain the boats and their cargoes, and when he has paid for the freight, the Consul will notify you officially, so that you may write to the Commissioner to release the goods. He entreats you most earnestly to oblige him by doing this, and we shall be most deeply grateful.

b. Well, as to that, *officially* speaking, when Liu Yün-fa has paid the full duties, the Customs have really no right to detain the boats and their cargoes; but as the Consul asks me a favour, I will, merely from private regard for him, ask the Commissioner to temporarily detain Liu Yün-fa's boats with their cargoes. And as soon as he has paid the freight, please let the Consul send me word of it, so that I may notify the Commissioner, and the boats and cargo be released. But this is only done on this occasion by way of obliging, and must not be used as a precedent for the future.

a. If you will be so obliging as to do so, we shall really be infinitely grateful.

b. Not at all! In a short time I will send a note to the Commissioner.

a. Then I shall say good-bye.

  b. Good-bye, good-bye.

  a. Au revoir.

No. 8 *a.* I have been sent here to-day by the Taotai to see you, Sir, on business.

  b. What business is it?

  a. You wrote to the Taotai some time ago about a native firm dealing in foreign goods here, called Ch'ing Ch'ang, the head of which, Chao Hsi-san, had bargained to buy sixty bales of Russian cloth from the foreign firm of T'ien Shêng. You said that a written agreement had been made, and that when the goods arrived last month, the foreign merchant pressed Chao Hsi-san to take delivery, but he would not do so, and tried to find fault with the goods. And you asked the Taotai to give orders to the Chih hsien to summon Chao Hsi-san before him for examination. Since then the Chih hsien has reported on the case. He says the man has now been summoned, and this is what he states. Last year, before the river closed, he bargained with the foreign firm of T'ien Shêng for sixty bales Russian cloth, and signed a written agreement. He paid a hundred taels deposit, and it was distinctly stated that the goods were to be delivered and the price paid without delay on either side in the first ten days of the third moon of this year. When this date arrived the goods had come to hand, and the T'ien Shêng hong sent a message to him. He then took his muster to the foreign hong, and opened the bales and compared them; among them were ten not up to muster, and for that reason he refused to receive the goods, and demanded to be paid back his deposit, telling the foreign merchants to dispose of the goods elsewhere, but they would not give him back his deposit. Well, they separated without coming to any agreement, and to his surprise, the foreign merchants have actually laid a complaint against him for refusing to take delivery, which he has done simply because the goods are not up to muster, and not in the least because he wants an excuse to get out of his engagement. The Taotai wrote to you giving the substance of the Chih hsien's report, and afterwards received your reply that what Chao Hsi-san stated in his evidence before the Magistrate was an *ex parte* statement and was insufficient as proof, and asking that the Chih hsien might be instructed once more to make Chao Hsi-san take delivery of the goods and make payment of the money. Now the Taotai says that although Chao Hsi-san's statement is an *ex parte* one, yet, unfortunately, as he affirms that he has refused to take delivery on account of the goods not being up to muster, if he is now compelled to receive and pay for them, it will not make him feel he has been treated with justice. If we accept Chao Hsi-san's statement as the truth, then the foreign merchant will perhaps not be contented.

Now the Taotai has thought of a good plan, and has sent me to discuss it with you. He proposes that, some day this month, he and you should hold a joint investigation and summon the two parties, telling the foreign merchant to hire some men to carry the sixty bales into Court, and that you, Sir, and himself should hold a sitting, and have a public inspection of the goods, and then and there give judgment as to which is in the right. I don't know what you will think of this proposal.

b. I had not made up my mind about this matter, but as the two parties each have their own version, it will be difficult to decide. The Taotai's scheme is very satisfactory, still in my own opinion it would be well that the Taotai should instruct Chao Hsi-san to invite two Chinese merchants, and I should instruct the T'ien Shêng hong to procure two foreign merchants, and for them all to meet at the Mixed Court, where the four merchants would inspect the goods, and see whether they do or do not correspond with the samples, and make their verdict authoritative. If these four should decide after inspection that the goods and the sample córrespond, the Taotai could then make an order that Chao Hsi-san should take delivery and make due payment. If they should not correspond, I could then examine the head of the T'ien Shêng hong, and then decide on some action in consultation with the Taotai. That is my own view; what do you think of it?

a. The way you suggest, Sir, is still more perfectly satisfactory in every respect. I will go back and report this to the Taotai before sending you a reply.

b. Won't you stay a little longer?

a. I cannot stay long, because I have official duties to attend to. I will pay my respects to you another time, Sir.

b. You are very good.

a. Pray don't come out, Sir.

b. Au revoir.

No. 9 *a.* The Consul has sent me here to-day to consult with you on a matter of business.

b. What is the business?

a. It is the case of the debt due by Chu Hsiao-shan, the Compradore of the —— firm of Pao Ch'ang.

b. I have already written a despatch to the Consul about that case. I don't know what the Consul's opinion upon it is.

a. The Consul's view is this. When Chu Hsiao-shan was first engaged by the Pao Ch'ang firm, written security was given by four firms—Hsiang Li, Jên Ho, Fu Shun, and Chin Ch'ang. The security-paper expressly said that, in case of defalcation, etc., on the part of Chu Hsiao-shan, besides reimbursement being made by realising his private effects, whatever sum remained unpaid, the four guarantors would share the liability for equally. This they all agreed to abide by. The other day the Consul received your despatch, in which you say, that besides reimbursing Tls. 1,000 by realising Chu Hsiao-shan's private property, the guarantor Chin Ch'ang, the silk piece-goods firm, must be made liable for the payment of Tls. 2,000 of the Tls. 4,000 remaining unpaid, and the three guarantors, Hsiang Li, Jên Ho, and Fu Shun, proprietors of foreign-goods warehouses, must share the liability equally between them for the remaining Tls. 2,000. The Consul finds it really difficult to understand your dealing with the case in this way, and he therefore sent me here to inquire for what reason you do not keep to the provisions of the security-paper, and make all the four guarantors share and share alike, instead of singling out the Chin Ch'ang hong to pay more, and the other three hongs less, than their shares.

b. The reason why I make the Chin Ch'ang hong pay more, and the other three hongs less, is this. When I summoned the four guaranteeing firms before me the other day for an investigation, three of the proprietors of the shops, Hsiang Li, Jên Ho, and Fu Shun, pleaded that although when the security-paper was originally drawn up it did provide that in case of future defalcations on the part of the Compradore Chu, besides his private effects being realised for the repayment of the debt, the amount of the debt then left outstanding should be paid in equal proportions by the four guarantors, yet for some years past the Chin Ch'ang hong had constantly borrowed money from Chu Hsiao-shan to trade with, and that for these loans Chin Ch'ang paid no interest. Consequently, for some years he has derived a good deal of benefit from Chu Hsiao-shan, while we three guarantors have had no monetary dealings with Chu Hsiao-shan during these years, and have never derived any benefit from him. If you now make us all equally responsible for his defalcations, it will be most unjust to our three firms.

Very well. Then I asked the head of the Chin Ch'ang hong whether what the other three said was a fact. He admitted that he had constantly borrowed money from Chu Hsiao-shan to trade with, and that it was quite true he had benefited to a considerable amount by him; and that is why I gave judgment for Tls. 2,000 to be paid by the Chin Ch'ang hong, and for the other three guarantors to pay the Tls. 2,000 between them.

All four parties signed a formal statement that they were willing to accept this award, — indeed, I exercised no great pressure in the matter. In what way do you consider this decision unjust?

a. Well, I hope you will excuse me, but I will take the liberty of making one remark upon it.

b. Pray don't hesitate to speak out plainly, whatever you have to say.

a. Then in my opinion, such a decision hardly seems quite fair.

b. In what way not quite fair?

a. Your view is that because the Chin Ch'ang hong has for some years derived benefit by Chu Hsiao-shan, you should now adjudge them to be bound to pay more, while the other three guaranteeing firms, Hsiang Li, Jên Ho, and Fu Shun, not having derived such benefit, are to be called upon to pay less. Now, in my humble opinion, in deciding this case you should be guided by what was said in the security-paper, and as that expressly mentions that the four guarantors should share the same degree of liability in making good any future deficit on Chu Hsiao-shan's part, if you now single out the Chin Ch'ang hong to pay more, it is not only a departure from the original agreement of the security-paper, but the other three guarantors will probably think it a lucky escape, which they were scarcely entitled to. As for the argument that the Chin Ch'ang hong constantly borrowed money from Chu Hsiao-shan to trade with, without paying interest, and that as they have enjoyed a considerable amount of benefit from him for some years, therefore you adjudge them liable for a larger amount, why, the loans from Chu Hsiao-shan to the Chin Ch'ang hong were affairs of purely private friendship, and have nothing to do with this case, and you have no right to import their private transactions into this case at all. As for the three other guarantors, who are trying to pay less than their share, let them give whatever untrue evidence they choose, but as far as you are concerned there certainly can be no occasion to decide in accordance with their assertions. Suppose, for instance, that among the four guarantors two had derived benefit from Chu Hsiao-shan, and two had not, ought the two who had be made to pay, and the other two, who hadn't, to hold themselves aloof altogether? And, therefore, in the interests of justice, you are bound to call upon all four guarantors, as the security-paper provides, to make payment in equal proportions, and not make any distinctions as to paying more or paying less.

b. Your argument is founded on the strict rule, and mine is a modification to meet the circumstances.

a. You may speak of "a modification to meet the circumstances," but such modifications are permissible only when a strictly regular decision would be impracticable. Now in this case there can be no obstacle to a strictly regular decision being given, so why should there be such a modification?

b. Well, since you consider my award not quite fair, will you, when you get back, consult with the Consul, and later on there is no reason why we should not devise some thoroughly well-considered scheme.

a. In that case we will discuss the matter again, and I will say good-bye to you, and go back.

b. What is your hurry? Stay and chat for a little while longer.

a. I have some other work to do, so I will wish you good-bye for the present.

b. Good-bye to you.

a. Au revoir.

No. 10 *a.* My visit to your Yamên to-day is to confer with you on a matter of business.

b. Ah! Pray tell me what it is.

a. It is about the case in which the Chinese foreign-goods hong, Hsin Ch'êng, are indebted to our nationals, the Hêng Yü firm, for goods supplied. When the Hêng Yü firm the other day laid a complaint against the Hsin Ch'êng hong, I first of all called Wang Pao-shan, the principal of the Hsin Ch'êng hong, before me and questioned him. His statement was that a native firm of general dealers of this place, called the Fu Shun Chan, owed him some Tls. 10,000 and more for goods supplied, which he had repeatedly pressed them for, but which they had not yet paid; that if he could recover this sum, he would, besides paying back their Tls. 5,000 to Heng Yü, have a balance over and above of Tls. 5,000, and he begged me to address you officially, so that you might give orders to the District Magistrate to summon the principal of the Fu Shun Chan before his Court and recover this amount, when he could repay his debt for goods supplied by the Hêng Yü firm. As I was afraid that the debt to Hêng Yü would not be settled, I wrote to you officially to ask you to instruct the District Magistrate to have up and examine the principal of the Fu Shun Chan and recover from him the sum he owed Hsin Ch'êng, with the object of rendering possible the repayment of their liability to the Hêng Yü hong. Yang *ta-laoyeh*, the deputy whom you sent to my office yesterday, said it was suspected that the principal of Hsin Ch'êng had induced the principal of the Hêng Yü foreign hong to bring forward a false charge, and to sue the Fu Shun Chan for their debt, in Hsin Ch'êng's interest, and that if the steps asked for were taken, it would be the beginning of a system of foreign merchants taking up and interfering in legal proceedings; and he begged me, before proposing anything further, to find out as to this by making close enquiries. Accordingly I sent for the principal of the Hêng Yü firm again, and I did closely question him. He declared that it was perfectly true that the Hsin Ch'êng hong owed his firm Tls. 5,000 for goods supplied, as their books would show. He knew nothing about the Fu Shun Chan being indebted to the Hsin Ch'êng hong for goods supplied. With regard to his request that I would move you officially to direct the District Magistrate to summon the principal of the Fu Shun hong for examination and the recovery of the amount owing, it was quite true that that was Wang Pao-shan's suggestion, and not a plan arranged between them two. So now, having clearly ascertained that there is no sharp practice in the matter, I have again to ask you to ask as I requested.

b. Yes, but though you have ascertained that there is no dishonest dealing in this matter, all the same, the only proper course is, that the foreign merchant should sue Hsin Ch'êng, and that the latter should lay his complaint against Fu Shun, each account being separately settled. If the parties were to be involved at discretion, although there might be no sharp practice in this case, it would be difficult to prevent abuses arising in the future, and precautions against them *must* be taken; do you not think so yourself, Sir?

a. Yes, I think what you say is very reasonable. There's only one point, and that is, that I would ask you to direct the District Magistrate, when Wang Pao-shan comes to the Magistracy with his plaint against Fu Shun, and the Magistrate recovers the money owing to Hsin Ch'êng, not to let Hsin Ch'êng take away the money for the present. The Magistrate should detain the Tls. 5,000 that Hsin Ch'êng owes to Hêng Yü, and let Wang Pao-shan take the rest. Do you think that plan feasible?

b. Why, yes, I could give instructions to the Magistrate to take that course.

a. In that case, I will send you a despatch to that effect to-morrow, meanwhile I will take my leave, if you will allow me.

b. Good-bye then till I next see you.

a. Good-bye to you.

b. Au revoir.

PART IV   THE GUIDE TO KUAN-HUA.   115

No. 11   *a*. My best congratulations to you.

b. The same to yourself.

a. Seeing, in the *Peking Gazette* yesterday, the news of your selection, I have come to-day to express my congratulations.

b. I am much obliged to you for your trouble. Please take a seat.

a. After you.

b. Have you been much occupied with official business lately?

a. For some time, yes, I have had a great deal of business; I have had no time to myself at all.

b. What makes you so busy?

a. It is all the business connected with the Autumn Assize.

b. Why, the Autumn Assize is nearly over, is it not?

a. Yes, at least it will be by the end of this month.

b. Ah! When will you be presented to the Commission of Scrutiny?

a. Probably on the tenth of this month.

b. What sort of a post is it?

a. Well, it is a medium post.

b. With your talents, Sir, it won't be long before you are transferred to the leading Magistracy.

a. Oh, I don't venture to aspire to that. This is my first official appointment. I am quite contented to get an easy post and be saved from the fear of making some blunder. If it had been one of the laborious and difficult posts, I should feel I was not competent for the position and that I should excite general ridicule.

b. Ah, you are too diffident, Sir.

b. Then about what date is your departure?

a. Well, it will be about the first week or so of the 11th moon.

b. And how many days do they allow you?

a. The time allowed is three months properly, and if anything of importance happened I can apply for another month's leave. My own idea is that, if, when the time comes, there is nothing special, why I needn't apply for leave.

b. Do you take your family with you on this occasion?

a. Well, I think travelling in the winter will be so very cold that there would be all sorts of inconveniences if I took my family, so I intend this year to go first to my post, and next spring to send one of my household to come and meet my family, which will be more convenient.

    b. Yes, if you arrange that way, it will be better, no doubt. Well, I must be going off to the Yamên. We will have some more talk another day.

    a. Well, I shouldn't like to detain you long, as you have official engagements. After I have been presented to the Commission, I shall call at your house and make my compliments.

    b. You are really too good. Pray don't move.

    a. Please don't stop; of course I must see you to the door.

    b. Pray go indoors, Sir.

    a. As soon as you are mounted.

    b. Thanks, many thanks.

No. 12   *a.* How do you do? I haven't seen you for a long time.

    b. Nor I you. My best wishes to you, Sir.

    a. And mine to you.

    b. I returned home the day before yesterday, saw the list of the successful candidates, and found you had passed, so I've come to-day on purpose to express my congratulations.

    a. Many thanks for your trouble.

    b. Not at all.

    a. Pray take the seat of honour.

    b. Please be seated, Sir.

    a. I hope that everything went very well on your journey.

    b. Thank you, yes, everything went smoothly. You have taken such a high place, Sir, on this occasion, that it is evident your scholarship is of the soundest.

    a. You flatter me; it is a piece of good fortune only.

    b. You are too modest. Who was the Assistant Examiner this time?

    a. It was the Hanlin Compiler Chang.

    b. Have you made all your calls?

    a. Yes, yesterday I made my calls upon the Chief and Assistant Examiners.

    b. Your brother has quite failed to meet with his deserts this time.

    a. Not at all, Sir, indeed.

    b. Was he "sent up"?

a. Yes, his papers were sent up for approval; it was his verse that ploughed him.

b. A mere momentary check in his literary career; he is sure to get his degree at the next Provincial Examinations.

a. I hope he may, thanks to your good auguries.

b. What is the employment that has brought you to Peking on this occasion?

a. I am escorting a consignment of copper.

b. Have you finished handing it over?

a. Yes, I handed it over in full yesterday.

b. Then on your return to the Provincial Capital, I suppose you will be able to take up your post.

a. This year, on my return, I shall be able to hold some acting appointment, but probably it will be next year before I take up my post.

b. Now, when are the Test Examinations?

a. On the 23rd of this month.

b. Then after your Test Examination is over, we will have some more conversation; and now I will bid you good-bye.

a. Why not stay a little longer, Sir?

b. Well, to-day I have other calls to make.

a. Then, when the Test Examination is over, I shall come and pay my respects to you.

b. You are too good. Don't come out.

a. Good-bye till we meet again.

No. 13 *a.* I have called upon you to-day, Sir, to ask you to do me a favour.

b. Thank you. What can I do for you?

a. It is this. A fellow-countryman of mine is importing some ten or more chests of Ssŭ-chuan opium, and he has asked me to arrange as to paying the duties for him. *I* being quite at sea about it myself, I have come to beg you to manage this for me.

b. When are the goods likely to arrive?

a. They will probably reach Peking the day after to-morrow.

b. That's easily managed.

a. Who can you get to manage it?

b. Has your friend from the country come to Peking?

a. Yes, he arrived yesterday evening. He intends, as soon as he has made proper arrangements with regard to paying the duties, to leave the city and meet the goods.

b. I see, yes. Well, I will go out of the city to-day and ask the good offices of the Commissioner of Customs' chief clerk, and get him to depute two men to go very early the day after to-morrow to your lodgings, and to accompany your friend from the country out of the city to meet the goods, and afterwards to go with the goods-carts in their charge to the Customs' Office. And will you tell your friend to make out an invoice beforehand and give it to me, to be handed in by me for verification on the same day. After it has been verified the opium will be stamped and released. And when the General Office has calculated the amount of duty, and let me know it, I will draw it from your friend from the country, and take it to the Commissioner of Customs. There will only be a little "rice-money" to be given to the understrappers on duty, that's all.

a. Oh, but my friend isn't afraid of spending a little extra cash, provided he can make sure of being fortunate enough to have no trouble. The plan you now propose is very satisfactory indeed.

b. Pray let your friend from the country make himself perfectly easy; as I undertake to manage the matter, I will guarantee absolute safety.

a. You know, with my friend it is a case of "a burnt child fears the fire."

b. How so?

a. Why, the year before last, he imported ten chests of Ssŭ-chuan drug. When they reached the Chang I Mên, the city gates were closed, and he put up in an inn. The carters were seen unloading the opium from the carts by the city police, who laid an information against him for unlawfully unloading goods, and he was fined a considerable sum of money, so that he's very nervous this time; and that is the reason of his asking me to make previous arrangements.

b. Tell him to have no fear whatever; there shall certainly be no mistake.

a. Well, I am really very much obliged to you for your trouble. To-morrow I shall await news from yourself at my lodgings.

b. Precisely.

No. 14 *a.* I have come to thank you for the honour of your visit the other day.

b. Thank you, but you are really too punctilious, Sir.

a. Not at all, I could do no less.

b. How have your official duties been lately?

a. For the last few days they have been rather slacker.

b. It is a case of "a capable man is always busy" with you.

a. You are too complimentary indeed; it is only "making up for dulness by industry" with me, you know.

b. You are too modest.

a. I came to-day to bring you an invitation for the 5th, at the T'ung Ch'ing T'ang; please don't decline, but let me have the honour of your company.

b. Oh, why should you put yourself to so much trouble; we have become so intimate at once, that such etiquette seems unnecessary.

a. It is only a slight piece of attention on my part, meant to fulfil in some measure one's duties as a resident of the place. Besides, the other guests are all men of high character and principles, with whom I am on very good terms, and all meeting together for the sake of conversation.

b. Well, since you are so exceedingly kind, I shall do as you bid me.

a. Thank you, you will do me a distinguished honour; then to-morrow I shall write you a note of invitation.

b. Oh, but as we have spoken of it verbally there is no occasion to send a written invitation; please tell me at what time, that's all.

a. Well then, I will do as you say and not send the note, and we shall meet at the T'ung Ch'ing T'ang at 11 o'clock on the 5th.

b. Yes, when the day comes, I shall not fail to be there in good time.

a. Good.

b. And there is something else, in which I wish to beg the honour of your assistance.

a. In what way can I be at your service?

b. You see, this is my first visit to Peking, and I am a total stranger here. I want to hand in my statement of Particulars of Antecedents, but I have nowhere to procure an Official Sponsor. I shall be much obliged should you have any friends well known to yourself that are sending in Statements of Antecedents, if you could find a Sponsor for me.

a. Why this is quite a coincidence. I have a friend, a chüjen, who, including this year's Metropolitan Examination, will have been up for his Three Examinations, and he is just now intending to hand in his Statement of Antecedents and await employment. It will be just the thing for both of you to prepare a mutual Security. This gentleman will be one of those present at my party on the 5th, and you can talk over the thing with him personally then.

b. Really, that is an extraordinary coincidence, and I shall rely on you entirely in the matter.

a. Thank you, it will be my duty to do all that I can to serve you ; and now I must say good-bye until we meet on the 5th.

b. You are going home then?

a. Au revoir.

No. 15 *a.* Let me introduce you two gentlemen,—This is Chu Yu-yuan,—this is Mr. Huang I-ch'ên.

b. I am delighted to make your acquaintance.

c. The pleasure is mutual, Sir.

b. Please take a seat, Sir.

c. After you, Sir.

b. I have often heard my friend here, Mr. Li Chih-hsien, speak of your wide and brilliant scholarship, and I have a great admiration for it. Our meeting to-day is a predestined event.

c. Thank you. Mr. Chih-hsien is far too flattering to my slight capacity and scanty learning ; I feel really quite overpowered.

b. You are too modest. May I ask, Sir, when you lost your father ?

c. In the spring of this year.

b. When your father was living, what had his appointments been?

c. My father had been transferred from the Hanlin to a Censorship, afterwards promoted to a Supervising Censorship, then, having gained a First Class at the Metropolitan Scrutiny, was selected for the appointment of Grain Intendant of Kuangtung ; last year he was promoted to be Financial Commissioner of Honan, and this spring, on the 5th of the 2nd moon, while in office as Financial Commissioner of Honan, he vacated his post [*i.e.,* he died].

b. What age was your father this year ?

c. He was sixty-six.

b. And what age is your mother?

c. My mother is just sixty.

b. Is she still vigorous?

c. Thank you, yes, she is quite hale and hearty.

b. You are serving in the Han Lin Yüan, are you not?

c. Yes, after passing successfully at the examinations in the Kuei Wei year, and entering as a Student Bachelor in the Hanlin, I "went down" last year, and was granted rank as a Hanlin Compiler. This spring I lost my father, and came to my native place here to keep my mourning.

b. How many brothers have you, Sir?

c. I have a younger brother,—there are two of us.

b. What posts has your brother held?

c. He has not held office. He was a Proxime accessit in the Jên Wu year, and while my father was alive, he accompanied him in attendance to his post, and he is at home now studying.

b. Yes. Now this is my first visit to your neighbourhood, Sir, and as I am quite unacquainted with anything here, I hope you will be my adviser in different matters.

c. Thank you. Where were you before as Private Secretary?

b. I had gone as Law Secretary, the year before last, to the Department Magistracy at I Chou, but last winter my Chief, owing to certain proceedings, left his post, and I gave up my engagement and went home. Then this spring our friend here was allotted this post, and as he was bent on inviting me to accompany him, I was morally bound not to refuse, and consequently came here with him.

c. From what position did our Prefect here enter the public service?

b. He was "favourably mentioned" as a chüjen by the State Historiographer's Office.

c. Indeed! And now I must be saying good-bye, and returning home. I shall call again another day to enjoy the benefit of your conversation.

b. You are very good. I shall pay my respects to your mother personally soon, meanwhile please present my compliments to her.

c. It is extremely kind of you. Please stay where you are, don't come out.

b. Good-bye to you.

No. 16 *a.* Some time ago I heard Mr. K'ung Chu-an mention your well-known name, and as I could not venture to intrude upon you unceremoniously, I asked Mr. K'ung to arrange for an interview, and have come to-day to pay my respects.

b. Thank you, I am much obliged to you for your trouble. I, too, have known you, Sir, by reputation, for a long time, and it is only my being so greatly occupied by domestic matters that has prevented me from calling upon you, so that our first meeting to-day affords me great gratification.

a. This being my first visit to your neighbourhood, and I being a stranger in the place, I shall trust in all matters entirely to your advice.

b. You are very kind. I shall not fail to try and be of service to you whenever occasion offers. Pray when did you arrive here?

a. I have only been here two months.

b. I heard from Mr. K'ung that you are in charge of the Lekin Collectorate here.

a. Yes; after being received by the Governor at the Provincial Capital, I had the honour to be deputed to assist in the management of the Lekin Collectorate here.

b. How long did you stay in the Provincial Capital?

a. I stayed a month only.

b. Are you likely to obtain a substantive appointment?

a. An appointment? Probably not before three years are passed.

b. How many other Expectants are there of your standing?

a. Five, including myself.

b. And which place have you in the scale?

a. My name comes fourth.

b. Indeed!

a. When do you go out of mourning, Sir?

b. In the first month of the year after next.

a. You are lecturer, are you not, at the Ch'ung Chêng College?

b. Yes, I was publicly elected lecturer at the College by the gentry of the place, but, to tell the truth, I am quite conscious of my unfitness for the post, and that I have gained a reputation I do not deserve.

a. Indeed, no.

b. A short time ago I asked Mr. K'ung to come and make a personal application to you, and I am here to-day expressly to make bold to respectfully press my request.

a. It is about your brother, is it not?

b. Yes, it is about that matter.

a. My attainments and scholarship are so slight and superficial that I-hardly like to engage myself off-hand, lest I should be a hindrance to his literary successes.

b. You are too modest, Sir. Should my brother become a pupil of yours, and familiarise himself with your teaching, his scholarship would improve daily, and he will be fortunate indeed.

a. Well, Sir, as you desire that your brother should seek instruction from my imperfect speculations, I must perforce obey your wishes.

b. I am deeply obliged to you for your consent. I shall bring my brother to make his student's obeisance to you on an auspicious occasion.

a. You are too good, indeed. When did your brother take his first degree?

b. The year before last; and I am afraid of his scholarship deteriorating at home, so I shall bring him out and present him to a celebrated instructor, to study hard with a view to his making progress. Now that you have condescended to undertake the task of polishing and refining, should my brother hereafter make a name for himself, you will have the gratitude of the whole family, and I shall remember it to the last day of my life.

a. You are very good. Then when you have fixed on a suitable day, your brother and I shall meet?

b. As soon as I have selected a date, I shall first ask Mr. K'ung to come and acquaint you.

a. Very well.

No. 17 *a.* What has been your occupation that I haven't seen anything of you lately?

b. I have been a trip to the Western Hills with some friends.

a. How long were you away?

b. We were ten days living at the Hills.

a. Ten days! Why you must have had enough sightseeing.

b. Sightseeing,—Well, no, we didn't go and see many places, we just stayed there a good many days.

a. And what were you doing during your stay?

b. Why, our party constituted themselves into a Literary Club, at a Temple to the God of War, in the Western Hills.

a. Excellent form! And the meetings are, every how many days in a month?

b. The 1st to the 5th, 11th to 15th, and 21st to 25th are our Club days.

a. If that is so, then each meeting lasts five days, and you have fifteen days every month.

b. Exactly, fifteen days every month.

a. That's a great many Club days in the month. How many members are there altogether?

b. Including myself there are five of us in Peking, and two who are people of the place,—seven in all.

a. Then you five here have to sleep there on the Club days?

b. Yes, whenever the Club meets, we go out the day before and come back when it's over.

a. Where do you stay at the Hills?

b. We stay in the same temple.

a. Then how do you manage about food?

b. We take a cook from the city with us, and we buy our provisions in the city and take them with us too. Wine and meat you can also buy at a small market-place there.

a. If the thing is like that, I should like to join this Club.

b. If we can get you to go, it will be an additional distinction to the Club.

a. You are too complimentary; but I am not good at writing poetry; I shall just go and rub the ink for you all, you know.

b. You are too modest.

a. And about the food,—I will only go if I subscribe an equal share.

b. Oh, as to that, you need not give yourself the slightest bother about it; that will be for me to see to.

a. Unless we come to an arrangement, indeed I could not think of doing as you wish.

b. If that is the way of it then we will mess together, each of us subscribing his share.

a. Yes, on that understanding I will go.

a. But who is the President of the Club?

b. We came to the conclusion to take it in turns to act as President.

a. That's a capital arrangement.

b. Very well, on the 21st, in the morning, I'll invite you, and we will all start together.

a. So be it then.

No. 18   *a.* From which district [ken] of your country do you come, Sir?

b. I am a Nagasaki man.

a. Oh, then you are close to China.

b. Yes, indeed, quite close.

a. How many years have you been in China?

b. Three years.

a. To speak *kuan hua* as well as you do, after living three years in China, you must be exceptionally clever. I am much impressed by it.

b. You are too complimentary. My knowledge is only a rough, general acquaintance, I don't pretend to have mastered it.

a. I am not paying you a mere compliment when I say that there is not the slightest difference between your pronunciation and that of my own countrymen. I assure you, such intelligence as yours is rare.

b. Oh, indeed, no.

a. What position in the public service do you hold here?

b. I am now Interpreter here.

a. Capital! And in our respective positions there are constantly matters to be jointly managed, so when I'm at a loss I shall beg you for your advice.

b. You are too good, but as this is my first appointment, I am quite unpractised, and it is from you I shall have to learn in everything.

a. No, I assure you. However, by constant consultation together we shall both be mutually improved.

b. Certainly, what you say is perfectly true. May I ask from what position you entered the service?

a. I was a graduate, and was drawn for this place.

b. How many years is it since that?

a. I have only been here rather more than a year.

b. What is your native place?

a. Chiang Hsia hsien in Hupei.

b. Is your family with you?

a. No, I have not brought my family with me, for my mother being aged could not have undergone the fatigue of a journey, and therefore did not come, so that I am here by myself.

b. Yes, I see. I hear from our Consul that you have inspired general respect since your arrival, by your very sympathetic intercourse with the foreign officials.

a. Not at all. At first I had no great experience in foreign matters, so having had the honour to be sent here by the High Authorities to assist in carrying on the duties of Mixed cases, I have simply treated bonâ-fide matters in a bonâ-fide spirit, hoping sincerely that there should be no distrust on either side, but an unreserved mutual confidence, thus leading to mutual consideration ; that is what my motive has been.

b. If, Sir, you always entertain these views, your public action will naturally be satisfactory. And as I have to make other visits to-day, I shall come again to your residence on some future occasion and do myself the honour of a personal interview. If you should be at leisure I trust you will come to my quarters for a little conversation.

a. Since you do not think it beneath you, I shall certainly, after a day's interval, call upon you at your residence.

b. Thank you ; then I shall await the honour of your visit there.

a. You are very kind. Pray mount and go on your way.

b. Pray don't come out. Many thanks to you.

a. Au revoir.

No. 19   *a*. I have called upon you to-day in order to beg you to be good enough to give me some assistance.

b. Please tell me what I can do for you.

a. It is about the loan that my relative Ku Tzŭ-hêng borrowed last spring from your friend Ch'in Pao-ch'ên. He has dunned him lately for this sum, and the two have had a misunderstanding and quarrelled. I hear now that Ch'in Pao-ch'ên, means to take legal proceedings against my relative, and knowing that there is an unbroken friendship between yourself and Ch'in Pao-ch'ên, I have come to beg you to use your good offices to effect a reconciliation between them.

b. Do you know if there was any intermediary at the time the money was borrowed ?

a. Yes, I know there was an intermediary ; Hao Wu was his name ; he died last winter.

b. How many taels did your relative borrow from Ch'in Pao-ch'ên, and was there any interest ?

a. My relative borrowed 200 taels, and it was distinctly stated that interest would be charged at the rate of 1½ candarins.[1] A promissory note was drawn up, in which it was provided that the amount should be repaid in two years. It is just a year and a-half up to now, and two months ago Ch'in Pao-ch'ên said to my relative that he wanted to purchase a house, and he was waiting for this money to use; he didn't want the interest, but interest was to cease and the principal to be repaid. My relative said he shouldn't be able to repay the principal all at once, and Ch'in Pao-ch'ên told him to do all in his power to raise the money, and after that they separated. A short time ago Ch'in Pao-ch'ên went again to my relative's house and wanted repayment at once. My relative said it was really impossible to raise the money immediately, and that a few months must be allowed him to repay the whole amount, he continuing as before to pay interest monthly. But Ch'in Pao-Ch'ên wouldn't consent to this, insisted on the repayment of the capital, and declined interest. Owing to this, they had an altercation and quarrelled violently. I now hear that Ch'in Pao-ch'ên is going to take legal proceedings. My relative, for his part, owing to the time agreed upon not having arrived, cannot pay the capital sum. Moreover, he is not in arrears with his interest. As for going to law, that would be reasonable enough, but he having an official position, to do so would interfere with his duties. And so I thought I would beg your good offices to reconcile them, and get them not to carry the thing farther. Don't you approve of that?

b. How do you think I can reconcile them if I came forward?

a. I would ask you to see Ch'in Pao-ch'ên and suggest that the principal should be repaid for certain at the end of two months, interest being paid meanwhile by the month, and that if at the due date my relative is unable to repay the principal, I will be personally responsible myself.

b. On that understanding, then, I will go and see Ch'in Pao-ch'ên to-morrow and speak to him.

a. I am very much obliged to you. When the matter is settled, I shall bring my relative to thank you for your trouble.

b. You are very good.

No. 20 *a.* We have both of us come to-day, Sir, with the express intention of paying our respects to you.

b. Thank you both for your trouble. Please sit down.

a. After you, Sir.

b. And how are you two gentlemen named?

[1] Equivalent to 18 per cent.

a. My name is Tao, and his Ching.

b. When did you reach here?

a. We arrived yesterday.

b. Where are you stopping?

a. At the Tê Yüan Inn, in the eastern suburb.

b. How many years have you spent, Sir, in our country?

a. I have been four years.

b. And this gentleman, how long?

a. He has been here only just half-a-year.

b. Is he acquainted with our language?

a. He is not; he has never learnt it.

b. Have you gentlemen travelled here for pleasure or on official business?

a. Not on official business,—for pleasure merely.

b. What part of your country do you come from, Sir?

a. I am an Osaka man.

b. And this gentleman, is he from the same neighbourhood?

a. No, he is not, he is from Yokohama.

b. Pray tell me, Sir, do you know a gentleman named Fu, of of the same place as yourself, who was formerly Interpreter at Shanghai?

a. Indeed I do; our families have been friends for generations.

b. What post has he now in your country?

a. He is not there at present. After his return to Japan, he was sent by Imperial orders to England.

b. Oh, indeed!

a. Were you a friend of his, Sir?

b. Yes, we were great friends.

a. Where was it you knew him?

b. I knew him when I was a Deputy in Shanghai, where we contracted a literary friendship which became a very close and lasting one. Afterwards, when Mr. Interpreter Fu had returned home, and had reached Nagasaki, he sent me a letter. After that, when I had the honour to be sent on duty here in Chihli, we quite lost sight of each other. But now that I have heard from you that he has received an appointment in England, I will get a letter to him ready within the next day or two, which I will hand to you, Sir, and beg you, when a convenient opportuntity occurs, to send to him in England.

a. Certainly. We shall be staying here a few days yet; if you will write it at your convenience and despatch someone with it to our inn to give it to me to send.

b. I must return you two gentlemen's visit at your lodging within the next day or so.

a. Indeed we cannot permit that. Your duties are too numerous. Besides, your friendship with Mr. Interpreter Fu renders us still more intimate, so that such etiquette is scarcely required.

b. It is indispensable.

a. And now we must take leave.

b. Thank you both for your visit.

a. Not at all. Please don't come out.

b. Well, I will do as you wish, and will not come far.

a. Thank you. Good-bye for the present.

TONE AND ACCENT IN PEKINESE.

The Glossary appended to this translation follows Sir THOMAS WADE's system of transliteration and tone-marks, adapted however, in the latter respect, by a modification designed to show at a glance the exact fall of the accent according to Pekinese pronunciation in each of the twenty-two hundred phrases inserted.

At the risk of appearing to travel needlessly over well-worn ground, I propose to examine briefly the nature of the Pekinese tones, both as they exist in their normal form, that is, in isolated words, and also as affected by contact with others in conventional combinations, under which conditions the all-important element of accent is developed and brought into play.

The Pekinese tones have been treated of by Sir T. WADE in the *Tzŭ Êrh Chi*,* and even more fully by Dr. EDKINS,† who has moreover described them in terms, and from the point of view, of a system of "natural tones." It will be convenient to summarise the main heads of EDKINS' observations on the subject at this stage.

In the *shang p'ing*, the first of the four recognised Pekinese tones, he finds three forms; (1) before another word in combination with it, it is an upper level tone moderate in length; (2) if second in a combination of two, it is the upper falling tone, when accented; and (3) if unaccented and in the same position, it drops to a low pitch and becomes level without being much prolonged. The *hsia p'ing* is heard as the upper quick rising intonation, which it keeps whether standing first or last, except when an unaccented final in a combination, in which case it becomes the same as the third form of the preceding tone. The *shang shêng* has the lower rising intonation pronounced with moderate quickness. This tone also when last and enclitic becomes the low level unaccented form of the *shang p'ing*. When two *shang shêngs* occur together with the accent on the last, the first rises to the pitch of the *hsia p'ing* with which it becomes identical. Of the *ch'ü shêng* there are, Dr. EDKINS considers, two intonations, one a compound tone or circumflex, falling and rising again quickly, which is the accented variety and prefers the first place in a combination of two; the second, or unemphatic form, is a low quick falling tone, and is heard when standing

---

* See that work, Colloquial Series, 2nd Edit., Part I, pp. 7-9, and Part VII, pp. 420-422.

† See his *Grammar of the Shanghai Dialect*, 2nd Edit., pp. 6 *et seqq.*; also his *Mandarin Grammar*, 2nd Edit., pp. 10 *et seqq.*; but especially *China Review*, Vol. V, pp. 140-142.

last in a combination. There is, besides, as in each of the three preceding tones, the same unaccented, low, level variety. Otherwise put, the unaccented word is heard with a low level intonation whatever its proper tone may be, if coming last.

After an independent and careful examination of the whole subject, made in Peking itself for the most part, and constantly checked and tested, I find my results agree in the main with Dr. EDKINS' conclusions, to which however I take certain exceptions to be presently specified.

But before recurring to the tones, it will be convenient to consider the nature and effect of accent in this dialect.

What is Accent? The word is thus derived and defined in the New English Dictionary of the Philological Society: "Accent, adopted
"from French *accent*, Old French *acent*, extant representative of Latin
"*accent-um*, formed on *ad* to + *cantus* singing, a literal rendering of
"Greek προσῳδία from Greek πρός to + ᾠδή song, literally 'song added
"to' sc. speech: see note under sense I. [Definition] 1. A pro
"minence given to one syllable in a word, or in a phrase, over the
"adjacent syllables, independently of the mode in which this prominence
"is produced. [Note by Mr. A. J. ELLIS] Accent in Greek (προσῳδία)
"is explained by DION. HAL. * * * as a distinct difference of
"musical pitch in pronouncing the syllables of a word, those having the
"*grave* or heavy accent * * * being spoken at a comparatively low
"pitch, those having the *acute* or sharp accent * * * being spoken
"as nearly as possible a musical Fifth higher . * * *, and those
"having the *circumflex* accent * * * beginning in the high pitch
"and descending a Fifth during the pronunciation of the same syllable.
"The same three varieties occurred in Latin, but their position in a word
"followed very different laws. This variety of pitch disappeared for
"both Latin and Greek towards the end of the Third Century A.D.
"when the feeling of quantity was lost, and the high pitch in Greek and
"Latin became merely greater force, and this stress accent has remained
"the substitute for musical accent in modern Greek, in Italian and
"Spanish, and is also found in German and English. In Swedish and
"Norwegian a musical syllabic accent remains in use; in Danish it is
"replaced in some circumstances by a peculiar catch, and in others by
"stress, as in English. In French, where probably stress was at one
"time strongly marked, the difference for at least three centuries has
"been so light that writers have disputed as to its nature and the
"position of the stress syllable. In all languages having the stress, a
"variable alteration of pitch and quality of tone always prevails, and is
"used to express varieties of feeling. This expression belongs to
"rhetoric. The grammatical varieties of accent in English are great,
"but are all varieties of stress. The position is fixed in words of more
"than one syllable. Monosyllables have various degrees of stress
"according to circumstances. Hence the distinction of *syllabic* accent
"for the first, and *verbal* accent, *phrase* accent, or *emphasis* for the
"second."

The above note is so interesting and suggestive that I have not hesitated to quote it in full. It seems hard to resist the conclusion that the accent or 'song added to' the speech of ancient Greece and Rome was, in the measure that it existed, nothing but what in Eastern Asia we now call *tone* in general, and the three accents distinguished, three varieties of tones in particular. Indeed from the description, we might hazard a guess that the grave, acute, and circumflex were a lower even, an upper even, and a falling tone, or Pekinese *ch'ü shêng*, respectively. But, it may be asked, if the "musical accent" of Greek and Latin is identified with tone, what meaning is to belong to accent, as distinct from tone, in dealing with a Chinese dialect? The answer is that, in Chinese, *accent is emphasized tone*. Hence it is by emphasizing the characteristic musical modulation of a given syllable, (known for want of a better term as its tone,) that there is produced alike in Pekinese and other dialects that prominence over the adjacent syllables, in which as we have just seen all accent consists.

Much the most numerous and important compound words in Pekinese are dissyllabic combinations,—"binomials" as LEGGE appropriately calls them. On such words the accent falls in one of three different ways. The compound may be *monotonic*, that is the accent may fall exclusively on one of the syllables, as for instance on the first in $t'a^1$ *mên* they, ya^2 *mên* a Yamen, $shu^1 fu$ comfortable, in which case the unaccented syllable becomes atonic: secondly, it may be *ditonic*, having the accent more or less evenly divided between the syllables, as in ta^4 $mên^2$ a principal gate, $shu^1 fu^2$ to accept a decision, where both tones are distinctly heard: or thirdly, it may be *metatonic*, that is, the accent may be in a state of unstable equilibrium as it were, so that words of this character might be classified as sometimes belonging to the first and sometimes to the second of the above divisions,—between which they form an intermediate and connecting link,—while again at other times the accent though greatly preponderating on one of the syllables, yet leaves a faint remnant of tone perceptible in the other. Such for example are $wên^3$ $chung^{(4)}$ dignified, hao^2 $shou^{(3)}$ a good hand at, $su^4 jih^{(4)}$ habitually.

Accordingly, all monotonic binomials in this Glossary are marked only with the tone of the single accented syllable, the unmarked half of the compound being strictly atonic, that is, destitute of all tone properly so called. As EDKINS well observes, "The tendency of the local accent is to forsake the last syllable whenever the process of dissyllabification is complete, that is, whenever the last of two words loses special significance, and can be treated as a syllable of a compound word." This atonic variation bears the same relation to its accented or fully toned companion as does the unaccented syllable to the accented in an English dissyllabic word. In our adjective *human* and the Chinese pronoun $t'a$ *mên* the latter portions of each are identical both in sound and tone— or rather tonelessness. The voice sinks in both instances to the "low level intonation" which EDKINS, following the native view, names the third variety of the *shang p'ing*, but which, it seems to me, can only be so called negatively and constructively, as referable to none of the other three classes, and to which therefore the term atonic appears more appropriate.

With ditonic words the tones of the component syllables are both marked because both are distinctly pronounced, though usually somewhat greater stress is laid upon the last.

In metatonic binomials both tones are marked, but one is inclosed in brackets. From the words so distinguished the tone often withdraws altogether, especially in rapid and familiar speech, and then the binomial becomes simply monotonic. At other times, when the speaker is enunciating with precision and accuracy, the bracketed tone reasserts itself, and the phrase hardly differs from a ditonic. More commonly the intermediate stage occurs, where the tone has almost, but yet not quite, deserted the weaker syllable.

So much for accent. It remains only to examine the character of the tones singly, and of the sixteen tonic combinations of which binomial phrases may consist.

The *shang p'ing* or "upper even" tone.

In the first place the normal Pekinese *shang p'ing*,—the *shang p'ing*, that is, when isolated,—is not an upper even tone at all. EDKINS has described this form (which is also heard when final and accented,) as the upper falling tone, or upper quick falling, but I cannot concur in the description for this reason. In his *Mandarin Grammar*, p. 18, writing on the Pekinese tones, he says, "When a word in *ch'ü shêng* "follows another in *ch'ü shêng* it rises in pitch, so that the intonation "l.q.f. [lower quick falling] becomes u.q.f. [upper quick falling]." *
He thus identifies a normal *shang p'ing* with an accented *ch'ü shêng* following another *ch'ü shêng*. Beyond question this is an error, as will at once be seen by making the necessary tests. Were it correct, the combinations 大刀 *ta tao¹* and 大道 *ta tao⁴*, for example, would be undistinguishable, which most certainly they are not. It is nevertheless true that the normal *shang p'ing* does terminate in a sort of rapid descent or "dying fall,"† and to my ear this normal form seems an even tone sustained on a somewhat high level until, just at the termination, the voice, relieved of the tension, drops suddenly as the sound ceases. In default of a better description, and to mark its distinction from the accented final *ch'ü shêng*, I would suggest its definition as the "upper deflected" tone. The *shang p'ing* when standing first in combination is, as Dr. EDKINS has pointed out, a true upper even tone, but it is observable that it tends to be of rather higher pitch when followed by an

---

* I have corrected the obvious slips or misprints l.q.r. [lower quick rising] and u.q.r. [upper quick rising] of the original.

† Mr. GOH in his introduction to the *Kuan Hua Chih Nan* speaks of this tone as 自上落下而止聲音較短, "descending from above and stopping, sound and tone comparatively short."

atonic final than when the final carries part of the accent, higher for example on *shan* in *shan¹ tung*, 山東, than in *shan¹ tung⁴*, 山洞.

The *hsia p'ing* or "lower even" tone also belies its name, not being either low or even, but, as EDKINS says, an upper, quick, rising intonation.

The *shang shêng* or "rising" tone is a low, slow, rising tone, prolonged on a low level and rising only towards the end. The Pekinese *hsia p'ing* and *shang shêng* do in fact constitute what in southern dialects would be upper and lower series of a single natural tone, distinguishable, however, not solely by difference of pitch, but by duration and manner of rising.

The fourth and last conventional Peking tone is the *ch'ü shêng*, a "quick falling" tone, varying considerably in pitch. The so-called circumflex variety described by EDKINS as falling and rising again quickly I do not regard as a distinct form, but simply as the effect of the necessary rapid elevation of the voice from the bottom of this descending tone to the higher point at which any succeeding accented tone (except the *shang shêng*) must begin.

To recapitulate: the Pekinese have five distinct natural tones grouped under four conventional names. There are an upper deflected, (normal), and an upper even tone, both classed under the *shang p'ing*; an upper rising,—the *hsia p'ing*; a lower rising,—the *shang shêng*; and a falling tone,—the *ch'ü shêng*; and further there is an atonic variety into which any of the four traditional tones may degenerate when final and unaccented.

We come lastly to the tones in the 16 groups of binomial combinations. These require to be dwelt on at no great length, and except in those commencing with a *shang shêng*, the monotonic groups do not demand special notice. The accented first syllable having its proper tone emphatically pronounced, and the second being atonic, a speaker has, so to say, only to take care of the first and the last will take care of itself.

(1). Double *shang p'ing*. In monotonics the accented first syllable is in a high even tone. In ditonics the first syllable is also of the upper even tone, with a tendency to be somewhat lower in pitch than when followed by an atonic; the second syllable is in the normal, or upper deflected tone, and, as pointed out by Sir T. WADE, is higher in pitch than the first. Examples, Monotonic, 山西 *shan¹ hsi*, Ditonic, 西山 *hsi¹ shan¹*.

(2). *Shang p'ing + hsia p'ing*. Monotonics as in (1). Ditonics, tones respectively upper even, and normal. Ex. M. 姑娘 *Ku¹ niang*, D. 官名 *kuan¹ ming²*.

(3). *Shang p'ing + shang shêng*. Monotonics as in (1). Ditonics, tones upper even, and normal. Ex. M. 清楚 *ch'ing¹ ch'u*, D. 拘禮 *chü¹ li³*.

(4). *Shang p'ing + ch'ü shêng.* Monotonics as in (1). Ditonics, tones upper even, and normal. Ex. M. 差事 *ch'ai¹ shih*, D. 生氣 *shêng¹ ch'i⁴*.

(5). *Hsia p'ing + shang p'ing.* Monotonics in this and the next three groups demand no remark. Ditonics require attention, for the tone of the initial syllable scarcely sounds like an ordinary *hsia p'ing*, being pitched unusually low; the second is in the upper deflected tone. Personally I find more difficulty in distinguishing between this group and ditonic double *shang p'ings* than between any two others. Ex. M. 人家 *jên² chia*, D. 回家 *hui² chia¹*.

(6). Double *hsia p'ing.* Ditonics, tones normal. Ex. M. 石頭 *shih² t'ou*, D. 革職 *ko² chih²*.

(7). *Hsia p'ing + shang shêng.* Ditonics, tones normal. Metatonics occur very commonly in this group. Ex. M. 雲彩 *yün² ts'ai*, D. 台甫 *t'ai² fu³*.

(8). *Hsia p'ing + ch'ü shêng.* Ditonics, tones normal. Ex. M. 顏色 *yen² sê*, D. 隨便 *sui² pien⁴*.

(9). *Shang shêng + shang p'ing.* Monotonics. It deserves noting that in all monotonic groups where a *shang shêng* is the first element, the pitch of the atonic word is perceptibly higher than in the corresponding syllable in any of the twelve other groups commencing with a *shang p'ing*, *hsia p'ing* or *ch'ü shêng*. So, for example, the same word *hsi* is higher in 陝西 *Shan³ hsi* (Shensi) than in 山西 *Shan¹ hsi*. What is the reason of this? Probably the following. As we have seen, the *shang shêng* is a tone prolonged on a low level, rising only towards its end. The stress of accentuation, which usually tends to raise the pitch of the voice, does in this case, (and analogous effects are produced by certain modes of emphasis in our own language,) still further *depress* the level of the tone, so much so that on the relaxing of the accentual strain the voice at once seeks relief by rising to a higher and more normal point and there leaving the atonic syllable stranded. Ditonics, tones normal, and upper deflected. Ex. M. 陝西 *Shan³ hsi*, D. 請安 *ching³ an¹*.

(10). *Shang shêng + hsia p'ing.* Ditonics, tones normal. There is less difference apparent between monotonics and ditonics in this combination than in any of the other groups. Ex. M. 敢情 *kan³ ch'ing* (actually!), D. 感情 *kan³ ch'ing²* (gratitude).

(11). Double *shang shêng.* Monotonics. Owing doubtless to the intimate natural relation between the Pekinese *hsia p'ing* and the *shang shêng*, in many instances the accented syllable, instead of bearing its normal tone, is heard in the *hsia p'ing*, as in 火把 *huo² pa* a torch, 死鬼 *ssŭ² kuei* a dead man, 打掃 *ta² sao* to sweep clean. In other cases the accented syllable is pronounced at one time in the *shang shêng*, at another in the *hsia p'ing*, as in 早起 *tsao³ ch'i* or *tsao² ch'i*, 晌午 *shang³ huo* or *shang² huo*, 寫法兒 *hsieh³ farh* or *hsieh² farh*. Others again are always normal, as 耳朵 *erh³ to*, 姐姐 *chieh³ chieh*. Ditonics,

Unless pronounced slowly, the tones are *hsia p'ing* and *shang shêng*, and are so marked in the Glossary. Ex. M. see above, D. 久仰 *chiu² yang³*, 馬尾兒 *ma² irh³*.

Although there is a general agreement as to the fact of this modification, it has not been quite unchallenged. On the one hand we have, amongst others, Dr. EDKINS, Sir T. WADE (partially) and Mr. GOH; on the other, Mr. E. H. PARKER. It will be useful to examine the opinions expressed.

I have quoted already Dr. EDKINS' statement, "When two *shang* "*shêngs* occur together with the accent on the last, the first rises to the "pitch of *hsia p'ing* with which it becomes identical." Sir T. WADE (*Tzŭ Érh Chi*, Colloquial Series, 2nd Edit., Vol. II, p. 422) observes, "Under the 3rd, [tone, viz., the *shang shêng*] the change is more "remarkable: the first syllable is changed nearly, if not quite, to the "2nd tone ; still there is a manifest limitation proper to particular "vowels." Mr. GOH affirms, in his Chinese introduction to the *Kuan Hua Chih Nan*, "Whenever in colloquial two connected *shang shêng* "words occur, the first must be read in the *hsia p'ing*, the second in the "*shang shêng*, as the saying runs 逢上必倒 *fêng shang pi tao*, which "means (he adds in a note) when two *shang shêng* words meet, the tone "of one must be overthrown."

Mr. PARKER, on the other hand, (*China Review*, Vol. VII, p. 183) considers such a rule to be too rigidly stated. He thinks the tonic modification described by EDKINS is "optional, unconscious and elastic ; "and a complete disregard of it in no way tends to make the speaker "less comprehensible than he otherwise would be." Further on he quotes a sentence from the "Hundred Lessons," where three successive *shang shêng* words occur, and points out, very truly, that it is immaterial whether each of them is separately clearly pronounced, or whether the first or the second is changed to a *hsia p'ing*.

So far as the statements of the four writers really conflict, I agree with the majority, and the more readily as Mr. PARKER seems not to have fully appreciated one element in the question which is in fact essential. The modifications described by Dr. EDKINS apply strictly only to recognised and *permanent* combinations. Such combinations or compound words, formed by the union of two members in an intimate and lasting alliance, are altogether distinct from the mere accidental and momentary juxtaposition of syllables, such as those in the sentence Mr. PARKER quotes. It is only in the former case that the mutual action and reaction of the tones are afforded opportunity to have full play. Where no such dissyllabification has been developed, as it has not in the above instance, or in one adduced by Sir T. WADE,* the accent will be regulated entirely in accordance with temporary and varying conditions, with, in fact, the relative prominence given by the speaker

---

* *Ma hsiao* "the horse is small," which is a complete sentence, not a compound word.

at his option to any one of the constituent and co-ordinate terms of the expression. Then, and only then, in my judgment, can this tonic modification be considered without system or significance.

Before leaving this group it will not be out of place to glance at what seems to be the reason why the *shang shêng* when modified becomes a *hsia p'ing* rather than any other tone. Although in ditonics neither syllable is destitute of tone, in many, perhaps most cases, the accent preponderates on one rather than the other. When therefore it falls on the latter syllable in a binomial of double *shang shêngs* the effect is to strengthen the tone of this at the expense of the first, so that the length and comparative lowness of the more accented tone are unusually marked, in contrast with the forced compression and elevation of the other, which in thus becoming a high and short rising tone, has been simply converted into a *hsia p'ing*, or in other terms, has been transferred from the lower into the higher series, a change of constant occurrence in those dialects where a regular double series of tones exists.

(12). *Shang shêng + ch'ü shêng.* Ditonics, tones normal. Ex. M. 買賣 *mai³ mai*, D. 滿地 *man³ ti⁴*. Metatonics are common in this group.

(13). *Ch'ü shêng + shang p'ing.* Ditonics, tones normal. Ex. M. 弟兄 *ti⁴ hsiung*, D. 用心 *yung⁴ hsin¹*.

(14). *Ch'ü shêng + hsia p'ing.* Ditonics, tones normal. Ex. M. 太陽 *t'ai⁴ yang*, D. 向前 *hsiang⁴ ch'ien²*.

(15). *Ch'ü shêng + shang shêng.* Ditonics, tones normal. Ex. M. 豆腐 *tou⁴ fu*, D. 要緊 *yao⁴ chin³*.

(16). Double *ch'ü shêng*. Ditonics, tones normal, but when the accent is thrown more strongly on the second word, as often happens, the latter, though in other respects unaltered, rises in pitch. Owing to this, the voice is compelled to rise suddenly from the low level where the first word terminates, to the higher one at which the second commences, and thus, as Mr. PARKER has pointed out, "the ear detects a change "which produces an effect approximate to that of a *shang shêng*," though the similarity is only superficial. Ex. M. 肚帶 *tu⁴ tai*, D. 拜客 *pai⁴ k'o⁴*.

138   THE GUIDE TO KUAN HUA.

GLOSSARY OF PHRASES

SHOWING THE TONES AND ACCENT OF EACH PHRASE AS
PRONOUNCED IN THE PEKINESE DIALECT.

ai⁴ nan²	碍難	to be unable, or impossible, to	IV, 7
ai⁴ shih⁴	碍事	to matter, be of harm	III, 13
an¹ ch'an	鞍韂	saddle and saddle-cloth	III, 16
an⁴ chao⁴	按照	according to, in accordance with	IV, 5
an¹ chia¹	安家	to give, or to serve, as alimony to one's family	III, 20
an¹ chih	安置	to put in position, III, 9. To establish one (in business) II, 9	
an¹ hsin¹	安心	free from anxiety, quiet, I, 7. Deliberately	II, 27
an¹ k'ang¹	安康	in good health	IV, 3
an¹ shang	安上	to fix on, or together	II, 14
an¹ tzŭ	鞍子	a saddle	III, 16
an⁴ tzŭ	案子	a table, work-bench	II, 14
ao² yeh⁴	熬夜	to work at night	I, 39
cha¹ ch'ih(4)	札飭	to officially instruct	IV, 6
ch'a² chirh¹	茶几兒	a teapoy	III, 2
ch'a² ch'ien	茶錢	"Tea-money," a fee on taking a house	II, 1
ch'a² ch'uarh²	茶船兒	a saucer	III, 2
ch'a² hsün	查訊	to investigate, examine judicially	IV, 8
ch'a² hu²	茶壺	a tea-pot	III, 2
ch'a⁴ i(4)	詫異	surprised	II, 33
ch'a² p'arh²	茶盤兒	a tea-tray	III, 2
ch'a¹ pieh²	差別	difference, distinction	IV, 18
ch'a¹ sung(4)	插訟	to intervene in legal proceedings	IV, 10
ch'a² tien(3)	查點	to check, go through, examine	II, 21
ch'a¹ ts'o(4)	差錯	a mistake, miscalculation	IV, 13
ch'a¹ tzŭ	叉子	a fork	III, 4
ch'a² wan²	茶碗	a tea-cup	III, 2
ch'a² wên	查問	to examine, interrogate	IV, 5
ch'a² yeh⁴	茶葉	tea	I, 9
ch'a² yen⁴	查驗	to inspect, verify	IV, 13

GLOSSARY OF PHRASES.

Romanization	Chinese	Meaning	Ref.
chai¹ kei	給	to lend (money) temporarily to	II, 21
chai² mêrh²	摘宅	a mansion, large establishment	II, 37
ch'ai¹ k'ai	拆開	to tear open	II, 36
ch'ai¹ shih	差事	official duties	I, 34
chan¹ ch'ieh³	暫且	temporarily	IV, 6
chan¹ fang²	棧房	a warehouse, godown	II, 2
chan¹ kuang¹	沾光	to receive benefit or profit from (a man)	IV, 9
chan¹ lien(²)	粘連	to append	II, 19
chan² pu	揩布	a duster	III, 4
chan¹ tzŭ	氈子	felt, also foreign woollen materials	III, 5
chang¹ ch'êng	章程	regulations	IV, 6
chang¹ fang²	賬房	a counting-house, accountant's office	III, 8
chang¹ fang²	帳房	a tent	III, 8
chang² jou⁴	長肉	to put on flesh	III, 16
chang⁴ mu	賬目	accounts	II, 19
chang² têng¹	掌燈	to light the lamps	II, 29
chang¹ tzŭ	帳子	curtains	III, 9
ch'ang² chiu(³)	長久	enduring, permanent	II, 23
ch'ang⁴ hsi⁴	唱戲	(of actors) to act, give a performance	III, 11
ch'ang² kung	長工	a labourer, etc., permanently employed	II, 12
ch'ang² yü	長於	good [or] clever, at	IV, 17
chao² chi²	着急	excited, disturbed	II, 22
chao⁴ fu²	照覆	to reply officially (on equal terms)	IV, 6
chao⁴ hui(⁴)	照會	to address officially (on equal terms)	IV, 1
chao⁴ k'an	照看	to look after, attend to	III, 8
chao⁴ li⁴	照例	legally	IV, 6
chao² liang²	着涼	to get a chill	I, 5
chao⁴ pan¹	照辦	to take action as requested	IV, 7
chao² pu	找補	to find a way to make it up to one	II, 7
chao³ shih⁴	找事	to seek employment	II, 17
chao⁴ ting¹	招定	to make a full confession	II, 38
chao¹ tsu¹	招租	to Let	II, 1
chao⁴ tzŭ	罩子	a shade, cover (e.g. a lamp-shade)	III, 13
chao⁴ yangrh⁴	照樣兒	like the pattern	II, 7
chao⁴ ying	照應	to look after, attend to	II, 9
ch'ao¹ fan	吵翻	to dispute	II, 32
ch'ao¹ hsieh(³)	抄寫	to copy	II, 38
ch'ao² nao	潮腦	camphor	III, 10
ch'ao³ nao⁴	吵鬧	to quarrel	IV, 19
chê² chiang	浙江	province of Chekiang	II, 24
chê² fu	折服	to satisfy, pacify, mollify	IV, 8

chā² kei	給 折	to make over to (in composition for a debt)	II, 26
chê² tzŭ	子 摺	a folded slip of paper	III, 4
chā¹ yen	掩 遮	to make excuses	III, 15
ch'ê⁴ chou²	肘 掣	hampered, embarrassed	II, 24
ch'ê¹ hsiangrh¹	箱 車 兒	the body of a cart	III, 6
ch'ê¹ irh¹	尾 車 兒	a cartstail	III, 17
ch'ê¹ tzŭ	子 車	a wheelbarrow	II, 21
ch'ê¹ yüarh² (sic)	沿 車 兒	the shaftboard of a cart	III, 6
chên¹ cho	酌 斟	to deliberate, think or talk over	II, 38
chên¹ chiu³	酒 斟	to pour out wine	III, 7
chên⁴ tien(4)	店 鎭	a market-place, market-town	II, 12
chên² t'ou	頭 枕	a pillow	III, 3
ch'ên⁴ yüan¹	願 趁	to exult over	II, 30
chêng⁴ ch'ien²	錢 掙	to make money [or] a profit	II, 17
chêng⁴ ching³ (sic)	經 正	proper, right, correct	I, 33
chêng⁴ fang(2)	房 正	the main range of a house	III, 9
chêng¹ lun	論 爭	to dispute, argue	IV, 6
chêng⁴ pan⁴	辦 正	a regular or correct course, proceeding	IV, 10
chêng¹ yüeh(4)	月 正	the first month of the year	IV, 16
ch'êng² chia¹	家 成	(of men) to marry	II, 17
ch'êng² chien¹	見 成	a fixed resolve, a resolution, a mind made up	IV, 8
ch'êng² cho¹	桌 成	dinners ready laid	III, 11
ch'êng² chuang	狀 成	a written plaint or charge	II, 19
ch'êng² ch'ün²	群 成	in crowds, in bodies	II, 23
ch'êng² hsin(1)	心 誠	an attention	IV, 14
ch'êng¹ hu	呼 稱	to address by name, to style	I, 16
ch'êng² i¹	衣 成	ready-made clothes	II, 35
ch'êng² kuan³	管 承	to hold oneself responsible	II, 13
ch'êng² ming²	名 成	to make a name	IV, 16
ch'êng² shang	上 乘	to mount (a horse)	IV, 18
ch'êng² ti¹	遞 呈	to hand in, deliver	IV, 1
ch'êng² wên⁴	問 承	to be obliged for (your) kind inquiries	IV, 2
chi² chih⁴	至 及	upon proceeding to, as soon as	IV, 6
chi⁴ fang(4)	放 寄	to deposit at	II, 15
chi⁴ hsia	下 記	to bear in mind, take note of	II, 39
chi⁴ hsing	性 記	memory	III, 15
chi⁴ i⁴	議 計	to devise	IV, 9
chi² jan²	然 既	since, as	II, 16
chi¹ jou(4)	肉 雞	fowl (as food)	III, 4
chi¹ mi	密 機	secret	I, 16
chi² p'in³	品 祭	sacrificial vessels	II, 40

GLOSSARY OF PHRASES.

chi³ shih(2)	時	at what time	IV, 11
chi¹ t'ang¹	雞湯	chicken broth	III, 4
chi⁴ tsai	載	inserted in, mentioned in	I, 19
chi¹ tzŭrh²	子兒	an egg	III, 3
chi² yen²	吉言	auspicious words, good auguries	IV, 12
chi⁴ yen¹	戒烟	to give up smoking opium	II, 25
ch'i² ch'a²	沏茶	to make tea	II, 29
ch'i² chi(2)	齊集	to assemble, meet together	IV, 8
ch'i² chieh²	截	in full readiness	III, 20
ch'i² ch'u¹	初	at first	II, 23
ch'i³ chung¹	中	in this, therein	IV, 7
ch'i⁴ chung⁴	重	to highly appreciate or value (a man's services)	II, 5
ch'i³ fêng¹	封	to remove the official seals	II, 22
ch'i⁴ fu²	服	to go out of mourning	IV, 16
ch'i⁴ hou⁴	厚	(of friendship) close and lasting	IV, 20
ch'i⁴ hsien²	嫌	to disdain	IV, 18
ch'i² huo⁴	貨	to take delivery of goods	IV, 8
ch'i² jên²	人	a Bannerman	II, 24
ch'i² kan³	敢	you are very good!	II, 1
ch'i³ lai²	來	to rise	I, 25
ch'i² ma³	馬	to ride a horse	III, 16
ch'i² nei⁴	內	therein, included	II, 9
ch'i² pei⁴	俻	ready prepared	IV, 17
ch'i⁴ sê⁴	色	one's looks, appearance	I, 5
ch'i¹ shang	上	(of tea) to make it	III, 2
ch'i¹ shên¹	身	to start on a journey	II, 3
ch'i¹ shêng¹	生	to impose on one's ignorance	II, 24
ch'i² shih²	實	as a matter of fact, the truth is	II, 33
chia¹ chien³	剪	sycee shears	II, 36
chia⁴ ch'ien²	錢	a price	III, 3
chia⁴ chih²	值	a price	II, 2
chia¹ chü⁴	具	fittings of a house	II, 9
chia¹ chüan	眷	one's wife	II, 3
chia¹ hao⁴	號	to cangue	II, 6
chia¹ huo⁴	伙	utensils	III, 8
chia¹ i⁴	意	with all possible (care, zeal, etc.)	IV, 5
chia¹ jên²	人	a member of one's household	II, 22
chia¹ k'ai¹	開	to cut open with shears	II, 36
chia¹ li³	理	in the house, at home	II, 3
chia¹ mu³	母	my mother	IV, 15
chia¹ pei⁴	倍	twice as much	I, 21

chia² pei⁴	被	a double coverlet	III, 17
chia³ pi³	比	for example, for instance	II, 39
chia¹ shih⁴	事	domestic affairs	IV, 16
chia¹ ssŭ¹	私	private effects	IV, 9
chia² tzŭ²	子	year of one's birth	I, 3
chia⁴ tzŭ	子	a frame, stand	III, 3
chia¹ yin¹	音	"glad tidings," news from you	IV, 13
chiang³ chiu	究	neat, tasteful	I, 30
chiang¹ hsi	西	province of Kiangsi	II, 24
chiang¹ lai²	來	in future	II, 17
chiang³ shu¹	書	to explain the text	I, 30
chiang¹ su	蘇	province of Kiangsu	II, 21
chiang⁴ tzŭ	子	paste	III, 14
chiang³ yü (²)	譽	to praise	IV, 4
chiang⁴ yu²	油	soy	III, 4
ch'iang² chien (⁴)	健	vigorous, robust	IV, 1
ch'iang³ ling⁴	令	to force, compel	IV, 6
ch'iang³ liu²	留	to detain by force	IV, 2
ch'iang¹ tiao	調	accent	I, 17
chiao³ cha (⁴)	詐	dishonest	II, 32
chiao¹ chi⁴	際	on occasions of intercourse	IV, 18
chiao¹ ch'ing	情	intimacy	I, 9
chiao¹ ch'ing¹	清	to hand over in full	IV, 7
chiao² ch'ing	情	stubborn	III, 15
chiao¹ fa	法	way, or system of teaching	I, 30
chiao³ hsia (⁴)	下	the present moment	II, 1
chiao¹ hsieh¹	卸	to give over charge	II, 3
chiao³ hsing¹	倖	a piece of good fortune	II, 5
chiao¹ huan²	還	to hand back	II, 22
chiao¹ huarh¹	花	to water flowers	III, 18
chiao¹ huo⁴	貨	to deliver goods	II, 19
chiao⁴ k'ai¹	開	to call to one to open a door	II, 29
chiao⁴ kei	給	to hand or give over to	I, 19
chiao¹ kei	給	to show how	III, 10
chiao¹ nun	嫩	fragile	III, 18
chiao¹ shê	涉	international, "mixed" (cases, etc.)	IV, 4
chiao¹ shou	手	scaffolding	III, 14
chiao¹ tai	代	to hand over to	III, 13
chiao² tzŭ	子	a bit (for horses)	III, 16
chiao⁴ tzŭ	子	a sedan chair	III, 8
chiao¹ wang	往	dealings, transactions, with	IV, 9

GLOSSARY OF PHRASES. 143

ch'iao⁴ huo(4)	俏貨	good bargains	II, 9
ch'iao² ping⁴	瞧病	to see patients	II, 87
chieh⁴ ch'i²	屆期	at the due date	IV, 19
chieh² chieh	姐姐	an elder sister	II, 17
chieh¹ chien⁴	接見	to receive (a visitor)	IV, 5
chieh⁴ ch'ien²	借錢	to borrow money	II, 17
chieh² chüeh¹	截絕	to break off relations or intimacy with	
chieh¹ fang	街坊	a neighbour	II, 15
chieh⁴ i⁴	介意	the slightest anxiety or thought	IV, 17
chieh⁴ kei	借給	to lend to	II, 9
chieh² mei	姐妹	sisters	II, 17
chieh⁴ mo	芥末	mustard	III, 4
chieh⁴ pan⁴	借辦	to procure, raise, (money)	IV, 7
chieh¹ shang	街上	in the street	II, 27
chieh⁴ shao⁴	介紹	to be one's introducer	I, 19
chieh⁴ shih²	屆時	when the time comes	IV, 14
chieh² shou³	解手	to make water	III, 16
chieh¹ shu⁴	接署	to take over charge	II, 5
chieh⁴ t'ung²	解銅	to escort a consignment of copper	IV, 12
chieh⁴ tzŭrh⁴	借字	a promissory note	IV, 19
chieh⁴ tz'ŭ²	藉詞	to make an excuse	IV, 8
chieh⁴ yüeh¹	借約	a promissory note	II, 31
chieh⁴ yung⁴	借用	to borrow for one's needs	IV, 9
ch'ieh⁴ shih²	切實	trustworthy, exact	II, 8
chien³ chêng	見証	a witness	II, 32
chien⁴ chiao⁴	教請	(your) instructions, wishes, desires	IV, 13
chien¹ ch'ing³	堅請	to press one to	IV, 6
chien⁴ chu(3)	主	a person to recommend one	II, 10
chien⁴ chuang⁴	健壯	hale and hearty	IV, 15
chien⁴ chüan⁴	薦卷	to send up a candidate's examination papers for the approval of the Chief Examiner	IV, 12
chien² ch'üeh(1)	鈌	an easy post	II, 3
chien³ fa	簡發	to select by lot for a post	IV, 18
chien³ fang⁴	簡放	to select for appointment	IV, 15
chien⁴ hsin⁴	薦信	a letter of recommendation	II, 24
chien⁴ hsing⁴	賤姓	my surname	I, 1
chien⁴ kei	薦給	to recommend	III, 20
chien¹ ku	堅固	strong, substantial	II, 10
chien⁴ kuai⁴	見怪	to think strange, to mind	IV, 1
chien¹ kuan³	兼管	to administer in addition to one's proper duties	IV, 2
chien¹ lin⁴	慳吝	miserly, stingy	II, 31
chien³ man⁴	簡慢	unceremonious, cavalier	IV, 1

chien⁴ shurh(⁴)	數兒	the number of articles	III, 14
chien⁴ t'ien¹	天	every day	II, 14
chien⁴ yü⁴	諭	to signify (your) wishes	IV, 5
ch'ien⁴ an¹	秋安	indisposed, unwell	I, 10
ch'ien¹ ch'iu	行	(your or his) birthday	I, 32
ch'ien² hang	錢	a cash-bank	II, 9
ch'ien² hou⁴	前後	first and last	II, 18
ch'ien² jên⁴	前任	the former incumbent	II, 5
ch'ien² jih(⁴)	前日	the day before yesterday	IV, 9
ch'ien⁴ k'uan²	欠款	a sum owed, indebtedness	IV, 10
ch'ien² liang	錢糧	the land-tax	II, 22
ch'ien² mi³	錢米	money and food	II, 31
ch'ien² nien	前年	the year before last	I, 18
ch'ien² p'u⁴	錢舖	a cash-bank	II, 9
ch'ien¹ shê	牽涉	to introduce, import, bring forward (into a discussion)	IV, 9
ch'ien² shih	前失	a stumble (of horses)	III, 16
ch'ien² shurh(⁴)	錢數	the number of copper cash	III, 12
ch'ien² t'ien	前天	the day before yesterday	I, 19
ch'ien² t'ou	前頭	in front	II, 29
ch'ien² ts'ai²	錢財	money	IV, 9
ch'ien¹ tzŭ	簽子	slips of wood, labels	III, 14, 17
ch'ien² tzŭ	鉗子	pincers	III, 9
ch'ien² tz'ŭ⁴	前次	the last [or] a previous, occasion	IV, 8
ch'ien¹ wan	千萬	(also ch'ien¹ wan (⁴)), on no account	I, 16
ch'ien² yung(⁴)	錢用	money for an outlay	II, 8
chih² chao	執照	a warrant, written authority	III, 20
chih⁴ ch'i	志氣	resolution, strength of will	II, 25
chih¹ ch'ih	支持	to manage to struggle along	II, 23
chih¹ chou³	掣肘	(or ch'ê⁴ chou³), hampered, embarrassed	II, 24
chih⁴ ho⁴	致賀	to convey congratulations	I, 32
chih¹ hsien⁴	知縣	a District Magistrate	II, 5
chih¹ hui	知會	to officially inform, notify	IV, 7
chih² i⁴	執意	resolved, bent upon	IV, 15
chih¹ kei	支給	to advance (wages, etc.)	III, 13
chih² k'o³	只可	can only, the only thing is to—(also tzŭ² k'o³ and tzŭ⁴ k'o³)	II, 34
chih⁴ kuan³	只管	just, merely, (also tzŭ⁴ kuan³)	IV, 4
chih² li	直隸	province of Chihli	IV, 20
chih¹ ming	職名	a visiting card	III, 18
chih³ ming²	指名	by name, specifically	IV, 5
chih¹ shang	搘上	to prop up, stretch upon	III, 9

GLOSSARY OF PHRASES. 145

chih¹ shên¹	身	solitary, quite alone	IV, 18
chih¹ shih	使	to indicate, instruct as to	IV, 4
chih¹ tao	道	(also chih¹ tao⁴) to know	I, 6
chih¹ tsui⁴	罪	to punish	II, 35
chih⁴ tu	度	social system, state of society	IV, 4
chih³ wang(4)	望	hope, aspiration	IV, 11
chih² yao⁴	要	provided that (also tzŭ² yao⁴)	II, 24
chih² yü	於	to go and — (do some prejudicial act), I, 16, II, 13, to go so far as to	
ch'ih¹ fan⁴	飯	to eat, take food	III, 4
ch'ih⁴ ling¹	令	to give official orders to	IV, 6
ch'ih² p'ing²	平	guided by justice, impartially	IV, 1
ch'ih¹ shih	食	provisions, eatables	III, 8
ch'ih² ts'un	寸	measurement, dimensions	II, 7
ch'ih² tzŭ	子	a spoon	III, 4
ch'ih¹ yen¹	烟	to smoke opium	II, 25
chin⁴ ch'êng²	城	to go into the city	II, 18
chin³ chi²	急	urgent, hurried	IV, 3
chin¹ chih²	職	one's present post or rank	II, 5
chin⁴ ching¹	京	to go into Peking	II, 17
chin¹ chirh	兒	just (enough, etc.), neither too — nor too —	III, 3
chin⁴ ch'ü	去	to go in, enter	II, 8
chin⁴ hsüeh²	學	to take a Licentiate's Degree	IV, 16
chin⁴ i⁴	益	progress, advance, improvement	I, 30
chin¹ jih(4)	日	to-day	IV, 4
chin⁴ kung¹	宮	to go into the Palace	II, 39
chin⁴ lai²	來	lately	I, 16
chin⁴ li⁴	力	with all one's power	IV, 5
chin¹ nien	年	this year	I, 2
chin⁴ shêng³	省	to go into the provincial capital	II, 4
chin⁴ shih	士	a Metropolitan Graduate	IV, 2
chin¹ tzŭ	子	gold	II, 28
chin³ tzŭ	自	to do nothing but —, to be for ever	I, 37
chin³ yao⁴	要	important, urgent	IV, 1
chin⁴ yeh⁴	謁	to present oneself to, pay a visit to	IV, 16
ch'in¹ ch'ai	差	an Envoy, an Imperial Commissioner	IV, 1
ch'in¹ ch'i	戚	a relative of another name	II, 1
ch'in¹ p'ei⁴	佩	to respect deeply	IV, 18
ch'in¹ shên¹	身	in person	II, 18
ch'in¹ tzŭ	自	personally	II, 12
ch'in¹ yu(3)	友	relatives and friends	II, 11
ching¹ ch'a²	察	the Metropolitan Scrutiny	IV, 15

20

ching¹ ch'êng	承	a Chief Clerk	IV, 13
ching¹ chi	紀	a salesman	II, 12
ching² chih	致	scenery	I, 20
ching¹ hsia⁴	嚇	frightened, scared	II, 28
ching⁴ i⁴	意	respect for, mark of respect	I, 9
ching¹ kuan	官	Peking officials	I, 35
ching¹ kuan (3)	管	to manage, deal with	IV, 7
ching⁴ kuan³	管	just, simply	III, 15
ching¹ k'ung²	恐	(also ching¹ k'ung (³)), to startle	II, 28
ching¹ mi³	米	upland rice	III, 7
ching¹ pao⁴	報	the Peking Gazette	IV, 11
ching¹ shên	神	spirits, energy	II, 25
ching⁴ tzŭ	自	to be always —, to do nothing but —	II, 33
ch'ing¹ an¹	安	to present one's compliments	I, 3
ch'ing² chiao	教	May I ask, I, I (also, ch'ing³ chiao¹)	IV, 10
ch'ing³ chien⁴	見	to ask to see, or, for an interview	IV, 5
ch'ing³ chih³	旨	to request the issue of a Decree	II, 22
ch'ing¹ ch'u	楚	distinct, clear	I, 15
ch'ing¹ chung⁴	重	degree of gravity or importance	IV, 5
ch'ing¹ fêng¹	風	the cool breeze	II, 22
ch'ing¹ hsien	閑	elegant leisure	II, 24
ch'ing² hsing	形	circumstances, state of affairs	IV, 5
ch'ing² i (4)	意	feeling, sentiment	I, 9
ch'ing³ k'o⁴	客	to invite guests	III, 11
ch'ing³ shang¹	上	please take the place of honour	II, 4
ch'ing¹ shêng	省	better, not so severe (of an illness)	I, 7
ch'ing² shih²	實	as a matter of fact, the truth is	IV, 9
ch'ing³ shih⁴	示	to request instructions	IV, 6
ch'ing¹ tan	淡	(of food), plain, without dressing	III, 11
ch'ing¹ tan¹	單	a detailed list, an Invoice, etc.	IV, 13
ch'ing¹ tsao (3)	早	very early in the day	III, 12
ch'ing³ tso⁴	坐	please take a seat	II, 4
ch'ing² tsou³	走	please proceed	IV, 11
ch'ing³ wên⁴	問	may I ask	I, 3
ch'ing² yüan⁴	願	willing	IV, 9
chiu³ chêng	城	the 9 divisions of the Tartar city Peking	III, 12
chiu³ ch'ien	錢	wine-money, a pourboire	III, 6
chiu¹ ching (sic)	竟	after all	I, 13
chiu¹ chu	住	to catch hold of with the hand	II, 32
chiu³ hsing¹	興	(of wine) exhilaration	III, 2
chiu² i (3)	已	long since	IV, 1

GLOSSARY OF PHRASES. 147

chiu⁴ jih⁴	日		former days	II, 31
chiu⁰ liu²	留	舊	to detain long	IV, 11
chiu³ pei¹	杯	久	a wine-glass	III, 4
chiu³ p'ei²	陪	酒	to stay long with	IV, 8
chiu⁴ ping⁴	病	久	an old complaint	II, 24
chiu⁴ shourh³	手	舊	while about it	III, 2
chiu⁴ sui⁴	歲	就	the old year	II, 40
chiu³ tsuan¹	鑽	舊	a corkscrew	III, 7
chiu⁴ tzŭ	子	酒	a wife's brother	II, 10
chiu³ wei²	逢	舅	I am delighted to meet you again (and chiu³ wei¹)	I, 4
chiu² yang³		久	I am delighted to make your acquaintance	I, 1
chiu² yen²	仰	久	to delay, loiter	IV, 3
ch'iu¹ shên³	延	秋	the autumn assize	IV, 11
ch'iu¹ shou¹	審	秋	the autumn harvest	II, 11
ch'iu¹ t'ien	收	秋	autumn	II, 22
cho² lo	天	着	a settlement, termination	IV, 7
cho² pi³	落	拙	suppose for the sake of argument (or cho¹ pi³)	II, 11
cho¹ tzŭ	比	棹	a table	I, 18
cho² tzŭ	子	鐲	a bangle, bracelet	II, 36
ch'o¹ tzŭ	子	戳	a stamp, die	II, 34
chou¹ ch'ê¹	車	舟	carriage by land and water	IV, 18
chou¹ chêng	正	周	proper, correct	III, 5
chou¹ chih¹	知	周	to be perfectly informed	IV, 4
chou¹ chuan (3)	轉	周	enough to go round, adequate	II, 9
chou¹ hsien⁴	縣	州	Department and District Magistrates	IV, 5
chou¹ hsüan	旋	周	to pass the dishes to	IV, 1
chou⁴ mei²	眉	皺	to frown	III, 2
ch'ou⁴ t'i	屉	抽	a drawer	III, 3
ch'ou² tzŭ	子	綢	silkstuffs	III, 10
chu² ai⁴	碍	阻	to impede, obstruct	IV, 6
chu⁴ cha²	箚	駐	stationed, resident, at	IV, 1
chu⁴ chia¹	家	住	to have one's private residence	II, 8
chu² chiang³	講	主	a Lecturer	IV, 16
chu⁴ chih	址	住	an address	IV, 7
chu² ching⁴	徑	竹	a path through a bamboo-grove	I, 20
chu¹ chu	蛛	蛛	a spider	III, 14
chu⁴ fang²	房	住	a dwelling-house	II, 11
chu³ fu	咐	主	to get, or, ask one to	II, 30
chu⁴ hsia	下	住	to stop, lodge at	II, 15
chu² i	意	主	notion, idea, plan	II, 17
chu⁴ tien⁴	店	住	to stop at an inn	III, 8

chu¹ to¹	多	a number of, numerous	IV, 11
chu⁴ tzŭ	柱子	a pillar	III, 10
ch'u¹ ch'êng²	出城	to go out of the city	II, 11
ch'u¹ chien	出間	the first part of a month	IV, 8
ch'u¹ ch'ü	出去	to go out	I, 25
ch'u¹ ch'üeh¹	出缺	to die in office	IV, 15
ch'u² fang	廚房	a kitchen	III, 9
ch'u¹ hai³	出海	to put to sea	II, 30
ch'u¹ hsi	出息	(of children) usefulness	I, 33
ch'u¹ kung¹	出恭	to relieve nature	II, 29
ch'u¹ lai	出來	to come out	II, 4
ch'u¹ ma³	出馬	to visit patients	II, 2
ch'u¹ mên²	出門	to go out of doors	I, 10
ch'u¹ ming²	出名	to become celebrated	II, 37
ch'u¹ shên	出身	mode of entering the public service	IV, 15
ch'u³ shih⁴	處事	to administer affairs	IV, 1
ch'u⁴ shou⁴	出售	to dispose of by sale	IV, 8
ch'u⁴ so³	處所	a spot, locality, place	IV, 6
ch'u² ti¹	鋤地	to hoe	II, 11
ch'u¹ t'ou²	出頭	to come forward, appear (in a matter)	IV, 19
ch'u¹ tsu¹	出租	to let	II, 1
ch'u² tzŭ	廚子	a cook	II, 20
ch'u¹ tz'ŭ	初次	the first occasion	IV, 18
ch'u¹ wai⁴	出外	to go abroad, leave home	II, 15
chü¹ chang³	居長	to be the eldest	I, 3
chü³ chia¹	舉家	the entire family	IV, 16
chü² chien	薦	to recommend	II, 10
chü⁴ hui(⁴)	會	to assemble, make a party	IV, 14
chü³ jên	舉人	a Provincial Graduate	II, 5
chü¹ li³	禮	to stand on ceremony	I, 8
chü¹ t'ing¹	停	a patron	II, 24
chü² tzŭ	子	a workroom, factory	II, 7
ch'ü³ ch'ien²	取錢	to fetch money, to cash	II, 26
ch'ü³ chung⁴	取中	to obtain one's degree	IV, 12
ch'ü¹ hsin¹	心	rascality	II, 16
ch'ü⁴ jên⁴	任	to leave one's post	IV, 15
ch'ü⁴ nien	年	last year	II, 16
ch'ü⁴ shih⁴	世	to die	IV, 19
chuai³ wo	窩	a hole or rut in the road	III, 6
chuan⁴ chang⁴	賺	profits, makings	II, 27
chuan¹ ch'êng²	專誠	with the express intention, expressly for	IV, 20

GLOSSARY OF PHRASES.

149

chuan⁴ ch'ien²	賺錢	to make money or, a profit	II, 19
chuan³ chih⁴	轉致	to transmit the information to	IV, 7
chuan³ ch'ih⁴	轉飭	to transmit orders to	IV, 5
chuan² mai⁴	轉賣	to resell	II, 19
chuan¹ wa²	磚瓦	bricks and tiles	II, 10
ch'uan² an⁴	傳案	to summon to a Court	IV, 8
ch'uan² chia⁴	船價	passage-money	III, 20
ch'uan² chih	船隻	shipping, boats	IV, 3
ch'uan² chih²	傳旨	to issue a Decree	II, 39
ch'uan² chu(3)	船主	the master of a ship	IV, 6
ch'uan² fei⁴	船費	passage-expenses	III, 20
ch'uan² hsün⁴	傳訊	to summon and examine	IV, 10
ch'uan² hu⁴	船戶	the master of a native vessel	IV, 6
ch'uan² pang¹	船幫	the side, or beam, of a vessel	IV, 6
ch'uan¹ shang	穿上	(of clothes) to put on; to run or pass something with a hole, or opening, over a stick, string, etc.	III, 5, 10
ch'uan² to⁴	船柁	a rudder	IV, 6
ch'uan¹ t'u²	川土	Szechuen opium	IV, 13
chüan³ shang	捲上	to roll up	III, 17
ch'üan¹ k'ai	勸開	to intervene between	II, 32
ch'üan² pien(4)	權變	a modification to meet the circumstances or exigencies	IV, 9
chuang¹ chia	莊稼	crops	II, 10
chuang¹ chia³	裝假	to make pretence	IV, 1
chuang⁴ huai⁴	撞壞	to injure by collision	IV, 6
chuang¹ shang	裝上	to load on or into	IV, 7
chuang¹ tsai⁴	裝載	to load or be loaded with	IV, 7
chuang¹ tso	裝做	to pretend	II, 30
chuang¹ tzŭ	樁子	a post	III, 16
ch'uang¹ hu	窗戶	a window	I, 23
chüeh² chiao¹	絕交	to break off an intimacy, or relations	II, 25
chüeh² ting³	絕頂	exceptionally, pre-eminently	IV, 18
ch'üeh¹ fên	缺分	class or sort of post	IV, 11
ch'üeh⁴ tsun¹	恪遵	to conform scrupulously, strictly, to	IV, 5
chui¹ shang	追上	to catch, catch up, recover (a runaway)	II, 32
ch'ui² tzŭ	鎚子	a hammer	III, 9
chun² chien⁴	準見	shall meet	II, 1
ch'un¹ ch'iu¹	春秋	spring and autumn, (but ch'un¹ ch'iu¹ as title of the Classic)	I, 27
ch'un¹ hsin¹	春心	sexual passion	I, 44
ch'un¹ lien²	春聯	New year scrolls	II, 40
ch'un¹ t'ien	春天	Springtime	II, 16

chün¹ t'an¹	攤臣	to pay equal shares or contributions	IV, 9
ch'ün² ch'ên²	均	the Ministry	II, 39
chung¹ chiu¹	終	eventually	II, 15
chung¹ ch'ieh	中	a medium or average post	IV, 11
chung¹ fan⁴	中	the midday meal	II, 39
chung¹ hou(4)	忠	honourable	II, 24
chung¹ jên	中	an intermediary	II, 1
chung⁴ jên⁴	重	an onerous post	IV, 1
chung¹ kuo(2)	中	China, Chinese	I, 17
chung⁴ li⁴	重	high or heavy interest	II, 27
chung⁴ ping⁴	重	a severe illness	II, 16
chung¹ t'ang	中	a Grand Secretary	IV, 10
chung⁴ ti⁴	種	to farm	II, 11
chung¹ yung¹ (sic)	中	useful, of use	I, 31
ch'ung² lo	重	to have a relapse	I, 5
ch'ung⁴ shurh⁴	充	to be one of, to be of the number	IV, 2
ên¹ tien	恩	kindness from a superior	III, 13
erh² ch'ich²	而	moreover	III, 5
erh⁴ lai²	二	in the second place	IV, 4
erh³ to	耳	the ear	I, 16
fa¹ hsin⁴	發	to send a letter	IV, 7
fa¹ hun¹	發	to be dizzy	II, 26
fa¹ juan²	發	to be tender or weak	III, 16
fa⁴ lan²	法	cloisonné	II, 7
fa⁴ ming²	法	religious name (Buddhist)	I, 31
fa¹ ts'ai²	雜	to grow rich	II, 23
fa² tzŭ	法	a device, means	I, 24
fan⁴ ch'ao²	犯	to become damp or mildewed	III, 14
fan⁴ ch'ien	飯	money for food	III, 6
fan⁴ ch'üeh(1)	煩	an arduous post	II, 3
fan⁴ huo⁴	販	to be a dealer	II, 2
fan⁴ i²	犯	to become suspicious	II, 29
fan² jung²	煩	busy, much occupied	IV, 5
fan⁴ shih	飯	food, provisions	IV, 17
fan⁴ ssŭ	藩	a Provincial Treasurer	IV, 15
fan² tsa	煩	much occupied, greatly engaged	IV, 16
fan⁴ wan²	飯	a rice-bowl	III, 4
fang² ch'an(3)	產	house property	II, 11
fang² ch'i(4)	契	a title-deed of a house	II, 11
fang² ch'ien	錢	house-rent	II, 1
fang² fan	防	to provide, take precautions	IV, 10

GLOSSARY OF PHRASES. 151

fang² fu	彿	for example, supposing, as if	II, 1
fang⁴ hsin¹	彷 心	to be at ease about, make one's mind easy	I, 19
fang⁴ hsing²	放 行	to release	IV, 7
fang⁴ niu²	放 牛	to tend cattle	II, 11
fang¹ pien	方 便	convenient	I, 14
fang² shih¹	房 師	an assistant examiner	IV, 12
fang² tung¹	房 東	the landlord of a house	II, 1
fang¹ tzŭ	方 子	a prescription	II, 25
fang² tzŭ	房 子	a house	II, 10
fang⁴ yang²	放 羊	to tend sheep	II, 11
fei⁴ hsin¹	費 心	thank you for your trouble	I, 32
fei⁴ wu	廢 物	a useless or worthless thing	III, 10
fên¹ chia¹	分 家	to set up a separate establishment	II, 11
fên¹ fu	分 法	mode of dividing	II, 11
fên¹ fu	吩 咐	to instruct, order	II, 19
fên¹ kei	分 給	to give a share to	II, 27
fên⁴ liang	分 兩	weight	III, 19
fên¹ pieh	分 別	to distinguish, a distinction	I, 12
fên³ tzŭ	粉 子	powder	III, 5
fêng¹ ch'êng	奉 承	to flatter	IV, 18
fêng⁴ chih³	奉 旨	to receive a Decree	IV, 5
fêng⁴ chih⁴	奉 致	to have the honour to acquaint	IV, 4
fêng¹ ching (3)	風 景	the scene	I, 21
fêng¹ ho²	風 河	(of rivers) to freeze up	II, 23
fêng¹ huo⁴	封 貨	to tender for articles at a pawnbroker's	II, 20
fêng⁴ k'ên²	奉 懇	to beg, entreat	IV, 13
fêng⁴ kuan¹	封 官	officially appointed	II, 12
fêng⁴ man³	俸 滿	expiry of an official appointment	II, 5
fêng⁴ ming⁴	奉 命	to be honoured by orders	IV, 20
fêng¹ shêng	風 聲	reputation, rumours	II, 16
fêng¹ shou¹	豐 收	an abundant harvest	II, 11
fêng⁴ sung⁴	奉 送	to take the liberty to send or present	III, 18
fêng¹ t'u	風 土	manners and customs	IV, 4
fêng⁴ wei³	奉 委	to be deputed	IV, 16
fêng¹ wên²	風 聞	to hear reports of	IV, 4
fêng¹ yin⁴	封 印	to close (for the New Year)	II, 4
fêng⁴ yin²	俸 銀	salary	II, 39
fu² ch'i	福 氣	prosperity	I, 2
fu² chien	福 建	province of Fuhkien	II, 21
fu⁴ ch'in	父 親	a father	II, 17
fu⁴ ch'ing¹	付 清	to pay over in full	IV, 7

fu¹ jên	人夫	(polite) a wife	I, 10
fu⁴ kuei (4)	富	wealthy	II, 23
fu⁴ pang²	副榜	a Proxime Accessit	IV, 15
fu² p'i¹	庇	auspicious influence	IV, 3
fu³ shang (4)	府上	your residence	I, 1—
fu² shih	服侍	to wait, attend, upon	III, 5
fu² shih⁴	覆試	the Test Examinations	IV, 12
fu³ t'ai	撫台	the Governor of a province	II, 5
fu¹ tzŭ	麩子	bran	III, 16
fu⁴ yü	富餘	to remain over and above, surplus	IV, 10
fu² yüarh²	復元兒	to look oneself again	I, 5
hai³ ch'uan²	海船	a seagoing ship	II, 29
hai⁴ hsiu¹	害羞	bashful, modest	I, 44
hai³ kuan	海關	the Maritime Customs	IV, 7
hai⁴ p'a⁴	害怕	to be frightened	II, 16
hai² tzŭ	孩子	a child	I, 33
hai³ wei (4)	海味	marine delicacies	III, 19
han³ chien⁴	罕見	rarely seen, exceptional	IV, 18
han² chih⁴	函致	to inform by note	IV, 7
han² fu²	函覆	to reply by note	IV, 7
han² hu	糊糊	indistinct, I, 15, scamped	II, 10
han⁴ lu (4)	旱路	by land	II, 28
han¹ san³	傘	a sunshade, umbrella	III, 17
han¹ t'arh¹	汗衫兒	a shirt	III, 5
hang² chan⁴	行棧	house of business, mercantile house	IV, 7
hang² ch'ing	行情	market-rates	II, 2
hang² chu (3)	行主	head of a firm	IV, 8
hang² hua	行話	technical terms, "shop"	II, 40
hang² shih	行市	market-rates	II, 2
hao³ ch'u	好處	advantages, good points, merits	I, 27
hao³ haorh¹ (sic)	好好兒	properly, thoroughly	I, 5
hao³ k'an⁴	好看	(also, hao³ k'an), goodlooking, beautiful	I, 21
hao³ shih⁴	好事	a good, charitable, or philanthropic, act	II, 29
hao³ shou (3)	好手	a good hand at	III, 6
hao³ shuo¹	好說	thank you for saying so!	I, 9
hao² ssŭ³	好死	a peaceful or honourable death	II, 16
hao² tai³	好歹	(also, hao² tai(³)), good and evil	I, 29
hao² tarh (3)	好在	a mortal illness	III, 13
hao³ tsai⁴	好子	it is a good thing that —	II, 39
hao¹ tzŭ	耗下	a rat	I, 43
hei¹ hsia	黑	nightfall	II, 13

GLOSSARY OF PHRASES. 153

hei¹ sé	色 黑	black colour, blacking	III, 15
hei³ tou¹ (sic)	豆 黑	black pulse	III, 16
ho¹ ch'a²	茶 喝	to drink tea	II, 4
ho¹ chiu³	酒 喝	to drink wine	I, 18
ho¹ chou¹	粥 喝	to eat gruel or porridge	III, 7
ho² chung (1)	衷 和	a spirit of fairness	IV, 1
ho² fang¹	妨 何	what objection is there to —	IV, 1
ho² hao³	好 和	friendly relations	IV, 1
ho² hsi	息 和	a formal reconciliation	II, 19
ho⁴ hsi³	喜 賀	to congratulate	IV, 2
ho¹ hu	呼 喝	to exclaim at, shout out at	II, 39
ho² i²	宜 合	suitable	II, 24
ho² i (3)	以 何	how, in what manner	IV, 5
ho² ju²	如 何	how, of what sort	IV, 9
ho² k'u³	苦 何	what is the use of —	I, 42
ho² mu	睦 和	amity, friendly relations	II, 11
ho² nan	南 河	province of Honan	I, 1
ho² pao	包 荷	a pouch, purse	III, 5
ho² pi¹	必 何	what need is there to (also ho² pi²)	III, 18
ho² p'ing	平 和	kind	II, 24
ho² po²	泊 河	a Harbour or River Inspector	IV, 6
ho² shang	尙 和	a Buddhist priest	I, 31
ho² shang	上 合	to fit on	III, 10
ho² shih⁴	式 合	suitable, suited to	II, 2
ho² t'ung	同 合	an agreement	II, 10
ho² tzŭ	子 盒	a small box	II, 7
hou¹ ch'êng²	乘 候	to wait while you mount	IV, 2
hou⁴ hsüan¹	選 候	to be an Expectant	II, 9
hou⁴ lai (2)	來 後	afterwards	II, 6
hou⁴ mien	面 後	behind, at the back	IV, 6
hou⁴ nien	年 後	the year before last	IV, 16
hou⁴ pu (3)	補 候	to be an Expectant	II, 3
hou⁴ t'ou	頭 後	behind	I, 22
hou⁴ yen⁴	驗 候	to await inspection	IV, 7
hsi¹ ch'êng	城 西	the Western city in Peking	II, 10
hsi² ch'i	氣 息	a habit, way, characteristic	III, 19
hsi¹ hsin¹	心 細	careful	I, 30
hsi³ huan	歡 喜	to like, be fond of	I, 20
hsi⁴ k'an (4)	看 細	to closely examine	I, 12
hsi² lu	鑞 鍚	pewter	III, 2
hsi¹ lan⁴	爛 稀	in pieces, to pieces	I, 43

hsi² lien³	洗臉	to wash the face	II, 29
hsi¹ pei³	西北	north-west	II, 31
hsi¹ pierh	西邊兒	the western side	III, 1
hsi¹ shan¹	西山	the Western Hills	III, 8
hsi⁴ t'ai²	戲臺	a theatrical stage	III, 11
hsi² tsao³	洗澡	to wash	III, 8
hsi¹ t'u²	希圖	to aim at, with a view to	IV, 9
hsi⁴ tzŭ	戲子	an actor	III, 11
hsia⁴ chien	下賤	mean, base, wretched	I, 34
hsia⁴ ch'ien⁴	下欠	a debit balance, balance unpaid	IV, 7
hsia⁴ ch'ü	下去	to go down	II, 19
hsia⁴ ch'uan²	下船	to disembark	II, 21
hsia⁴ huai²	下懷	the feelings, sentiments	IV, 16
hsia⁴ hui	下回	next time	II, 26
hsia⁴ hsing³	嚇醒	to startle out of sleep	II, 25
hsia⁴ lo	下落	a place to go to, or be found at	II, 32
hsia¹ mi	蝦米	dried shrimps	III, 19
hsia⁴ pao³	下保	to deposit security	II, 13
hsia⁴ shan¹	下山	to go down the hill	I, 31
hsia⁴ shang	下上	to put down into [or] on	III, 10
hsia⁴ shêng⁴	下剩	the remainder	II, 1
hsia² shih²	暇時	leisure	IV, 18
hsia⁴ t'a⁴	下榻	to sleep, pass the night, at	IV, 17
hsia⁴ t'ien	夏天	summer	II, 12
hsia⁴ tsou³	瞎走	to go blundering along	II, 29
hsia¹ tzŭ	瞎子	a blind man	III, 15
hsia² tzŭ	匣子	a small case or box	III, 18
hsiu⁴ tz'ŭ	下次	next time	IV, 12
hsia⁴ yü²	下餘	remaining over, surplus	II, 1
hsia¹ yü³	下雨	to rain	I, 23
hsia¹ yüeh (4)	下月	next month	II, 9
hsiang⁴ ch'i (2)	象棋	chess	II, 40
hsiang⁴ ch'ien²	向前	to get on, come to the front	I, 34
hsiang¹ ch'in	鄉親	a fellow-countryman	II, 31
hsiang¹ fang	廂房	the side buildings of a house	III, 9
hsiang¹ fu²	相符	to correspond, tally, to	IV, 8
hsiang¹ hao³	相好	on good terms, friendly	I, 3
hsiang² hsi	詳細	in detail, fully	IV, 4
hsiang¹ hsia	鄉下	the country	III, 13
hsiang¹ hsin⁴	相信	confidence, good faith	IV, 18
hsiang¹ hui¹	相會	to meet	IV, 1

GLOSSARY OF PHRASES. 155

hsiang¹ kan¹	干公	to concern, affect	II, 6
hsiang¹ kung	相公來	a boy actor	III, 11
hsiang¹ lai²	相向	hitherto	II, 2
hsiang² liang (4)	响詳	resonant, clear	I, 15
hsiang² pao¹	詳禀	to report to a Superior	IV, 6
hsiang¹ shang	鑲	to put on a border	III, 14
hsiang¹ shih¹	鄉試	the provincial examinations	IV, 12
hsiang¹ shih⁴	像事	the right or proper thing	II, 4
hsiang¹ t'an	鄉談	local dialect	I, 17
hsiang¹ tang¹	相當	suited to, suitable	II, 24
hsiang¹ tê⁴	相得	to take a liking to, congenial	II, 25
hsiang¹ tzŭ	箱子	a box, case	I, 4
hsiang¹ yangrh²	向陽兒	towards the light	III, 1
hsiao² ch'êrh (1)	小吃兒	"extras," small dishes not in the menu	III, 11
hsiao² ch'ü (3)	小取	mean, grasping	II, 27
hsiao³ hao¹	小號	my Firm	I, 3
hsiao³ hsin	小心	careful	III, 9
hsiao² hua⁴	小學話	(also, hsüeh² hua¹), to learn to speak a language	IV, 20
hsiao⁴ huarh	笑話兒	a joke, good story	II, 33
hsiao⁴ lao²	効勞	to be of [or] do a service to one	I, 40
hsiao¹ t'ing	消停	(of work), slack, easy	IV, 14
hsieh² chüan¹	携眷	to take one's wife with one	IV, 11
hsieh¹ fa²	乏法	to rest oneself	II, 38
hsieh²·³ farh	寫法兒	mode of writing	III, 12
hsieh¹ ho	謝和	to reward (as for recovery of a lost article)	II, 6
hsieh⁴ hsin⁴	寫信	to write a letter	IV, 6
hsieh¹ hsü¹	些須	a little, some slight —	IV, 1
hsieh⁴ lou	洩漏	to divulge, let out	I, 16
hsieh⁴ pu⁴	謝步	to return (your) call	I, 4
hsieh³ tzŭ¹	寫字	to write	I, 30
hsien¹ ch'êng	現成	in hand, in store, available	II, 22
hsien¹ ch'i²	先期	beforehand	IV, 4
hsien⁴ ch'i (2)	限期	a limit of time, fixed period	II, 22
hsien⁴ ch'ien²	現錢	cash	II, 10
hsien³ chih²	顯秩	a distinguished appointment	IV, 2
hsien¹ fu⁴	先父	my late father	IV, 15
hsien¹ jung²	先容	to arrange the preliminaries for an interview	IV, 16
hsien² k'ungrh⁴	閒空兒	spare time	I, 10
hsien⁴ mu (4)	羨慕	to admire	I, 19
hsien² p'i (2)	涎皮	unabashed	I, 37
hsien¹ shêng	先生	Sir (to non-officials)	I, 2

hsien² shih⁴	事時	things that do not concern one	I, 43
hsien⁴ shih²	閒署	at the present time	II, 13
hsien⁴ shu³	縣談	a District Magistracy	IV, 8
hsien² t'an²	閒在	to chat, talk	II, 31
hsien² tsai	閒在	at leisure	II, 9
hsien⁴ tsai⁴	現菜	now	I, 40
hsien² ts'ai⁴	鹹近	salted vegetables	III, 4
hsin⁴ chin (4)	新煩	lately	II, 3
hsin¹ farh²	心喜	annoyances, vexations	I, 39
hsin¹ hsi³	新任	a Happy New Year	II, 4
hsin¹ jên⁴	新開	one's new post	II, 3
hsin¹ k'ai¹	信口	newly opened	II, 2
hsin¹ k'ou²	辛苦	(to speak) recklessly, without restraint	IV, 5
hsin¹ k'u	幸虧	to put one to trouble	II, 14
hsing⁴ k'uei	心領	luckily	II, 28
hsin¹ ling³	新手	to decline with thanks	IV, 2
hsin¹ shourh³	新聞	a new hand	III, 20
hsin¹ wên²	行跡	news	IV, 3
hsing² chi	行期	etiquette, formality	IV, 14
hsing² ch'i (2)	行鐘	time of starting	II, 5
hsing³ chung¹	醒席	an Alarum	II, 14
hsing² hsi²	刑醫	Law Secretary (in a Yamên)	IV, 15
hsing² i¹	行李	to practise medicine	II, 2
hsing² li	行敗	baggage	I, 4
hsing¹ pai⁴	興得	rise and fall, growth and decline	I, 29
hsing⁴ tê²	幸走	to be fortunate enough to	IV, 1
hsing² tsou³	行子	to do duty, be employed at, II, 1; to proceed	IV, 6
hsing⁴ tzŭ	性文	temper	I, 42
hsing² wên²	行裂	to send a despatch	IV, 5
hsiu¹ fei⁴	修涹	expense of repairs	IV, 6
hsiu¹ sê⁴	羞拾	(of circumstances), straitened	II, 22
hsiu¹ shih	修才	to put in order, prepare	II, 38
hsiu⁴ ts'ai	秀慚	a Licentiate	II, 40
hsiu⁴ ts'an	賽子	confused, abashed	II, 33
hsiu⁴ tzŭ	袖橫	a sleeve	III, 4
hsiung¹ hêng	兒手	desperate, truculent	II, 26
hsiung¹ shou	兇弟	a homicide, murderer	II, 22
hsiung¹ ti	兄台	a younger brother; used to one of same generation = I.	II, 11
hsiung⁴ t'ai	兄久	you Sir, (used to an equal of the same generation)	II, 3
hsü² chiu³	許	a long time	IV, 5

GLOSSARY OF PHRASES. 157

hsü¹ ming²	名 虛	an undeserved reputation	IV, 16
hsü⁴ shang	上 續	to replenish, fill up again	III, 2
hsü¹ tu⁴	度 虛	my age is —	I, 2
hsüan⁴ shang	上 選	to select for a vacancy	II, 9
hsüan⁴ shou⁴	授 選	to allot, assign, to a post	IV, 15
hsüeh² ch'ai¹	差 學	a Literary Chancellorship	IV, 2
hsüeh² ch'ien²	淺 學	scanty learning	IV, 16
hsüeh² fang	房 學	a school	I, 28
hsüeh² hsi²	習 學	to practise, learn	IV, 4
hsüeh² tzŭ	子 學	boots	III, 5
hsüeh² wên	問 學	learning, studies	I, 30
hsüeh² yeh⁴	業 學	stock of learning, scholarship	IV, 16
hsün² chien	檢 巡	a sub-district Deputy Magistrate	II, 32
hsün⁴ chui¹	追 訊	to recover a debt after formal exam. of debtor	IV, 10
hsün² fu	撫 巡	a Governor of a province	IV, 5
hsün² i⁴	役 巡	the City Police of Peking	IV, 13
hsün⁴ kuan	官 巡	Police officials	II, 6
hsün⁴ ming²	明 訊	to examine, interrogate	IV, 8
hu⁴ chao	照 護	a Passport	IV, 5
hu¹ hsiang¹	相 忽	mutually	IV, 18
hu¹ jan²	然 忽	suddenly	I, 23
hu² pei⁽³⁾	北 湖	province of Hupei	IV, 18
hu² shang	上 糊	to paste on	III, 17
hu² shuo¹	說 胡	to talk nonsense	III, 16
hu⁴ sung	送 護	to escort	IV, 3
hu¹ tou³	斗 斛	measures of capacity	II, 12
hu² t'ung	衙 衚	(sometimes hu² t'ungrh¹) a side street	II, 1
hu¹ wei	衛 護	the Imperial Body guard	II, 39
hu² yen²	言 胡	wild, reckless, language	IV, 5
hua² chieh	稭 花	packing straw	III, 17
hua¹ ch'ien²	錢 花	to spend money	II, 17
hua² ch'üan²	拳 划	to play morra	II, 39
hua² la	拉 胡	to brush or sweep away	III, 14
hua¹ p'ing²	瓶 花	a flower-vase	III, 7
hua¹ shang¹	商 華	a Chinese merchant	IV, 8
hua⁴ shuo	說 話	something to say	II, 9
huai⁴ shih⁴	事 壞	to do harm, to mar	I, 16
huan² chiarh⁴	價 還 兒	to offer a price	III, 19
huan² ch'ing¹	清 還	to repay in full	IV, 7
huan² kei	給 還	to give back to	II, 22
huan⁴ nang	宦 囊	emoluments, private fortune	II, 22

†

huan⁴ shang	換上	(of clothes, etc.) to change, put on other —	III, 18
huang² chia⁴	謊價	an exorbitant price	III, 19
huang² chiu(3)	黃酒	yellow wine	III, 11
huang³ hu	恍惚	vague	II, 16
huang² kua	黃瓜	cucumber	III, 4
huang² shang	皇上	the Emperor	I, 35
huang¹ su	荒疎	dispersed, dissipated	IV, 16
huang⁴ tang	晃蕩	to jolt, shake	III, 17
huang¹ t'ang	荒唐	reckless, wild	II, 33
huang² ti⁴	皇帝	the Emperor	IV, 3
huang³ tzŭ	幌子	a shopsign	II, 29
huang² yu²	黃油	butter	III, 3
hui² chi²	回籍	to return to one's native place	IV, 15
hui² chia¹	回家	to go home	I, 35
hui⁴ ch'ien²	會錢	to club together a sum of money	IV, 17
hui² ch'ü	回去	to go back	II, 2
hui² fu	回覆	to give an answer to	II, 17
hui² hsin(4)	回信	a letter in reply	II, 16
hui⁴ hsün⁴	會訊	joint investigation	IV, 6
hui⁴ kai³	悔改	to reform	II, 16
hui⁴ kuan³	會館	a Guildhouse, a club	II, 17
hui² lai	回來	to come back	I, 21
hui⁴ mien⁴	會面	to meet one another	IV, 14
hui² ming²	回明	to give a message to	IV, 5
hui⁴ pai⁴	回拜	to return a visit	IV, 4
hui⁴ pan⁴	會辦	joint management or control	IV, 18
hui³ ping(3)	回稟	(of servants) If you please, Sir	II, 4
hui⁴ shih⁴	會試	the Metropolitan Examinations	II, 5
hui² shou²	回手	(a blow, etc.) in return	II, 35
hui⁴ shou²	會首	the President of a club	IV, 17
hui² ta	回答	to reply	II, 35
hui² t'ou²	回頭	in a minute, and then —	II, 14
hui⁴ t'ung²	會同	conjointly	IV, 6
hui⁴ tzŭ (sio)	會子	a while	II, 11
hui² wên²	回文	an official reply, a despatch in reply	IV, 8
hun² shên(1)	渾身	all over one's body	I, 5
hung² ch'a²	紅茶	black tea	III, 2
hung² ch'i⁴	紅契	a Stamped Title Deed	II, 8
hung² chiu¹	紅酒	red wine, claret	III, 7
hung³ p'ien(4)	哄騙	to swindle	II, 26
hung² yün²	紅運	good fortune	II, 20

GLOSSARY OF PHRASES. 159

huo⁴ ch'ê¹	車	火車	a wagon	IV, 13
huo³ chi	計	夥計	(vulg. huo³ ch'i), a shopman, assistant	I, 13
huo² pa	把	火把	a torch	II, 27
huo³ pan⁽⁴⁾	辦	夥辦	on joint account, jointly	II, 27
huo⁴ pao¹	包	貨包	a bale	IV, 8
huo³ parh⁴	件	夥件	a fellow-workman	III, 9
huo³ p'ên²	盆	火盆	a chafing-dish	III, 2
huo³ t'ung	同	夥同	to conspire	II, 26
huo⁴ wu⁽⁴⁾	物	貨物	goods	II, 2
huo⁴ yin²	銀	貨銀	money for goods supplied	IV, 10
i⁴ ch'i²	齊	一齊	all together	IV, 17
i⁽⁴⁾ ch'ich¹⁻³	切	一切	altogether	IV, 15
i³ chih⁴	致	以致	the result being	IV, 6
i³ ching	經	已經	already	I, 2
i² ch'üeh⁽¹⁾	鈌	遺鈌	a vacancy caused by promotion	II, 24
i¹ chun³	準	一準	for certain	IV, 4
i⁴ chung	中	意中	in one's thoughts, in the mind's eye	II, 24
i¹ fu	服	一服	clothing	I, 4
i³ hou⁴	後	以後	afterwards	I, 8
i⁴ hsü⁽⁴⁾	叙	議叙	favorably mentioned by the Board of Civil Office	IV, 15
i² huo	惑	疑惑	to doubt, suspect	II, 29
i² kai⁴	概	一概	entirely, altogether	II, 27
i² k'uairh⁴	塊兒	一塊兒	together	I, 14
i¹ lai²	來	一來	in the first place	IV, 4
i¹ liang³	兩	一兩	one or two	II, 1
i² lü⁴	律	一律	uniformly, equally	IV, 9
i¹ lun⁽¹⁾	論	議論	to criticise, discuss	II, 11
i¹ shang	裳	衣裳	clothes	II, 30
i¹ shih²	實	一實	heartily	IV, 1
i¹ shih²	時	一時	at once, all at once	II, 1
i¹ shu⁽⁴⁾	術	醫術	(of doctors) methods of treatment	III, 7
i¹ ssŭ	意	意思	meaning, intention	II, 10
i² sungrh⁴	送兒	一送兒	the single journey	III, 6
i¹ tao⁽⁴⁾	道	醫道	system of medicine	III, 7
i⁽⁴⁾ tierh³	點兒	一點兒	a little, somewhat	I, 7
i² ting⁴	定	一定	certainly	I, 11
i⁴ ting⁴	定	議定	to settle definitively	IV, 7
i⁴ tsai⁽⁴⁾	在	意在	with the intention of, to mean to —	IV, 5
i¹ tsao³	早	一早	very early	IV, 7
i¹ t'ung²	同	一同	together	I, 14
i² tzŭ	子	胰子	soap	III, 3

i³ tzŭ	椅子	a chair	II, 31
i¹ wai⁴	意外	unforeseen, unexpected	IV, 5
i¹ yao⁴	醫藥	treatment and medicines	III, 7
i³ yeh⁴	肄業	to prosecute one's studies	IV, 16
ian² erh (2)	然而	but yet, still, nevertheless	IV, 9
jan² hou⁴	然後	afterwards	II, 12
jao² shu	饒恕	to overlook, pardon	III, 4
jê⁴ nao	熱鬧	lively, bustling	II, 35
jên⁴ chang⁴	認帳	to confess, acknowledge a charge	III, 15
jên⁴ chên¹	認眞	zealous	I, 36
jên² chia	人家	people, others	I, 34
jên² ch'ing (2)	人情	popular character	IV, 4
jên² hsing	人性	disposition	II, 25
jên² hsing²	人行	human nature	II, 26
jên⁴ i⁴	任意	at will, at discretion	IV, 9
jên² min²	人民	the populace, population	IV, 5
jên⁴ p'ei²	認賠	to acknowledge a liability to pay	IV, 6
jên⁴ shih	認識	to recognise	IV, 20
jên⁴ so³	認所	place of appointment	IV, 15
jên² wu	人物	(also, jên² wu⁴), mankind, man	I, 29
jêng² chiu (4)	仍舊	as before, once more	IV, 8
jih⁴ chi⁴	日記	a diary	II, 38
jih⁴ ch'i²	日期	a date	IV, 16
jih⁴ ch'ien²	日前	on a former day [or] occasion	IV, 2
jih⁴ hou⁴	日後	in the future	IV, 5
jih⁴ hsin¹	日新	ever fresh	IV, 16
jih⁴ tzŭ	日子	a day	I, 7
jo⁴ hsü³	若許	a good many, a good deal	IV, 13
jo⁴ kan¹	若干	so much, a certain amount	IV, 9
ju² chin	如今	at present	I, 13
ju² ho²	如何	how	II, 29
ju² kuo (3)	如果	if	IV, 8
ju² shu (4)	如數	in full	II, 1
ju⁴ t'ao⁴	褥套	a mattress-cover	III, 17
ju⁴ tzŭ	褥子	a mattress	III, 6
ju² tz'ŭ³	如此	thus	II, 5
juan³ p'ien⁴	軟片	soft stuff things	III, 17
jung² hsia²	融洽	considerateness, consideration	IV, 18
jung² hsing²	融行	your departure	IV, 4
jung² i	容易	easy	I, 19
jung² jên⁴	榮任	your post	II, 5

GLOSSARY OF PHRASES.

jung² ying¹	榮膺	your incumbency (of a post)	IV, 2
ka¹ larh²	嘎喇兒	a corner	III, 9
k'a¹ la	哈喇	Russian cloth	IV, 8
kai³ jih⁴	改日	on another day	IV, 7
kai³ kuo⁴	改過	to reform	II, 25
kai⁴ shang	蓋上	to cover over	III, 10
kai¹ tang¹	該當	ought, should	II, 11
kai³ t'ien(1)	改天	another day	II, 2
k'ai¹ ch'uan²	開船	to set sail	II, 30
k'ai¹ fa	開發	to disburse, pay out	II, 10
k'ai¹ fan⁴	開飯	to serve dinner	III, 4
k'ai¹ hui⁴	開會	(of clubs, societies) to open, meet	IV, 17
k'ai¹ k'ai	開開	to open	II, 29
k'ai¹ shih⁴	開事	to begin business	II, 9
k'ai¹ shui³	開水	boiling water	III, 2
k'ai¹ ts'an¹	開參	to denounce specifically	IV, 5
k'ai¹ yin⁴	開印	to open an office after New Year	II, 4
kan³ chi	感激	to be grateful	I, 40
kan¹ ch'i	肝氣	an attack of spleen	II, 27
kan¹ chieh²	甘結	a voluntary Bond	IV, 9
kan² chin³	趕緊	at once, without loss of time	II, 12
kan¹ ching	乾淨	clean	II, 40
kan³ ch'ing	敢情	really! actually!	II, 14
kan³ ch'ing²	感情	gratitude	IV, 7
kan³ hsieh⁴	感謝	grateful	IV, 7
kan⁴ lien⁴	幹練	competent, skilled	II, 38
kan¹ su	甘肅	province of Kansu	II, 29
kan³ tai⁴	感戴	sentiment of gratitude	IV, 16
kan³ tang¹	敢當	to venture to accept (a compliment, etc.)	IV, 1
kan³ tao(4)	趕到	(of time) by, by the time that —	I, 23
kan¹ tzŭ	竿子	a pole, rod	II, 12
kan³ tzŭ	敢自	I daresay —	III, 1
k'an⁴ chien	看見	to see	I, 25
k'an³ chierh¹	坎肩兒	a waistcoat	III, 5
k'an³ k'ai	砍開	to hack or split open	II, 28
k'an⁴ ming²	勘明	to find by inspection	IV, 8
k'an⁴ p'o⁴	看破	to see through, discover	I, 11
kang¹ ts'ai²	纔	just, just now	I, 38
k'ang¹ chien	康健	robust	I, 2
k'ang¹ t'ai⁴	康泰	robust	IV, 3
kao⁴ chia⁴	告假	to apply for leave	IV, 11

THE GUIDE TO KUAN HUA.

Romanization	Chinese	Meaning	Ref
kao¹ chih¹	告知	to acquaint, inform of	IV, 4
kao¹ chung¹	中	(your) success at the examination	IV, 12
kao¹ hsing⁴	高興	enjoyable	I, 14
kao¹ liang	高粱	millet	III, 16
kao⁴ ping⁴	告病	to apply for sick-leave	II, 24
kao⁴ shou⁴	高壽	your age (to elderly or old persons)	I, 2
kao⁴ sung	告訴	(commonly also kao⁴ su) to inform, to tell	I, 42
k'ao³ shang	考上	to pass (an examination)	II, 24
k'ao³ ta (3)	考打	to apply corporal punishment	II, 38
kên¹ ch'ien	跟前	in the family of, a child of	I, 38
kên¹ jên²	跟人	a personal attendant	II, 21
kên¹ kuan¹	跟官	to be a private servant of an official	II, 17
kên! t'ou (sic)	跟斗	a tumble	I, 45
k'ên³ ch'iu (2)	懇求	to entreat, beg	I, 19
kêng³ chih	耿直	unyielding, stiff	I, 42
ko² chih²	革職	to cashier	II, 22
ko⁴ ch'u (1)	各處	each place, everywhere	I, 17
ko² chü²	格局	a standard, prescribed method or form	IV, 1
ko² hsia	閣下	Sir	I, 19
ko⁴ jên	各人	(also ko² jên), each one. oneself	I, 35
ko¹ ko	哥哥	an older brother	II, 17
ko⁴ kuo²	各國	all countries, all the Powers	IV, 5
ko² shan	屏扇	a screen	I, 16
ko⁴ shêng³	各省	all the provinces	IV, 5
ko¹ tzŭ	鴿子	a pigeon	II, 32
ko² tzŭ	格子	a shelf, partition	III, 2
ko⁴ tzŭ⁴	自	by oneself	IV, 17
k'o³ ch'i⁴	可氣	irritating, aggravating	II, 26
k'o² ch'iao³	可巧	by pure chance, as it happened	II, 21
k'o³ chien⁴	可見	apparent, obvious	IV, 6
k'o¹ fang	科房	the Board Office (in a provincial Yamen) IV, 5, the General Office (Peking)	IV, 13
k'o¹ fên	科分	the year of taking a Degree	II, 5
k'o² hên⁴	可恨	detestable, to detest	II, 27
k'o³ hsi¹	可惜	pitiful, a pity	I, 31
k'o² hsiang³	可想	to long for	I, 4
k'o² hsiao⁴	可笑	amusing	I, 44
k'o³ hsin⁴	可信	trustworthy, credible	IV, 6
k'o² i (3)	可以	can, may, will	I, 8
k'o⁴ jên (2)	客人	a stranger, visitor	II, 19
k'o¹ ming²	科名	literary reputation, honours	IV, 12
k'o³ lü⁴	可慮	to be feared or apprehended	II, 1

GLOSSARY OF PHRASES.   163

k'o⁴ po	薄	to be hard upon	I, 42
k'o² shih⁴	是	but, now	I, 7
k'o³ so	嗽	a cough	I, 7
k'o¹ ta	打	to knock out, clean by knocking	III, 10
k'o⁴ tien⁴	店	an inn	II, 31
k'o⁴ t'ing¹	廳	a drawing-room, reception-room	II, 9
k'o¹ t'ou²	頭	to kotow	IV, 2
k'o³ wu⁴	惡	detestable, hateful	II, 26
kou⁴ sung⁴	訟	to take legal action	IV, 19
kou¹ yerh³ 兒	眼	the mouth of a drain	III, 16
k'ou⁴ fa	法	mode of deducting	III, 20
k'ou⁴ hsia	下	to deduct, subtract	II, 6
k'ou⁴ liu²	留	to detain	IV, 7
k'ou⁴ mo²	蘑	mushrooms from beyond the Great Wall	III, 19
k'ou³ tzŭ	子	an arch, tunnel	III, 6
k'ou³ wei	味	taste	III, 11
k'ou² yin (1)	音	accent, pronunciation	IV, 18
ku³ chi	跡	historical objects, antiquities	IV, 8
ku⁴ chiao¹	交	a longstanding friendship	IV, 1
ku⁴ i¹	衣	second-hand clothes	II, 37
ku³ jên	人	the ancients	II, 27
ku¹ niang	娘	a girl	I, 38
ku¹ ting⁴	定	to hire, engage definitively	IV, 7
ku¹ tung¹	咚	noise of a heavy fall	II, 25
ku⁴ tz'ŭ³	此	for that reason	I, 3
ku³ wan²	玩	antiques, curios	II, 17
k'u³⁻² fa	法	degree of wretchedness	II, 23
k'u⁰ li⁴	力	a coolie	III, 9
k'uᴸ lung	窿	a hole	II, 30
k'u³ tzŭ	子	a misfortune, hardship	II, 34
k'u⁴ tzŭ	褲	trousers	III, 5
kua⁴ ch'ih³	掛	(worth) mention	IV, 1
kua¹ fêng¹	颭	to blow	II, 24
kua⁴ hsin¹	掛	kind regards, consideration	IV, 2
kua⁴ mien⁴	麪	strips of dough	III, 19
kua⁴ tzŭ	褂	a coat	III, 5
kua¹ tzŭrh³ 兒	瓜	melon-seeds	I, 41
k'ua¹ k'ou³	誇	to boast	II, 39
kuai³ narh¹	拐	a corner, round the corner	I, 28
k'uai⁴ tzŭ	筷	chopsticks	III, 4
kuan¹ ch'ai¹	官差	an official duty or mission	II, 18

kuan² chang⁴	管帳	to keep the accounts	II, 30
kuan¹ chao (4)	關照	kind attention	I, 7
kuan¹ hsi	關係	to relate to, affect	IV, 8
kuan¹ hua	官話	the "Mandarin" dialect	I, 17
kuan¹ k'an⁴	觀看	to view, gaze at, stare at	IV, 5
kuan¹ maorh⁴	官帽兒	official servants' hats	III, 6
kuan¹ min²	官民	officials and private persons	IV, 5
kuan¹ ming²	官名	official name (cognomen)	I, 3
kuan³ pao (3)	管保	no doubt (also pronounced kuam³ mo)	II, 16
kuan³ shih⁴	管事	to act as steward	II, 14
kuan¹ ssŭ	官司	legal proceedings	II, 12
kuan¹ ti⁴	關帝	the God of War	IV, 17
kuan¹ tsorh⁴	官坐兒	a Box at a theatre	III, 11
kuan⁴ tzŭ	罐子	a jar	III, 2
k'uan¹ shu	寬恕	to forgive, pardon	III, 15
kuang¹ ching	光景	circumstances, probably	III, 14
kuang¹ jun	光潤	lustrous	I, 12
kuang¹ ku⁴	光顧	the honour of your visit	IV, 2
kuang¹ lin²	光臨	your visit	IV, 7
kuang⁴ miao⁴	逛廟	to visit a temple	III, 5
kuang³ tung	廣東	province of Kuangtung	II, 2
k'uang⁴ ch'ieh³	況且	moreover	II, 5
k'uang¹ p'ien⁴	誆騙	to defraud	II, 26
kuei¹ ch'u⁴	貴處	your native place	I, 1 –
kuei¹ chü	規矩	rules, customary modes	I, 30
kuei¹ hang²	貴行	your Firm	II, 14
kuei¹ hsia	跪下	to kneel down	II, 35
kuei¹ hsing⁴	貴姓	your surname	I, 1 –
kuei¹ huan	歸還	to repay, reimburse	IV, 10
kuei¹ kan⁴	貴幹	your business, your object	II, 2
kuei⁴ kêng¹	貴庚	your age	IV, 2
kuei⁴ kuo (2)	貴國	your country, Government	IV, 1
kuei¹ pên³	歸本	to repay a capital sum	IV, 19
kuei¹ shang	歸上	to pay up, repay	II, 23
kuei¹ tzŭ	櫃子	a cupboard, press	III, 2
kuei⁴ yang⁴	貴恙	your illness	I, 7
kuei⁴ yü⁴	貴寓	your lodging	IV, 18
k'uei¹ k'ung	虧空	a deficit	II, 23
k'uei¹ tuan³	虧短	a deficit	II, 22
kun⁴ tzŭ	棍子	a stick	II, 25
k'un¹ chung	昆仲	(your) brothers	I, 1 –

GLOSSARY OF PHRASES.   165

k'un³ shang	綑上	to roll up	III, 9
kung¹ ch'êng	工程	building, construction	II, 10
kung¹ ch'ien	工錢	wages	II, 10
kung⁴ chih²	供職	to serve, fulfil duties	IV, 15
kung¹ ching	恭敬	respect, deference	IV, 1
kung⁴ ch'u¹	供出	to state in evidence	IV, 8
kung¹ chü²	公舉	to publicly elect	IV, 16
kung¹ fu	工夫	time, leisure	II, 4
kung¹ hou⁴	恭候	to await	IV, 18
kung¹ hsi²	貴喜	your position, status	I, 3
kung⁴ jên⁴	供認	to admit in evidence	IV, 9
kung¹ kuan³	公館	a residence, (in Peking, a Legation)	II, 7
kung¹ ming	功名	a title, decoration	II, 37
kung¹ p'ing	公平	impartial	IV, 1
kung¹ shih (4)	公事	public business	I, 35
kŭng⁴ shih	公事	an Official Writership	II, 24
kung⁴ shuo¹	供說	to state in evidence	IV, 6
kung¹ so³	公所	a public office	IV, 8
kung¹ tao	公道	fair, just	II, 11
kung⁴ tsung³	共總	in all, the total	II, 18
kung¹ t'ung²	公同	publicly and together	IV, 8
kung¹ wu⁴	公務	official business	IV, 20
kung¹ yün²	公允	just, equitable	IV, 9
k'ung⁴ chui¹	控追	to sue for	IV, 10
k'ung⁴ kao⁴	控告	to bring a charge against	IV, 10
k'ung³ p'a	恐怕	to fear that, expect that	II, 29
k'uo² chêng⁴	國政	politics, statesmanship	IV, 3
kuo² chia	國家	the State, the Imperial House	II, 22
kuo⁴ chiang (3)	過獎	to be too flattering	II, 5
kuo⁴ ch'ien²	過錢	transfer [or] passing of money	II, 27
kuo⁴ ch'ü	過去	to go over or across	I, 4
kuo²jan²	果然	actually, in the event	II, 22
kuo⁴ lai	過來	to come over or across	I, 4
kuo⁴ lu⁴	過路	to pass en route	II, 15
kuo⁴ nien²	過年	the New Year	II, 13
kuo² shu¹	國書	a Royal Letter, a Letter of Credence	IV, 1
kuo⁴ t'ang²	過堂	to hold a sitting of Court	II, 19
kuo³ tzŭ	果子	fruit	II, 13
kuo¹ yü	過於	too, excessive, over —	II, 24
la⁴ têng¹	蠟燈	a candle	II, 7
lai² hui²	來回	there and back	III, 6

†

Romanization	Characters	Meaning	Ref
lai¹ lien²	臉來	to have the face to	I, 37.
lai² wang (3)	往	intimacy, intercourse with	II, 25
lan² huo⁴	藍貨	cloisonné ware (the name in the trade)	II, 7
lan² kuei⁴	攔櫃	a shop-counter	II, 6
lan⁴ larh¹ (sic)	爛爛兒	pulpy, to a pulp	I, 41
lan² lü	襤褸	in rags, tattered	II, 31
lan³ tai	怠懶	disinclined to	I, 14
lao³ chia⁴	駕老	I am much obliged to you for your trouble	I, 4
lao² hsiung¹	兄老	you, Sir	II, 5
lao³ kung	公老	a eunuch	II, 29
lao² ping	病痨	consumption	II, 14
lao² shih¹	師老	a tutor, master	I, 10
lao² shou³	手老	an old or skilled hand	II, 39
lao³ ti⁴	弟老	you (to an equal younger than oneself)	II, 3
lao³ tung	動老	to trouble, disturb (polite)	I, 8
lao³ tzŭ	子老	a father (*lao³ tzŭ*, when = name of the philosopher)	I, 33
lao⁴ tzŭ	子落	means, something to live upon	II, 39
lao³ yeh	爺老	(an official title)	II, 4
lê⁴ ling¹	令勒	to compel	IV, 8
lei² chui	贅累	bother, trouble, annoyance	III, 6
lei⁴ hsin¹	心累	trouble, anxiety	II, 2
lei⁴ k'ên	肯累	(excuse me for) putting you to the trouble	II, 14
lei⁴ ssŭ	死勒	to strangle	II, 11
li² chien	間離	to estrange	II, 11
li⁴ ch'ien	錢利	interest on money	II, 9
li⁴ hai	害利	dreadful, also a common superlative	I, 23
li⁴ hsi	息利	interest on money	II, 9
li³ hui (4)	會理	to notice, observe	II, 39
li⁴ k'o⁴	刻立	(also *li⁴ k'o³*), at once	II, 32
li⁴ lien	練歷	trained, practised	III, 1
li⁴ lo	儷俐	tidy	III, 15
li³ mao (4)	貌禮	polite, courteous	II, 35
li⁴ tai⁴	代歷	dynasties	I, 29
li² tang¹	當理	(of a formality) Quite correct!	IV, 1
li³ t'ou	頭裡	inside	II, 11
li³ tzŭ	子李	plums	III, 19
li³ wu	物禮	a present	III, 17
liang² hsin	心良	conscience	II, 16
liang² k'uai	快涼	cool	I, 24
liang² shih	食糧	grain	II, 10
liang² shui³	水涼	(or *liang² shu'rh³*), cold water	III, 16

GLOSSARY OF PHRASES. 167

liang² tsao¹	兩造	the two parties to a case	II, 19
liao²li (sic)	料理	to attend to	IV, 1
liao² shih⁴	了事	to manage, transact, business	II, 9
liao² shou(3)	了手	an end of it	I, 33
lieh² lieh	咧咧	rubbish, nonsense	II, 40
lien² chieh²	連捷	a series of successes	II, 5
lien² p'ên²	臉盆	a wash-hand basin	III, 3
lien² tzŭ	簾子	a hanging screen, portière	III, 17
lien² yeh⁴	連夜	(to work on, etc.,) into the night	II, 17
lin² chin⁴	鄰近	close to	II, 29
lin² fêng¹	鄰封	the adjoining	II, 38
lin² shui⁴	臨睡	before sleeping	III, 7
lin² ssŭ²	臨死	at the point of death	II, 16
ling² chiao	領教	to learn from (you what, — etc.)	II, 2
		[Note.—So toned when followed by object, but ling² chiao⁴ when standing absolutely.]	
ling⁴ ch'in¹	親	your relative	I, 38
ling⁴ mei⁴	妹	your younger sister	II, 30
ling⁴ shu¹	叔	your uncle (father's younger brother)	I, 3
ling² sui	碎	odds and ends, miscellaneous	II, 21
ling⁴ ti⁴	弟	your younger brother	II, 11
ling³ tzŭ	子	a collar	III, 5
ling⁴ wai	外	besides, not included, extra	II, 17
ling⁴ yu²	友	your friend	II, 2
liu² hsia	下	to leave, leave behind	II, 16
liu² hsin¹	心	to be careful	II, 33
liu¹ hua²	滑	slippery	III, 16
liu² lo	落	vagrant, outcast	II, 31
liu⁴ lu⁴	路	the six directions	II, 39
liu² shên	神	careful	III, 4
liu¹ ta	達	to stroll	II, 11
lo² ma²	馬	horses and mules	II, 23
lo¹ so	瑣	bother, trouble	III, 20
lo² tzŭ	子	a mule	III, 6
lou³ tzŭ	子	a basket	III, 8
lu² tzŭ	子	a stove	III, 15
lun² liu(2)	流	to take turns	IV, 17
lung² pu	布	a cover of cloth (e.g., pillow-case)	III, 3
lung² t'ou	頭	a bridle	III, 16
ma² chang²	掌	a horse-shoe	III, 16
ma² irh²	尾兒	a horse-hair	I, 39

ma² p'êng²	馬棚	stables	III, 16
ma¹ sa	摩抄	to smooth, stroke	III, 10
ma² shêngrh²	麻繩兒	twine, hemp-cord	III, 14
ma³ têng⁴	馬鐙	stirrups	III, 16
ma² t'ou	碼頭	a landing-place	II, 28
ma² t'ung³	馬桶	a closetool	III, 8
mai³ hsia	買下	to buy oneself —	II, 23
mai³ huo⁴	買貨	to buy goods	II, 31
mai⁴ huo⁴	賣貨	to sell goods	II, 2
mai⁴ kei	賣給	to sell to	II, 32
mai³ mai⁴	買賣	trade (but mai³ mai⁴, when = to buy and to sell)	I, 3
mai² mo	埋沒	to ignore	I, 30
man² k'ou³	滿口	(of speaking) profusely	IV, 5
man⁴ marh¹ (sic)	慢慢兒	by and by	I, 13
man⁴ ti⁴	滿地	all over the place	I, 43
mang² jan²	茫然	at a loss	IV, 13
mao² fang	茅房	a w.-c.	II, 29
mao⁴ i⁴	貿易	trade, commerce	III, 12
mao⁴ mei⁴	冒昧	at random, inconsiderately	I, 18
mao² ping	毛病	a defect, blemish, fault	II, 17
mao² shaorh¹	毛梢兒	the fur of skins	III, 10
mao⁴ shih	冒失	hasty, incautious	II, 33
mao⁴ ssŭ	茅厠	a w.-c.	III, 8
mao⁴ tzŭ	帽子	a hat	III, 18
mei² ch'lurh²	煤球兒	coal-balls	III, 4
mei³ fêng (2)	每逢	every —, every time that	IV, 17
mei³ jih⁴	每日	every day	IV, 5
mei⁴ mei	妹妹	a younger sister	II, 30
mei³ nien (2)	每年	every year	II, 12
mei³ yüeh⁴	每月	every month	II, 1
mên² hsia	門下	under the tuition of	II, 39
mên² k'ou³	門口	gateway, doorway	I, 28
mên² mien⁴	門面	a frontage	II, 9
mên² mo	門脉	the pulses	II, 2
mên² ssŭ	悶死	(also mên⁴ ssŭ³), to bore or worry to death	II, 40
mên² ting	門丁	a door-keeper, porter	IV, 5
mên² tzŭ	門子	(in certain phrases) the family, household	II, 17
mi³ lirh⁴	米粒兒	grains of rice	III, 7
miao³ mang²	渺茫	far separated	IV, 20
mien³ ch'iang (3)	勉強	under constraint or compulsion	III, 18
mien⁴ chien⁴	面見	to see personally	IV, 5

GLOSSARY OF PHRASES. 169

mien¹ ch'iu²	求	to beg personally	IV, 5
mien² hua	棉花	cotton	II, 33
mien⁴ ling³	面領	to receive in person	IV, 18
mien⁴ pao¹	麵包	(foreign) bread	III, 3
mien² pei⁴	棉被	a lined coverlet	III, 17
mien⁴ shan⁴	面善	familiar by face	I, 18
mien⁴ shang¹	面商	to consult personally	IV, 10
mien⁴ t'an²	面談	to have a personal interview with	IV, 5
mien⁴ tzŭ	麵	meal, flour	III, 7
min² chieh²	敏捷	intelligent, quick	IV, 4
ming² jih (4)	明日	to-morrow	IV, 4
ming² pai	明白	clear, to understand	I, 35
ming² p'ien	名片	a visiting-card	III, 7
ming² shêng	名聲	reputation	II, 27
ming² shêng⁴	名勝	celebrated	I, 20
ming² shih¹	名師	a celebrated teacher	IV, 16
ming² t'ien	明天	to-morrow	I, 4
ming² tsao³	明早	to-morrow morning	IV, 4
ming² tzŭ	名字	a name	I, 31
ming² tz'ŭ (4)	名次	one's number in a series	IV, 16
ming² yen²	明言	to express, declare explicitly	IV, 9
mo⁴ fei¹	莫非	it is certain that	II, 11
mo⁴ jo⁴	莫若	better to, just as well to	II, 11
mo² shang¹	磨傷	to damage by rubbing or knocking	III, 9
mo² ts'êng	磨蹭	to dawdle	III, 4
mo² wei³	末尾	the end of, the last	II, 39
mu⁴ chiang	木匠	a carpenter	II, 10
mu³ ch'in	母親	a mother	II, 17
mu⁴ liao	木料	timber	II, 10
mu⁴ pan³	木板	planks	II, 13
mu⁴ tso	木作	carpentering	II, 17
na² chu	拿住	to catch hold of, hold fast	II, 30
na⁴ fu²	納福	to enjoy oneself	II, 23
na² h'ai	拿開	to take away	I, 22
na² lai	拿來	to bring	II, 7
na² tsei²	拿賊	to capture a thief	II, 22
nan² jên	男人	a man (as opposed to a woman), a husband	II, 30
nan² mien³	難免	inevitably	I, 6
nan² pien	南邊	southern	II, 9
nan² tao (4)	難道	do you mean to say—?	I, 44
nan² wei	難爲	to be hard on, ill-treat	II, 40

nao² tai	腦袋	the head	III, 7
nao⁴ tsei²	鬧賊	a robbery, brigandage	II, 30
nei⁴ li	內裡	the Palace	II, 39
nêng² kou	能殼	to be able	I, 34
ni² mên	你們	you	I, 38
niarh² mên	娘們兒	women	III, 8
nieh¹ tz'ŭ²	捏詞	to bring a false charge	IV, 10
nien² chi	年紀	age	II, 17
nien² ch'ing¹	年輕	young	IV, 4
nien² fên	年分	age	IV, 4
nien² hsia	年下	the end of the year	II, 25
nien² mai⁴	年邁	aged	IV, 18
nien⁴ shu¹	念書	to read a book	II, 25
nien² sui	年歲	age, years of age	IV, 2
nien² t'ourh	年頭兒	the harvest, year's yield	II, 10
niu² jou	牛肉	beef	III, 4
niu² nai²	牛奶	milk	III, 3
niu² tzŭ	鈕子	buttons, studs	III, 5
niu⁴ ying¹	謬膺	unfitted to undertake (a high post, etc.)	IV, 1
no² yung⁴	挪用	to misappropriate	II, 22
nu³ li⁴	努力	to make great efforts	I, 34
nü³ jên	女人	a woman	II, 27
nung⁴ ch'ien²	弄錢	to handle (that is, with Chinese, to make) money	II, 39
nung⁴ chü²	弄局	to hold a private gambling-club	II, 26
nung⁴ t'u³	弄土	to handle soil	III, 18
o² cha	訛詐	to swindle, defraud	II, 26
o³ hsin (sic)	惡心	nausea	III, 7
o⁴ ssŭ	餓死	to starve	I, 13
ou² fên²	藕粉	ground arrow-root	III, 19
ou² jan²	偶然	by chance, should it happen that	II, 13
pa¹ chieh	巴結	to push one's way (fig.), to strive	I, 34
pai² ch'i⁽⁴⁾	白契	an unstamped Deed	II, 8
pai⁴ fang²	拜訪	to call and inquire after	I, 4
pai⁴ hsia²	拜匣	a case for holding presents	III, 17
pai⁴ hui	拜會	to pay a visit to	IV, 1
pai² jih	白日	daytime, daylight	II, 13
pai⁴ k'o⁴	拜客	to pay visits or calls	I, 10
pai⁴ nien²	拜年	to make a New Year call	II, 4
pai² shih	白事	a death in the family	II, 27
pai⁴ shih¹	拜師	to make a student's obeisance to a teacher	IV, 16
pai⁴ shou⁴	拜壽	to make a birthday call	I, 32

GLOSSARY OF PHRASES. 171

pai² t'ang²	糖		white sugar	III, 3
pai² t'ien	天		daylight	I, 21
pai² ts'ai⁴	菜		cabbage	III, 4
pai⁴ wang	望		to make a call upon	IV, 3
pai² yen²	鹽		salt	III, 4
pai² yen⁴	宴		to give a banquet	II, 39
p'ai⁴ ch'ai¹	差		to send an official messenger	II, 15
p'ai⁴ kuan¹	官		to depute an officer	II, 22
p'ai² lou	白 機		a memorial gateway	II, 1
p'ai¹ mai⁴	白 賣		to sell by auction	III, 17
p'ai⁴ yüan²	拜 法		to appoint a deputy	IV, 6
pan⁴ fa	白 貨		a measure, proceeding	II, 11
pan⁴ huo⁴	擺 理		to purchase goods	II, 31
pan⁴ li³	派 事		to deal with, act	IV, 2
pan¹ pu² (sic)	派 樵		to drain a man of his money	II, 27
pan⁴ shih⁴	牌 天		to transact business	I, 36
pan³ têng rh⁴	拍 子		a bench	III, 6
pan⁴ t'ien¹	派 次		a good while, "some time"	II, 11
pan² tzŭ	辦 夜		blows with a bamboo	II, 32
pan² tz'ŭ	辨 運		relative rank	IV, 16
pan¹ yeh⁴	盤 查		midnight	II, 22
pan¹ yün (⁴)	辦 費		to spirit away	II, 31
p'an² ch'a	盤 盤		to examine, check	II, 22
p'an² fei	盤 盤		travelling expenses	II, 22
p'an² huan	盤 盤		to spend (a holiday)	IV, 4
p'an² huo⁴	盤 貨		to take stock	II, 28
p'an² suan	盤 算		to think over, turn over in the mind	II, 39
p'an⁴ tuan⁴	列 斷		a judgment, decision	IV, 9
p'an² tzŭ	盤 子		a dish	III, 4
pang¹ pan (⁴)	幫 辨		to act as Assistant	IV, 16
pang¹ tzŭ	梆 子		castanets	III, 11
yang⁴ tzŭ	棒 子		Indian corn	III, 16
yang² yang (⁴)	榜 樣		an example	I, 36
p'ang² changrh⁴	傍 帳	兒	the curtains of a cart	III, 6
p'ang² pierh¹	傍 邊	兒	at the side, close by	II, 33
pao³ chia	保 家		a security, guarantee	IV, 9
pao³ chieh²	保 結		a written security	IV, 14
pao⁴ chieh²	報 結		to finish, complete (a building, etc.)	III, 14
pao³ chü²	寶 局		a gambling-house	II, 17
pao⁴ ch'ü⁴	抱 屈		to be hardly treated	IV, 12
pao² ch'üan¹	寶 眷		your wife	IV, 18

pao⁴ fang	房	the Office of the *Peking Gazette*	II, 2
pao¹ fu	袱	a bundle, wrapper	II, 7
pao³ hao⁴	號	your Firm	I, 3
pao³ hu (4)	護	to protect, afford protection	IV, 5
pao³ jên	人	a security, guarantor	III, 1
pao¹ kei	給	to make over to under contract	II, 18
pao¹ kuan¹	官	to give notice to the authorities	II, 38
pao¹ lan	攬	to undertake the management of	IV, 10
pao¹ p'ei	賠	to make good (a sum, etc.)	II, 19
pao¹ piao¹	鏢	to escort Treasure	II, 29
pao³ sê⁴	色	the gloss	III, 10
pao¹ shang	上	to fold up	III, 9
pao² shêng¹	陞	to recommend for promotion	II, 5
pao³ t'a³	塔	a pagoda	I, 22
poo³ tan¹	單	a security-paper	IV, 9
pao¹ tsu¹	租	to guarantee, be security for, rent	II, 1
pao² tzŭ	子	hail	II, 13
pao¹ tzŭ	子	a poster	I, 28
pao⁴ ying	應	to recompense	II, 16
p'ao² hai³	海	(of carts) to go anywhere	III, 6
pei³ pierh	邊兒	northern	II, 1
pei³ shang⁴	上	to go north (to Peking)	IV, 3
pei⁴ ts'an¹	叅	to be denounced to the Throne	II, 22
pei⁴ wo	窩	a coverlet	I, 25
pei⁴ yirh¹	陰兒	in the shade	III, 10
pei⁴ yün	運	bad luck	II, 20
p'ei² ch'ang²	賞	to repay, indemnify	IV, 6
p'ei² ch'ien²	錢	to lose money by a transaction	II, 20
p'ei² chiu³	酒	to keep one company at one's wine	III, 11
p'ei⁴ fu (2)	服	to highly appreciate, be much impressed by	IV, 18
p'ei² huan²	還	to repay, reimburse	IV, 9
p'ei² k'o⁴	客	to entertain guests	III, 11
p'ei² pu³	補	to make good (a debt, loss, etc.)	IV, 9
p'ei² shang	上	to heap up	III, 15
p'ei⁴ t'ao⁴	套	to fit a book in boards	II, 18
pên³ chia	家	a blood relation	II, 9
pên³ ch'ien	錢	capital	I, 13
pên³ chiu (4)	就	would, should	I, 40
pên³ hsiang	鄉	one's native place	II, 26
pên³ i (4)	意	motive, desire, intention	IV, 18
pên³ nien (2)	年	this year	IV, 8

GLOSSARY OF PHRASES.   173

pên³ sê (4)	本色	in one's line	II, 40
pên³ shih	本事	talents	I, 36
pên³ ti (4)	本地	of this place	II, 15
pên³ yao (4)	本要	should have, would have	I, 4
pên³ yüeh⁴	本月	this month	IV, 8
p'ên¹ shang	噴上	to spirt water from the mouth on	III, 5
p'êng² yu	朋友	a friend	I, 9
pi³ ch'u⁴	彼處	that place	II, 5
pi⁴ ch'u⁴	敝處	my native place	I, 1
pi⁴ hang²	敝行	my Firm	II, 14
pi⁴ hsü¹	必須	must, obliged to	IV, 2
pi³ huarh⁴	筆畫兒	formation of a character	I, 30
pi⁴ jan²	必然	certainly, necessarily	IV, 4
pi⁴ kuan³	敝館	my residence (official), (in Peking) our Legation	IV, 10
pi⁴ kuo (2)	敝國	my country or Government	IV, 1
pi⁴ nan⁴	避難	to make one's escape	II, 25
pi⁴ ping	弊病	an abuse, act of dishonesty, "something wrong"	IV, 10
pi³ shang	比上	to compare with	II, 14
pi³ shih²	彼時	at that time	IV, 4
pi⁴ shu³	敝署	my Office	IV, 1
pi⁴ tang¹	必當	shall not fail to	IV, 4
pi⁴ tuan¹	弊端	an abuse	IV, 10
pi² t'ung²	筆筒	a pen-vase	II, 7
pi² tz'ŭ³	彼此	mutually, on both sides	II, 8
pi⁴ yao (4)	必要	will certainly, will not fail to	I, 35
p'i² ao³	皮襖	a fur-lined cloak	II, 37
p'i² ch'i	皮氣	temper, temperament	I, 6
p'i² hsiang¹	皮箱	a leather trunk	II, 21
p'i² huo	皮貨	skins, furs	II, 2
p'i⁴ ku (3)	屁股	the breech	III, 6
p'i² la	皮喇	tough, strong	III, 9
p'i¹ lei²	霹靂	a thunder-clap	I, 23
p'i¹ lo⁴	批落	to be plucked at an examination	IV, 12
p'i¹ p'ing	批評	to compare notes	II, 39
p'i¹ tan¹	批單	a Note of Contract of Sale	II, 19
p'i¹ ting⁴	批定	to bargain to buy or sell	IV, 8
piao¹ ch'ê⁴	鏢車	treasure-carts	II, 29
piao¹ chih	緻	handsome, elegant	I, 38
p'iao⁴ tzŭ	票子	a banknote	II, 34
pieh² chih	別致	queer, strange, curious	II, 25

†

pich² ch'u	處	elsewhere	I, 17
pich² jên	別人	other people	II, 6
pien⁴ chia⁴	價	to realise the value	IV, 9
pien¹ hsiu¹	修	a Hanlin Compiler	IV, 15
pien⁴ lun⁴	論	to discuss, debate, argue	IV, 6
pien³ o²	額	a presentation tablet	III, 17
pien⁴ tzŭ	子	the queue	III, 18
p'ien¹ ch'iao³	巧	by a coincidence, as it so happened	II, 22
p'ien² i (sic)	宜	cheap	II, 2
p'ien⁴ tzŭ	子	a card	III, 17
p'in⁴ ch'ing³	請	to engage the services of	IV, 9
p'in³ hsing	行	habits, character	I, 30
ping⁴ ch'ieh³	且	besides, moreover	II, 26
ping³ chien (4)	見	to have an official interview with (a superior)	IV, 16
ping³ chih¹	知	to tell (a superior)	III, 13
ping³ fu (2)	覆	to report in reply	IV, 8
ping³ k'ung⁴	控	to lay a complaint or charge against	IV, 8
ping³ ming²	明	to report to (a superior)	IV, 6
ping³ pao⁴	報	to report to (a superior)	II, 22
ping¹ pu	部	the Board of War	II, 1
ping¹ t'ang²	糖	sugar-candy	III, 19
ping³ t'ieh	帖	a Petition	II, 5
ping¹ ting	丁	a private soldier	II, 89
pin¹ tzŭ	子	a small, red, sourish, apple-like fruit	III, 19
p'ing² an (1)	安	(occ. p'ing⁴ an¹), quiet, prosperous, without mishap	II, 86
p'ing² ch'ang²	常	ordinary	I, 35
p'ing² chü	據	proof	II, 16
p'ing² hsi¹	西	westering, near setting	II, 15
p'ing² hsin⁴	信	to be believed, relied upon	IV, 6
p'ing² k'ou³	口	a mere verbal statement	II, 16
p'ing² kuo	菓	apples	III, 19
po¹ ch'uan²	船	a lighter, cargo-boat	IV, 7
po² hsing	姓	the people, population	II, 5
po¹ li	璃	glass	III, 14
po² li (3)	禮	a small present	I, 32
po² mu³	母	your mother (complimentary)	IV, 15
p'o⁴ huai⁴	壞	to damage by breaking	IV, 6
p'o¹ to¹	多	many, a large number of	IV, 9
pu⁴ chia	咖	Oh no! No, no!	II, 9
pu³ ch'üeh¹	缺	to obtain a substantive appointment	IV, 16
pu⁴ kuan³	管	never mind —	I, 16

pu² kuo⁴	過		only, merely	I, 9
pu² liao⁴	料	不	unexpectedly	IV, 8
pu² pao⁴	報	不	to repay (a kindness, etc.)	I, 40
pu³ shang	上	補	to patch up	III, 5
pu² shih	是	不	a fault	I, 42
pu³ ting	丁	補	a patch	III, 5
pu² ts'o⁴	錯	不	capital! I, 38. Quite right! Exactly!	II, 1
pu³ tzŭ	子	補	an official's distinctive badge	II, 39
pu³ yao⁽⁴⁾	藥	不	a tonic	I, 7
p'u¹ kai	蓋	鋪	bedding	II, 28
p'u⁴ kuei¹	規	鋪	rules of a shop	II, 17
p'u¹ k'ung¹	空	撲	to go on a fruitless errand	III, 7
p'u⁴ pao³	保	鋪	substantial security (*lit.* shop security)	II, 1
p'u² t'ao	葡萄	鋪	grapes	III, 19
p'u⁴ tzŭ	子	鋪	a shop	II, 2
sa¹ huang³	謊	撒	to tell lies	I, 11
sa² li	俐	撒	tidy, (scarcely known in Peking)	III, 18
san¹ k'o¹	科	三	Three Examinations (in separate years) for the Graduate's degree	IV, 14
san⁴ kuan³	館	散	to "go down" from the Hanlin Yuan	IV, 15
sang³ tzŭ	子	嗓	the throat, pitch of the voice	I, 15
sao³ t'a⁴	榻	掃	to prepare for a guest	IV, 4
sê⁴ k'o	刻	嗇	miserly, close	II, 30
sê⁴ ch'ü³	取	索	to press for, dun	IV, 19
sêng¹ jên	人	僧	a Buddhist priest	I, 31
sha¹ kao¹	槁	杪	building-poles	III, 14
sha¹ kuo¹	鍋	沙	an earthenware pot	II, 17
sha¹ ssŭ	死	殺	(sometimes *sha¹ ssŭ³*), to kill by violence, murder	II, 22
shai⁴ shang	上	晒	to put out in the sun	III, 10
shan⁴ fa³	法	善	a good measure, scheme, or plan	IV, 8
shan¹ hsi	西	山	Province of Shansi	II, 31
shan¹ tung	東	山	Province of Shantung	III, 1
shang⁴ ch'ê¹	車	上	to get, or put, into a cart	III, 6
shang⁴ ch'i⁴	氣	上	to lose one's temper	II, 35
shang³ chiao⁽⁴⁾	覺	晌	a siesta	II, 11
shang⁴ chieh¹	街	上	to go into the street	II, 36
shang⁴ chin⁴	進	上	to make progress, improve	IV, 16
shang⁴ ching¹	京	上	to go up to Peking	II, 16
shang⁴ ch'ü	去	上	to go up	I, 22
shang¹ ch'uan²	船	商	a merchant-vessel	IV, 6
shang⁴ ch'uan²	船	上	to go on board	II, 21

shang² fêng⁴h¹	賞 封 兒	a present, "tip"	III, 18
shang⁴ hsia⁴	上 下	above and below, upper and lower	II, 23
shang⁴ hsien²	上 憲	the High Authorities	IV, 18
shang¹ hsin¹	傷 心	grieved, distressed	II, 31
shang⁴ hsiu⁴	上 鏽	to get rusted	III, 15
shang⁴ hui	上 回	last time	II, 18
shang² huo	晌 午	(and shang³ huo), noon	I, 20
shang¹ i (4)	商 議	to arrange in consultation	IV, 8
shang¹ jên	商 人	a merchant	IV, 7
shang⁴ jên⁴	上 任	to go to one's post	II, 3
shang² kei	賞 給	(and shang³ kei), to bestow on, give to	III, 6
shang⁴ kung⁴	上 工	to commence work	III, 20
shang⁴ lai	上 來	to come up	II, 28
shang¹ liang	商 量	to confer or consult with	II, 8
shang² lien⁴	賞 臉	to do one the honour or favour to	I, 8
shang¹ min²	商 民	the mercantile classes	IV, 1
shang¹ pan⁴	商 辦	to consult and take action	IV, 1
shang⁴ piao¹	上 膘	to make flesh (of horses, etc.)	III, 16
shang⁴ pierh	上 邊 兒	above, the upper side	IV, 6
shang⁴ shan¹	上 山	to ascend a hill	II, 15
shang² shou (1)	賞 收	to do one the honour of accepting	I, 32
shang⁴ shui⁴	上 稅	to pay in Duties	IV, 13
shang⁴ so³	上 鎖	to turn the lock	III, 17
shang⁴ tang¹	上 檔	to be taken in	I, 6
shang⁴ t'ien¹	上 天	Providence	I, 13
shang⁴ t'ou	上 頭	above, on the top	II, 16
shang⁴ tso (4)	上 坐	to take the seat of honour	IV, 1
shang⁴ yu²	上 游	the higher official circles	II, 5
shao³ chien⁴	少 見	how do you do!	I, 5
shao¹ chiu (3)	燒 酒	common Chinese spirits	III, 11
shao¹ shang	燒 上	to light up	III, 15
shao⁴ yeh	少 爺	Master (So-and-so)	III, 2
shê⁴ chih²	舍 姪	my nephew	II, 9
shê⁴ ch'in¹	舍 親	my relative	I, 38
shê⁴ fa³	設 法	to take measures, find means	II, 31
shê⁴ hsia	舍 下	my house	II, 1
shê⁴ i²	設 疑	to become suspicious	IV, 7
shê⁴ ti⁴	舍 弟	my younger brother	II, 28
shêm² mo	甚 麼	what	I, 13
shên¹ chin	紳 衿	the gentry	IV, 16
shên³ hsün⁴	審 訊	to try, hear, a case	IV, 9

GLOSSARY OF PHRASES. 177

Romanization	Characters	Meaning	Ref
shên¹ shang	身上	on one's person	I, 4
shên¹ t'i³	身體	the person, bodily frame	IV, 15
shên¹ tzŭ	身子	the body	II, 14
shêng² ch'êng	省城	a provincial capital	I, 1
shêng¹ ch'i⁴	生氣	to get angry	I, 39
shêng⁴ chia⁴	聖駕	the Sacred Person (i.e. the Emperor)	IV, 3
shêng¹ fên	生分	to fall out, quarrel	II, 24
shêng¹ i	生意	calling, business	I, 13
shêng¹ jên⁴	生任	to be promoted	II, 5
shêng¹ k'ou	牲口	beasts (horses, mules, asses, etc.)	II, 12
shêng¹ lai²	生來	by nature, constitutionally	I, 15
shêng¹ lêng³	生冷	raw and cold (of food)	III, 7
shêng⁴ shê⁴	盛設	(of dinners) elaborate	IV, 1
shêng¹ shih⁴	生事	to create trouble or disturbance	IV, 5
shêng⁴ t'i³	聖體	the Sacred Person (i.e. the Emperor)	IV, 3
shêng² tzŭ	繩子	string, cord	II, 12
shêng¹ yin (1)	聲音	tone of voice	I, 15
shih⁴ ch'ai¹	試差	a Chief Examinership	IV, 2
shih² ch'ang²	時常	constant, chronic	II, 24
shih² ch'ên	時辰	the time	IV, 14
shih² ch'êng	實誠	truthful	I, 11
shih² chi (4)	實記	the Dynastic Histories	I, 29
shih⁴ chiao¹	世交	a hereditary friendship	IV, 20
shih⁴ chien (4)	事件	matters, affairs	IV, 2
shih⁴ ching	失敬	to owe an apology to	I, 1
shih⁴ ch'ing	事情	a matter, event	I, 16
shih⁴ chu (3)	事主	the person principally concerned in an affair	II, 30
shih² ch'üeh (1)	實缺	a substantive post	II, 3
shih² chung	實終	from first to last, all along	II, 22
shih² fên	十分	wholly, totally	II, 39
shih⁴ fou³	是否	whether or no	IV, 8
shih¹ fu	師傅	a school-master, teacher	I, 28
shih² hourh	時候	a time, the time when	I, 16
shih³ huan	使喚	to use, employ	II, 23
shih¹ hui (4)	詩會	a Verse Club, Literary Club	IV, 17
shih⁴ jih	是日	this day, or, on that (future) day	IV, 8
shih⁴ lang	侍郎	Vice-President of a Board	IV, 2
shih² ling	時令	a season of the year	II, 28
shih¹ p'ei²	失陪	excuse (my) leaving (you)	II, 7
shih¹ p'iao (4)	失票	a lost Banknote	II, 6
shih¹ tao⁴	失盜	a robbery committed	II, 30

shih² tou	摃頭	to put to rights, to tidy	I, 4
shih² t'ou	石	a stone	I, 20
shih² tsai	實	true, really	I, 4
shih⁴ tuan¹	事端	an affair, incident	IV, 5
shih² tzŭ⁴	識字	to be able to read	II, 36
shih⁴ wei²	視爲	to regard as, consider	IV, 5
shih¹ wên²	詩文	verse and prose	I, 30
shih⁴ wu (4)	事務	affairs	IV, 2
shih¹ yeh	師爺	a Secretary in a Yamên	II, 24
shih¹ ying²	失迎	to miss receiving you	IV, 2
shou² an	熟諳	well acquainted with	IV, 18
shou¹ ch'ang	收塲	the outcome, finale, result	II, 28
shou¹ ch'êng	收成	harvest	II, 12
shou³ chih⁴	守制	to observe one's mourning	IV, 15
shou⁴ chih²	授職	to confer official rank	IV, 15
shou³ chin	手巾	a napkin, towel	III, 16
shou³ fêngrh⁴	手縫兒	the spaces between the fingers	I, 44
shou¹ hao	收號	an endorsement, receipt mark	II, 34
shou³ hsien³	首縣	the Chief Magistracy of a Prefecture	IV, 11
shou¹ huo⁴	收貨	to receive goods	IV, 8
shou³ i	手藝	handicraft	I, 13
shou⁴ jê⁴	受熱	to get overheated, have a feverish attack	II, 28
shou² kung	熟工	handicraft	II, 14
shou¹ shih	拾等	to repair II, 14; to pay one out	II, 30
shou⁴ têng³	受等	to be kept waiting	II, 11
shu¹ chan³	舒展	smoothed out, opened out	III, 5
shu⁴ ch'ang¹	庶常	a Student Bachelor of the Hanlin	IV, 15
shu¹ ch'i³	書啟	a Despatch Writer, Secretary	II, 24
shu³ ch'i (4)	暑氣	heat of the sun	I, 24
shu² chieh	秫稭	millet-stalks	III, 14
shu¹ fang²	書房	a library	II, 4
shu¹ fu	舒服	comfortable, in health	II, 11
shu¹ fu²	舒服	to accept a decision	IV, 9
shu¹ hsiu	脩給	salary (of secretaries, etc.)	II, 24
shu¹ kei	輸口	to lose money to	II, 26
shu⁴ k'ou³	漱口	to rinse the mouth	III, 3
shu¹ pan	書辦	a clerk, Writer	IV, 5
shu¹ p'u⁴	書舖	a bookseller's	II, 18
shu⁴ shih (4)	術士	a magician, conjurer	II, 31
shu⁴ shih⁴	署事	to hold an acting appointment	IV, 12
shu¹ t'an	舒坦	easy, comfortable	II, 9

GLOSSARY OF PHRASES.   179

Romanization	Chinese	Meaning	Ref
shu² tang⁴	贖當	to redeem a pawn	II, 17
shu¹ t'ao⁴	書套	a book-cover	II, 18
shu¹ yüan⁴	書院	a college	IV, 16
shua³ ch'ien²	耍錢	to gamble	II, 25
shua⁴ pai²	刷白	(sometimes sha⁴ pai²), as white as a sheet	II, 27
shua¹ shang	刷上	to rub on	III, 15
shua¹ tzŭ	刷子	a brush	III, 5
shua¹ ya²	刷牙	to clean the teeth	III, 8
shuai² yün³	允	to consent off-hand	IV, 16
shuang⁴ k'uai⁽⁴⁾	快家	brisk, cheery	II, 30
shui² chia	誰家	what family?	I, 38
shui² chiao⁽³⁾	脚	freight	IV, 7
shui⁴ chiao⁴	覺	to sleep	II, 29
shui² chih¹	誰知	who would have supposed?	IV, 5
shui³ ching	水晶	crystal	III, 5
shui⁴ hsiang⁴	稅項	duties, dues	IV, 7
shui⁴ k'o⁴	稅課	duties, dues	IV, 7
shui² lu⁴	水路	by water, a water-route	IV, 8
shui³ mien⁴	水面	the surface of the water, sea, etc.	IV, 6
shun⁴ pien⁴	順便	on one's way	II, 18
shuo¹ chih¹	說知	to verbally inform	IV, 6
shuo¹ ho	說和	to reconcile	II, 19
shuo¹ hua⁴	說話	to speak, talk	I, 6
shuo¹ k'ai	說開	(sometimes shuo¹ k'ai¹) to come to, or, bring about an understanding	II, 29
shuo¹·li³	說理	to be reasonable, talk sense	II, 25
so² hsing	索性	just, simply	II, 17
so² i³	以	consequently, therefore, so	I, 15
so² shu³	所屬	the subordinates of	IV, 5
so² yu³	所有	all the —	I, 20
ssŭ⁴ chi⁴	四季	the four seasons	I, 27
ssŭ¹ ch'ing²	私情	private affairs or transactions	IV, 9
ssŭ⁴ ch'uan	四川	Province of Szechuen	II, 31
ssŭ⁴ hsiang¹	四鄉	the villages round	II, 39
ssŭ⁴ hu	似乎	to seem, seem somewhat	IV, 9
ssŭ³ jou⁴	死肉	dead flesh, fig. a wretched creature	I, 37
ssŭ² kuei	死鬼	a dead man	II, 16
ssŭ⁴ micyh⁴	四面兒	on all sides, all round	III, 14
ssŭ¹ shih	私事	private affairs	II, 18
ssŭ⁴ shu¹	四書	the Four Books	II, 40
su² chia	俗家	lay	I, 31
su⁴ jih⁽⁴⁾	素日	habitually	I, 40

su⁴ shih²	素識	to know well, be well acquainted with	IV, 14
su² yüerh (3)	俗語兒	a saying	I, 39
suan⁴ chang⁴	算帳	to cast up accounts	II, 23
suan⁴ ch'ing¹	算清	to reckon up in full	IV, 13
suan⁴ p'an	算盤	an abacus	II, 6
suan¹ t'êng²	酸疼	sore, aching	I, 5
sui² ho	隨和	conciliatory, agreeable	I, 42
sui¹ jan²	雖然	although, (also sui² jan²)	I, 7
sui² pien⁴	隨便	as one pleases, at will	I, 8
sui² shih⁴	隨侍	to accompany in attendance	IV, 15
sui¹ shurh	歲數兒	one's age	I, 44
sui⁴ yüeh⁴	歲月	months and years, lapse of time	II, 24
sung⁴ hsin⁴	送信	to send a letter	II, 36
sung⁴ hsing²	送行	to bid one farewell	II, 3
sung⁴ li³	送禮	to send a present	III, 18
sung⁴ t'ieh³	送帖	to send a card of invitation	IV, 14
ta⁴ ch'ê¹	大車	a wagon, baggage-cart	III, 9
ta⁴ chia¹	大家	everybody, the whole party	II, 1
ta⁴ chia⁴	大駕	your arrival, your visit	IV, 18
ta³ chia⁴	打架	to fight	II, 6
ta⁴ chiao⁴	大敎	your teaching, your words	IV, 16
ta⁴ chieh¹	大街	a main street, a high street	II, 1
ta³ chien¹	打尖	to take a meal when travelling	II, 38
ta³ fa	打發	to send (a messenger)	II, 14
ta⁴ hua (4)	大話	exaggeration	I, 6
ta⁴ i	大意	thoughtless, careless	III, 18
ta⁴ jên	大人	the title of the higher civil and military authorities; when preceded by the surname becomes ta jên², e.g. Li⁴ ta jên²	I, 32
ta⁴ kai (4)	大概	(also ta⁴ kai⁴), probably, in general	II, 3
ta³ k'ai	打開	to open (baggage, etc.)	I, 4
ta⁴ ko¹	大哥	lit. the eldest brother; you Sir	II, 8
ta⁴ mên²	大門	the front gate, principal gate	III, 9
ta⁴ ming²	大名	your name (cognomen), your reputation, I, 3, IV, 16
ta³ pan	打扮	mode of dressing	II, 37
ta¹ parh⁴	搭伴兒	to bear one company	I, 14
ta¹ pang¹	搭幫	to travel in company	II, 3
ta³ pao¹	打包	to make into a bundle	III, 17
ta³ p'ei	搭配	(of animals), coupled; (of things), joined together (ta¹ p'ei)	I, 44
ta³ sao	打掃	to sweep	III, 14
ta³ ssŭ	打死	(also ta² ssŭ²), to strike dead, kill by beating	II, 15
ta³ suan (4)	打算	to think, intend	I, 13

GLOSSARY OF PHRASES. 181

ta² tien	點	to sort out in readiness	III, 17
ta³ t'ing	打聽	to inquire	II, 1
ta⁴ ts'ai²	打財	great wealth	II, 5
ta⁴ wei²	大圍	to hunt or shoot	II, 15
ta² yen³	打眼	to make a bad bargain, be let in	II, 20
ta⁴ yen¹	打烟	opium	II, 25
ta¹ ying	打應	to consent, agree, assent	II, 6
ta³ yü³	答雨	a heavy rain	II, 12
ta⁴ yüch¹	大約	probably	IV, 3
t'a⁴ parh³	大板	a shelf	III, 7
tai⁴ fu	大夫	a doctor	I, 5
tai⁴ lao²	大勞	to take trouble for another	II, 38
tai⁴ lei	代累	to involve, get one into trouble	II, 38
tai⁴ ling³	帶領	at the head of, in command of	IV, 3
tai⁴ shang	帶上	to take with one	III, 8
t'ai² ai(4)	台愛	your kindness	I, 8
t'ai² chien(1)	太監	an Imperial eunuch	II, 39
t'ai² chierh¹	台墀	a flight of steps	I, 45
t'ai² fu³	甫	your Style	I, 1
t'ai⁴ shih⁴	太史	a Hanlin Compiler	IV, 12
t'ai⁴ shou(3)	太守	a Prefect	II, 5
t'ai⁴ t'ai	太太	a lady, wife of an official	II, 37
t'ai⁴ yang	太陽	the sun	I, 24
tan³ ta⁴	胆大	presumptuous	IV, 3
tan¹ tai	擔待	to make allowance, be tolerant to	IV, 4
tan¹ tsou²	單走	to travel alone	II, 3
tan¹ tzŭ	單子	a Note, memorandum	II, 18
tan³ tzŭ	胆子	the gall, courage	II, 23
tan¹ wu	耽誤	to delay, a delay	III, 6
t'an² horh²	痰盒兒	a Chinese spittoon	III, 2
t'an¹ p'ei²	攤賠	to contribute one's share of a payment, be proportionally liable for	IV, 9
t'an¹ tsang¹	貪贓	to be extortionate	I, 36
t'an² ya	彈壓	to keep or restore order	IV, 5
tang¹ ch'ai¹	當差	to be in an official position	II, 1
tang¹ ch'u¹	當初	at first	II, 2
tang¹ ch'üeh¹	當缺	a Chief or Managing Clerk	II, 40
tang¹ mien⁴	當面	to one's face, face to face	II, 6
tang¹ nien²	當年	in former years	II, 31
tang⁴ p'u	當舖	a Pawnbroker's	II, 20
tang¹ shih²	當時	at that (former) time	II, 16
tang² shih(4) (sic)	當是	to suppose it to be	II, 6

†

t'ang² huo⁴	倘或		if, in case of	II, 11
t'ang² kuan¹	堂官		(1) District Authorities, (2) Heads of Departments	II, 39
t'ang² shang⁴	堂上		in Court	II, 32
tao⁴ ch'u⁴	到處		anywhere, everywhere	IV, 5
tao⁴ fa³	道乏		to express thanks for a service	IV, 19
tao⁴ hsi³	道喜		to express congratulations	II, 9
tao⁴ hsieh⁴	道謝		to express thanks	II, 25
tao³ jao²	叨擾		to trespass on (your) hospitality	IV, 1
tao⁴ t'ai²	道台		an Intendant of Circuit	IV, 6
tao⁴ ti³	到底		(or tao⁴ ti(³)), as a matter of fact	I, 26
tao⁴ tsorh⁴	倒座兒		rooms facing the main range in a Chinese house	III, 9
tao¹ tzŭ	刀子		a knife	III, 4
t'ao² jao²	討擾		to take advantage of your hospitality	IV, 2
t'ao¹ jung²	陶鎔		to polish and refine	IV, 16
t'ao¹ kou¹	淘溝		to cleanse drains	II, 40
t'ao⁴ k'u⁴	套褲		leggings	II, 16
t'ao³ lun⁴	討論		to seek advice or counsel from	IV, 18
t'ao² p'ao³	逃跑		to abscond	II, 22
t'ao⁴ shang⁴	套上		to put up into its cover	III, 17
t'ao³ yen⁴	討厭		annoying, a nuisance	III, 11
tê² hsia²	得暇		to find leisure	IV, 18
t'ê⁴ i(4)	特意		(also t'ê⁴ i⁴), on purpose	I, 32
t'ê⁴ p'ai⁴	特派		to specially depute	IV, 2
têng¹ chaorh⁴	燈罩兒		a lamp shade or globe	III, 15
têng² hou⁴	等候		to await	IV, 5
têng¹ hurh³	燈虎兒		riddles	II, 40
têng¹ kuangrh¹	燈光兒		light of a lamp	II, 29
têng¹ lung²	燈籠		a lantern	II, 25
têng¹ miaorh²	燈苗兒		the flame of a lamp	III, 15
têng³ tzŭ	戥子		small weighing scales	II, 36
têng⁴ tzŭ	櫈子		a bench, stool	II, 37
t'êng² hsieh³	謄寫		to copy out	II, 38
t'êng² k'ung¹	騰空		to empty out	III, 17
ti⁴ ch'i⁴	地契		a Title Deed for land	II, 8
ti⁴ chu³	地主		the landlord, proprietor	IV, 14
ti⁴ fang	地方		a place	I, 20
ti³ hsia	底下		beneath, afterwards	II, 1
ti⁴ hsia	地下		on the ground	II, 13
ti⁴ hsiung	弟兄		brothers	I, 1
ti⁴ kei³	遞給		to hand to	III, 4

GLOSSARY OF PHRASES.

ti⁴ lin²	地隣	a neighbouring landowner	II, 12
ti⁴ mingrh²	地名兒	name of the place	III, 9
ti⁴ mu	地畝	land, land estate	II, 8
ti⁴ pan³	地板	a floor	III, 14
ti⁴ pao(3)	地保	a tipao	II, 39
ti⁴ shih	地勢	a site	II, 1
ti⁴ t'an³	地毯	a carpet	III, 9
ti¹ t'ou²	低頭	to bow or hang the head	II, 27
t'i² hsing	提醒	to remind	III, 4
t'i⁴ kung¹	替工	to act as a substitute for a servant, etc.	III, 13
t'i² mien(4)	體面	respectable	II, 25
t'i⁴ t'ou²	剃頭	to shave the head	III, 18
t'i⁴ tzŭ	梯子	a ladder, staircase	I, 22
tiao⁴ jên⁴	調任	to appoint to a post	II, 24
tiao⁴ tu(4)	調度	to arrange, dispose	III, 9
tiao⁴ ssŭ	吊死	to kill or die by hanging	II, 16
t'iao² fu²	條幅	a hanging scroll	III, 17
t'iao² so	咬剔	to incite, egg on	II, 11
t'iao¹ t'i⁴	挑剔子	to find fault with, disparage	IV, 8
t'iao² tzŭ	條子	a strip of paper	III, 11
t'iao² yang	關養	to take care of the health	I, 7
t'iao² yüeh	關約	a Treaty	IV, 5
tieh² fa	疊法	mode of folding	III, 10
tieh² shang	疊上	to fold up	III, 10
tieh² tzŭ	碟	a plate	III, 4
t'ieh³ huo²	鐵	ironwork	III, 16
tien⁴ chi	惦記	to bear one in mind, remember	III, 18
tien⁴ chia	店家	inn-servants	II, 29
tien³ hsin	點心	refreshments	II, 36
tien⁴ hu	佃戶	a tenant	II, 8
tien⁴ pan(4)	墊辦	to find, advance, provide (money) on account	II, 10
tien⁴ shang	墊上	to fill in with, fill up interstices with	III, 10
tien² shih	典史	a District Police Master	II, 39
t'ien¹ chia	天家	the day long	I, 83
t'ien¹ hsia	天下	the world, in the world	II, 25
t'ien¹ li³	天理	natural or divine justice	II, 16
t'ien¹ p'ing	天平	balance-scales	II, 36
t'ien¹ shang	天上	to add on	II, 39
t'ien¹ tan³	天胆	audacious, daring	III, 13
t'ien² yüan(2)	田園	fields and gardens	I, 31
ting⁴ an⁴	定案	to decide a case	IV, 8

tso⁴ shih⁴	作事	to be employed on business	I, 8
tso⁴ t'ang¹	作湯	to make soup	III, 4
tso⁴ t'ang²	坐堂	to hold a Court	II, 35
tso³ t'ien	昨天	yesterday	I, 4
tso⁴ tsei²	作賊	to thieve	II, 25
tsou³ lu⁴	走路	to make a journey	II, 29
tsou⁴ ming²	奏明	to memorialise the Throne	IV, 1
tsou⁴ ts'an¹	奏叅	to impeach to the Throne	IV, 5
tsou³ tung	走動	to relieve nature, to be moved	I, 25
ts'ou⁴ ch'iao³	凑巧	a coincidence	IV, 14
ts'ou⁴ pan⁴	凑辦	to raise, find (money)	IV, 19
tsu² chien⁴	足見	obvious, apparent	IV, 2
tsu¹ hsia	租下	to take on rent	II, 1
tsu² hsin⁴	足信	credible, to be believed	IV, 6
tsu¹ kei	租給	to rent or lease to	II, 1
tsu² p'ing²	足憑	reliable	IV, 6
tsu¹ tzŭ	租子	rents	II, 8
ts'u¹ chih¹	粗知	to be roughly acquainted with	IV, 18
ts'u¹ chung⁴	粗重	heavy	III, 9
ts'u⁴ hsia²	促狹	mean, ungenerous	I, 45
ts'u¹ huo²	粗活	heavy manual labour	III, 18
tsui³ pa	嘴巴	blows on the mouth	II, 35
tsui³ ying⁴	嘴硬	stubborn, argumentative	III, 15
ts'ui⁴ t'ao³	催討	to press for (a debt, etc.)	IV, 10
ts'ui⁴ tsaorh³	脆棗兒	dried and crisp "Chinese dates"	III, 19
tsun¹ chao⁴	遵照	in accordance with	IV, 5
tsun¹ hang²	尊行	your place in the family	I, 3
tsun¹ hsing⁴	尊姓	your surname	I, 3
tsun¹ hsün²	遵循	to follow, be guided by	IV, 4
tsun¹ i⁴	尊意	your view or opinion	IV, 8
tsun¹ kuei	尊貴	honoured, honourable	II, 39
tsun¹ ming⁴	遵命	to comply with (your) wishes	IV, 4
tsun¹ pan⁴	遵辦	to act as instructed	IV, 10
ts'un¹ chuang	村庄	a village	II, 30
tsung¹ chi	蹤跡	footsteps, whereabouts	IV, 20
tsung² li³	總理	general control or management of	IV, 2
ts'ung² ch'ang²	從長	permanent, thorough, well-considered	IV, 9
ts'ung² hsin¹	從新	anew, over again	III, 16
ts'ung¹ ming	聰明	able, clever	II, 26
ts'ung² ming⁴	從命	to obey orders, do as one is told	II, 9
ts'ung² tz'ŭ³	從此	from this time forward	II, 25

GLOSSARY OF PHRASES.

tu² chang⁴	帳局	a gambling-debt	II, 26
tu² chü²	賭局	a gambling-saloon	II, 26
tu¹ fu¹	督撫	Governors-General and Governors	IV, 5
tu² shu¹	讀書	to study	I, 29
tu⁴ tai	肚帶	girths	III, 16
tu⁴ tzŭ	肚子	the stomach	II, 33
tu² yao⁴	毒藥	poison, a poisonous drug	II, 25
t'u² fu²	徒負	to acquire undeserved —	IV, 16
t'u⁴ mo	唾沫	saliva, expectorations	III, 2
t'u² wurh⁴	土物兒	local products	III, 18
tuan¹ chêng (⁴)	端正	(and tuan¹ chêng⁴), correct	I, 30
tuan⁴ chiu⁴	斷就	to have foretold a thing	II, 17
tuan⁴ ling⁴	斷令	to adjudge that — shall	IV, 9
tui⁴ chiang²	對講	to discuss between (themselves, etc.)	IV, 7
tui⁴ chin⁴	對勁	agreeable to, having a liking for	II, 11
tui¹ fang	堆房	a store-room	III, 10
tui⁴ kei	對給	to transfer (something received) to	II, 32
tui⁴ lien²	對聯	scrolls	III, 9
tui⁴ shou²	對手	(of the game of morra), Quits!	II, 39
t'ui⁴ ch'êng²	推誠	to exhibit, display, the fullest	IV, 18
t'ui⁴ huan²	退還	to refuse and return (something) to	IV, 8
t'ui⁴ hui²	退回	to refuse and return (something) to	IV, 8
t'ui¹ k'ai	推開	to push open or apart	II, 29
t'ui⁴ p'iao (⁴)	退票	a bad or spurious Note	II, 34
t'ui¹ t'o¹	推托	to repudiate	IV, 8
t'ui¹ tz'ŭ	推辭	to decline (a present, etc.)	I, 32
t'un¹ yen¹	吞烟	to swallow opium	II, 16
tung¹ chia	東家	the master of a household	II, 9
tung⁴ ch'ing²	動情	to excite the passions	I, 44
tung¹ hsi	東西	a thing, object	I, 9
tung⁴ shou²	動手	to use force	II, 39
tung¹ t'ien	冬天	winter	I, 27
t'ung² ch'uang¹	同窓	schoolfellows	I, 28
t'ung² hsi²	同喜	(of congratulations) The same to you!	IV, 11
t'ung¹ hsiang²	通詳	to send an identical Report to one's various official superiors	II, 39
t'ung² hsiang¹	同鄉	a fellow-countryman, fellow-provincial	II, 31
t'ung² hsiao³	通曉	to be conversant with	IV, 20
t'ung¹ hsing (²)	通行	current everywhere	I, 17
t'ung² jên	同人	companions, colleagues	II, 24
t'ung¹ k'ai	通開	to clear, free from obstructions	III, 16
t'ung² nien²	同年	of the same year	II, 24

188　THE GUIDE TO KUAN HUA.

t'ung¹ p'an⁴	通判	an Assistant Sub-Prefect	II, 3
t'ung² shên¹	同身	the same body or person	IV, 4
t'ung¹ ta	通達	conversant with	II, 9
t'ung¹ yung²	通融	(or t'ung¹ jung², as a concession, by way of obliging	IV, 7
tzŭ⁴ chi (3)	已	oneself	I, 11
tzŭ¹ ch'ing³	諮請	to move (an official equal) to —	IV, 5
tzŭ⁴ chü	據	a written Agreement or other document	II, 14
tzŭ⁴ huarh⁴	字薔兒	scrolls of pictures and characters	I, 19
tzŭ⁴ jan²	自然	naturally, of course	I, 15
tzŭ⁴ korh²	自各兒	oneself, by oneself	III, 2
tzŭ⁴ k'uei⁴	自愧	self-shame, to feel painfully conscious of	IV, 1
tzŭ¹ pao (4)	咨報	to advise (an official equal) of	IV, 3
tzŭ¹ shêng¹	滋生	to give rise to, be the beginning of	IV, 10
tzŭ¹ shih¹	滋事	to breed, create, trouble	IV, 5
tzŭ⁴ t'ieh⁴	字帖	writing copies, rubbings from inscriptions	I, 29
tzŭ⁴ ts'ung²	從	from	IV, 2
tzŭ⁴ yin¹	字音	enunciation, pronunciation	I, 15, 17
tzŭ⁴ yerh³	字眼兒	a phrase, expression	II, 39
tz'ŭ² ch'i	磁器	crockery	III, 9
tz'ŭ³ ch'u⁴	此處	this place	IV, 7
tz'ŭ¹ hou	伺候	to attend on	III, 1
tz'ŭ² hsing²	辭行	to take one's leave	II, 3
tz'ŭ⁴ jih⁴	次日	the following day	IV, 5
tz'ŭ² kuan²	辭館	to throw up one's employment	II, 24
tz'ŭ⁴ kuang¹	賜光	to accord (one) the honour of (your) company	IV, 14
tz'ŭ² shih⁴	磁實	firm, strong	III, 17
tz'ŭ³ shih⁴	此事	this matter	IV, 8
tz'ŭ³ tz'ŭ⁴	此次	this occasion	IV, 6
wa¹ k'u	挖苦	to chaff, banter, ridicule	II, 39
wa¹ ti⁴	窪地	lowlying land	II, 12
wai⁴ hang²	外行	an outsider, not in the business	II, 13
wai⁴ hsiang	外鄉	another part of the country	II, 16
wai⁴ jên (2)	外人	outsiders, strangers	II, 26
wai⁴ jên⁴	外任	a provincial appointment	II, 8
wai⁴ kuan (1)	外官	provincial officials	I, 36
wai⁴ mierh⁴	外面兒	externally	I, 44
wai⁴ pierh	外邊兒	outside, out of doors	I, 5
wai⁴ shêng (3)	外省	the other provinces (viz., not that where the speaker is)	II, 16
wai⁴ t'ou	外頭	outside	II, 2
wan⁴ an¹	萬安	perfectly quiet, altogether at ease	IV, 13

GLOSSARY OF PHRASES. 189

Romanization	Chinese	Meaning	Ref.
wan² ch'ing¹	完清	to make full payment	IV, 7
wan⁴ fên¹	萬分	in the highest degree	IV, 14
wan⁴ i¹	萬一	1 in 10,000, just possible	II, 14
wan⁴ nan²	萬難	very difficult, impossible	IV, 9
wan³ shang	晚上	late, in the afternoon or evening	I, 4
wang³ hou⁴	往後	afterwards	III, 2
wang⁴ hsiang¹	妄想	to be over eager or anxious to	II, 23
wang⁴ k'an(4)	枉看	to go and see; to visit	II, 2
wang³ ku⁴	枉顧	the honour of your visit	IV, 14
wang³ lai²	往來	coming and going, to and fro	IV, 6
wang² yeh²	王爺	His (or Your) Highness the Prince	IV, 17
wei² ch'i²	圍棋	the game of *weichi*	II, 40
wei¹ i⁴	微意	a slight attention	IV, 1
wei⁴ li⁴	為力	to assist, be of service to	II, 31
wei⁴ mien³	未免	inevitably	II, 33
wei² nan²	為難	to be in difficulty or trouble	II, 11
wei³ p'ai(4)	委派	to depute, delegate	IV, 5
wei² shêng¹	為生	for a living, as a livelihood	II, 35
wei⁴ tao	味道	flavour	I, 9
wei² tzŭ	圍子	the cover of a cart	III, 6
wei³ yüan²	委員	a Deputy	II, 5
wên² chü⁴	文具	writing materials	III, 17
wên³ chung(4)	穩重	dignified	I, 38
wên⁴ hao³	問好	to ask after one's health	II, 3
wên² hsi⁴	文戲	a play of civil history	III, 11
wên² shu¹	文書	a despatch	IV, 3
wên³ tang³	穩當	safe, secure	II, 23
wên² tzŭ⁴	文字	written characters, literature	IV, 20
wo³ mên	我們	we	I, 13
wo¹ p'êng²	窩棚	a matshed	II, 13
wu⁴ ch'ai¹	誤差	to interfere with, prejudice one's official duties	IV, 19
wu⁴ chien(4)	物件	articles, objects	II, 7
wu³ hsi⁴	武戲	a play of military history	III, 11
wu² hsü¹	無須	needless to —	IV, 17
wu² lun(4)	無論	(and wu⁴ lun⁴); no matter —	I, 34
wu² nai⁴	無奈	unfortunately	II, 11
wu⁴ pi²	務必	must, must positively	III, 7
wu³ pien⁴	武弁	petty military officials	IV, 8
wu² ts'ai²	無才	want of ability	IV, 2
wu³ tso⁴	仵作	a corpse-examiner	II, 38
wu¹ tzŭ	屋子	a room	II, 29

†

wu² wei⁴	味	dull, "slow"	II, 39
ya² chu³	囑	your wishes, instructions	IV, 4
ya² mên	門	a Yamên	II, 1
ya¹ sharh¹	山	(of the sun) just setting over the hills	III, 10
ya² t'ieh	帖	a Government licence	II, 12
ya¹ t'ou	頭	a maid-servant	III, 5
ya² yi	役	a Yamên runner	II, 30
yang² chang⁴	仗	to rely upon, trust to	IV, 16
yang² ch'ien²	錢	foreign dollars	III, 12
yang² ch'ing²	情	foreign (non-Chinese) affairs	IV, 18
yang² fa	法	(and yang¹ fa), mode of preserving health	IV, 1
yang² hang²	行	a foreign firm	II, 14
yang² jên	人	foreigners	IV, 5
yang² mao²	毛	sheep's wool	III, 10
yang² ping⁴	病	to nurse (one or oneself) in sickness	II, 14
yang² shang¹	商	a foreign merchant	IV, 8
yang² shên¹	身	to take care of one's health	II, 11
yang⁴ tzŭ	子	a pattern	II, 7
yang² yao⁴	葯	foreign opium	II, 23
yao⁴ chan⁴	棧	a druggist's	II, 2
yao⁴ ch'ien²	錢	to take money, to be venal	I, 35
yao⁴ chin³	緊	important, material	I, 9
yao² ch'ün (2)	幗	cantankerous, surly	II, 24
yao² huang	搖	to shake, jolt	III, 17
yao⁴ huang³	謊	to ask exorbitant prices	III, 19
yao⁴ p'u⁴	舖	a druggist's	II, 17
yao⁴ shih	匙	a key	III, 10
yao⁴ ting⁴	定	to insist on having	II, 21
yao⁴ tzŭ	子	the uppers of a boot	III, 5
yeh³ chi¹	雞	a pheasant	II, 15
yeh⁴ ching⁴	靜	late at night	II, 28
yeh³ chu¹	猪	a wild boar	II, 15
yeh³ hsü	許	(also yeh² hsü²), very possibly, perhaps, it may be	II, 34
yeh³ mao¹	貓	a hare	II, 15
yeh⁴ tso	作	work at night	II, 14
yen¹ ch'i⁴	氣	the sallow complexion of an opium-smoker	II, 25
yen² ch'ih¹	飭	to give strict orders	IV, 5
yen² chin³	緊	strict	I, 30
yen² ching	睛	eyes	I, 44
yen¹ chüarh³	捲兒	cigars	III, 7
yen¹ fang⁴	放	to inspect and release	IV, 11

yen² horh²	盒兒	a salt-cellar	III, 3
yen³ lei⁴	醢淚	tears	II, 31
yen² lu⁴	沿路	a route	IV, 3
yen² ming²	言明	to state expressly	IV, 9
yen² mo⁴	研墨	to rub ink	IV, 17
yen¹ p'arh²	烟盤兒	a pipe-tray	III, 7
yen² sê	顏色	colour, colouring	I, 12
yen⁴ shih¹	驗屍	to hold an inquest	II, 16
yen¹ t'u³	烟土	opium, "drug"	II, 23
yen² t'u²	沿途	the road, journey	IV, 3
yen² yü³	言語	conversation, colloquy	IV, 19
yin³ chien (4)	引見	an Audience	II, 17
yin² ch'ien	銀錢	money	II, 19
yin¹ chuang⁴	陰狀	a dying declaration	II, 16
yin² hao⁴	銀號	a Bank	II, 6
yin¹ hsin (4)	音信	information, news, intelligence	IV, 5
yin² hsin	銀信	a letter of advice	II, 36
yin² liang	銀兩	money	IV, 13
yin² p'arh²	銀盤兒	the value of silver	III, 12
yin² p'iao⁴	銀票	a bank-note	II, 6
yin⁴ sê	印色	oil for sealing	II, 7
yin⁴ shih⁴	銀市	the silver market, Exchange	III, 12
yin² shurh⁴	銀數兒	amount of money	II, 8
yin² tzŭ	銀子	silver, sycee	II, 2
yin⁴ tzŭ	印子	a seal; also, in certain phrases, loans for short periods	II, 35
yin¹ tz'ŭ²	因此	owing to this, therefore	IV, 9
yin¹ wei	因爲	because	I, 4
ying¹ kuo (2)	英國	England, British	IV, 20
ying² shêng	營生	tricks	I, 34
ying¹ tang¹	應當	(also ying⁴ tang), ought	I, 42
ying¹ yang²	鷹洋	the Mexican Dollar	III, 12
ying¹ yün (3)	應允	to promise to do as asked	IV, 5
yu³ ai⁴	有碍	to impede, cause obstruction to	IV, 6
yu³ ch'i⁴	有氣	to be angry	I, 35
yu² chih (8)	油紙	oiled paper	III, 17
yu² chung⁴	尤重	to set a very high value on	IV, 1
yu³ hsien⁴	有限	limited, a limited number or amount	III, 19
yu³ jih⁴	有日	on an early day	II, 5
yu² li	遊歷	to travel, make a tour	IV, 5
yu² mu (4)	遊幕	to act as private secretary	IV, 15
yu² ni	油膩	greasy, sticky	III, 11

†

yu² ni²	泥	sweat and dirt	III, 16
yu² shou	手	to idle	I, 33
yu³ su⁴	素	(of scholarship), sound, thorough	IV, 12
yu³ wan	玩	to travel for pleasure	IV, 17
yu⁴ wang⁴	望	hopeful	II, 11
yu⁴ yüan²	緣	there is a predestined connexion	IV, 1
yü⁴ ch'i	器	objects of art	II, 17
yü² chien (4)	見	my opinion, view	IV, 8
yü⁴ chien	見	to meet with, come across	II, 20
yü⁴ hsien¹	先	beforehand	IV, 4
yü⁴ pei	俻	to prepare	I, 32
yü⁴ pien⁴	便	at a convenient opportunity	IV, 20
yü⁴ shan⁴	膳	an Imperial meal	II, 39
yü⁴ shih	史	a Censor	II, 39
yü⁴ shih	事	when a matter occurs	IV, 1
yü⁴ so (3)	所	a lodging	II, 22
yü⁴ ting⁴	定	to decide on beforehand	II, 5
yü⁴ t'ou	芋	taro	III, 4
yü⁴ yen⁴	宴	an Imperial Banquet	II, 39
yüan² ch'in¹	親	a distant relative	II, 20
yüan² ch'ing¹	青	dead black	III, 5
yüan¹ ch'ü	屈	a wrong, injustice	IV, 9
yüan² hsien (1)	先	in the first instance	II, 9
yüan² i (sic)	語	(to say) a word, " breathe a syllable "	II, 26
yüan⁴ i	意	(and yüan⁴ i⁴) willing	II, 8
yüan² ku	故	a cause, reason for	II, 2
yüan² lai (2)	來	originally, in fact	I, 25
yüan² liang	諒	to forgive, make allowance for	IV, 2
yüan² nien⁴	念	thoughts of those far away	IV, 4
yüan² pao⁴	報	the original statement	IV, 6
yüan² pên (3)	本	original	II, 24
yüan¹ po²	博	(of learning), profound and extensive	IV, 15
yüan⁴ shang	上	at the Governor's Yamên (or Viceroy's)	II, 38
yüan³ sung⁴	送	to accompany one far	IV, 20
yüan² tzŭ	子	a garden	II, 8
yüan⁴ tzŭ	子	a courtyard	II, 7
yüan² yang⁴	樣	the original sample	IV, 8
yüeh¹ ch'i²	期	the time agreed on, the due date	IV, 19
yüeh⁴ ch'u⁴	初	the beginning of the month	II, 18
yüeh¹ hui	會	to invite	III, 5
yüeh⁴ kuang¹	光	the moonbeams	I, 23

yüeh⁴ liang	月亮	moonlight	I, 21
yüeh¹ mo	約摸	to think likely, suppose	II, 8
yüeh¹ shang	約上	to invite	IV, 17
yüeh⁴ ti³	月底	the end of the month	II, 18
yüeh⁴ t'ourh²	月頭兒	the beginning of the month	III, 9
yün⁴ ch'i	運氣	luck	II, 15
yün² hsü³	允許	to consent	IV, 16
yün² liu	溜	viscous, semi-liquid	III, 7
yün² nan	雲南	province of Yunnan	II, 24
yün⁴ tou	斗	a box-iron	III, 5
yün² ts'ai	雲彩	clouds	I, 23
yung¹ chi³	擁擠	to crowd	IV, 5
yung⁴ ch'ien	用錢	a Salesman's fee	II, 12
yung⁴ hsiang	用項	an outlay, call for money	II, 21
yung⁴ 'hsin¹	用心	to take pains	I, 6
yung⁴ kung¹	用功	to work, study	III, 7
yung⁴ shan⁴	用膳	to "partake of refreshment"	II, 39
yung² yüan³	永遠	for ever	II, 27

www.ingramcontent.com/pod-product-compliance
Lightning Source LLC
Chambersburg PA
CBHW021734220426
43662CB00008B/844